ASPEN PUBLISHERS

D1541025

BASIC FEDERAL INCOME TAX

THIRD EDITION

Gwendolyn Griffith Lieuallen

Tonkon Torp LLP

The *CrunchTime* Series

Wolters Kluwer

Law & Business

AUSTIN   BOSTON   CHICAGO   NEW YORK   THE NETHERLANDS

Printed in the United States of America.

1 2 3 4 5 6 7 8 9 0

ISBN 978-0-7355-7893-7

This book is intended as a general review of a legal subject. It is not intended as a source for advice for the solution of legal matters or problems. For advice on legal matters, the reader should consult an attorney.

About Wolters Kluwer Law & Business

Wolters Kluwer Law & Business is a leading provider of research information and workflow solutions in key specialty areas. The strengths of the individual brands of Aspen Publishers, CCH, Kluwer Law International and Loislaw are aligned within Wolters Kluwer Law & Business to provide comprehensive, in-depth solutions and expert-authored content for the legal, professional and education markets.

CCH was founded in 1913 and has served more than four generations of business professionals and their clients. The CCH products in the Wolters Kluwer Law & Business group are highly regarded electronic and print resources for legal, securities, antitrust and trade regulation, government contracting, banking, pension, payroll, employment and labor, and healthcare reimbursement and compliance professionals.

Aspen Publishers is a leading information provider for attorneys, business professionals and law students. Written by preeminent authorities, Aspen products offer analytical and practical information in a range of specialty practice areas from securities law and intellectual property to mergers and acquisitions and pension/benefits. Aspen's trusted legal education resources provide professors and students with high-quality, up-to-date and effective resources for successful instruction and study in all areas of the law.

Kluwer Law International supplies the global business community with comprehensive English-language international legal information. Legal practitioners, corporate counsel and business executives around the world rely on the Kluwer Law International journals, loose-leafs, books and electronic products for authoritative information in many areas of international legal practice.

Loislaw is a premier provider of digitized legal content to small law firm practitioners of various specializations. Loislaw provides attorneys with the ability to quickly and efficiently find the necessary legal information they need, when and where they need it, by facilitating access to primary law as well as state-specific law, records, forms and treatises.

Wolters Kluwer Law & Business, a unit of Wolters Kluwer, is headquartered in New York and Riverwoods, Illinois. Wolters Kluwer is a leading multinational publisher and information services company.

**Dedicated
to
Spencer**

*Fix your eyes forward on what you can do,
not backward on what you cannot change.
—Tom Clancy*

Summary of Contents

Table of Contents

FLOW CHARTS

CAPSULE SUMMARY

EXAM TIPS

Preface

Thank you for buying this book.

This book is built on the foundation of the *Emanuel Law Outline* on *Basic Federal Income Tax*. The full-length *Outline* is intended as your guide as you study tax during the term. Then, as exams approach, this book can help you organize the large amount of material you've studied, as well as test yourself on your knowledge. In this book, the Capsule Summary is a bird's-eye view of the major concepts introduced in the basic tax course, and the problems and questions in this book will help you practice your test-taking skills. Use the Glossary to make sure you know tax terms and how to use them. The indexes in this book—Cases, Code, and Subject Matter— can help you as well. Use these to test your recall: Can you quickly identify what these statutes address? Can you recall the principles of the major cases?

The *CrunchTime* series is unique because it includes many flow charts. How can they help you? Many students are daunted by the "forest" of tax law and get lost in the trees of all the statutes and regulations that they must study. Let the flow charts help you get oriented in tax. Each flow chart guides you through the series of questions that must be asked in the five big areas of tax: income, deductions, character, timing, and rates/credits. You can use the charts to review what you've learned throughout your course and to help you see how all the concepts you've studied fit together. You can see how this is done in the Essay Exam Answers, which guide you through the applicable charts.

To use the flow charts to solve problems, you should first determine which charts are applicable to a particular problem. Many problems will require reference to multiple charts. Then you can use the flow charts to guide yourself through the "right questions to ask" in analyzing typical tax problems. If you develop the habit of asking these tax questions in the order in which they appear in the flow charts, you will not be likely to miss an important issue on the exam. (Of course, some of the detailed analysis, such as special rules or exceptions, is necessarily omitted from the charts, and you should refer to the full-length *Emanuel Law Outline* on *Basic Federal Income Tax*, your class notes, and the Code and Regulations for this detail.)

A few words about using the charts: Each flow chart is a series of choice questions, which are in rectangles or squares connected by straight lines. Sometimes the choice questions lead to a need for a calculation, and these are indicated with a triangle; curved lines direct you to the results of the calculation. The final conclusions are in circles or ovals. When you see dotted lines, you will be "netting" two calculations. Dashed lines lead to related questions that must be asked even after a conclusion is reached.

Each choice question is numbered with brackets, like this: [#]. The bracketed number allows you to identify the choice question as you make notes. It also makes it easier to discuss these guiding questions with your study partners. Some choice questions have endnote numbers attached to them. The endnote numbers reference explanatory notes following the chart, which give supplementary information and cross-references to the text and to material in the *Emanuel Law Outline* on *Basic Federal Income Tax*. The first time a term of art is used in a chart, it is italicized.

No book can replace the hard work of studying for exams, but the Aspen Publishers editors and I hope that the *CrunchTime* series will make the process just a little easier. Of course, no book is ever brought to press without a patient and understanding editor on the other end of the telephone. Many thanks to Barbara Lasoff, especially for tackling all these flow charts with such enthusiasm.

Good luck on your tax exam!

Gwendolyn Griffith Lieuallen
Portland, OR
June 2009

FLOW CHARTS

SUMMARY OF CONTENTS

FLOW CHART KEY

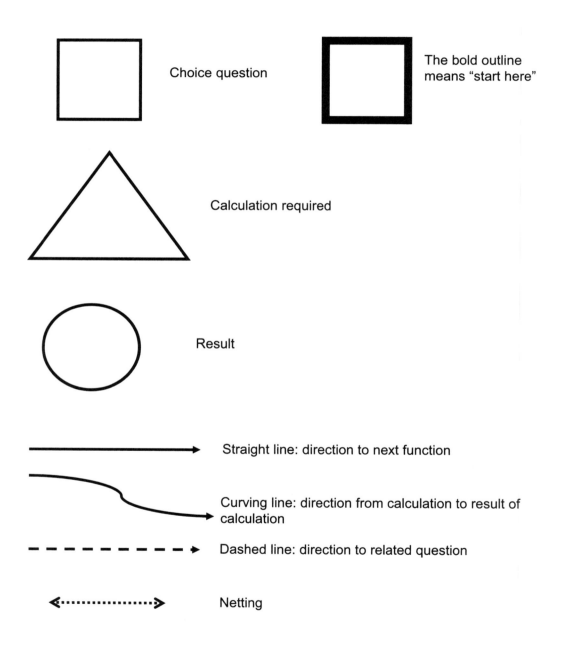

Choice question

The bold outline means "start here"

Calculation required

Result

Straight line: direction to next function

Curving line: direction from calculation to result of calculation

Dashed line: direction to related question

Netting

FIGURE 1

THE BIG PICTURE

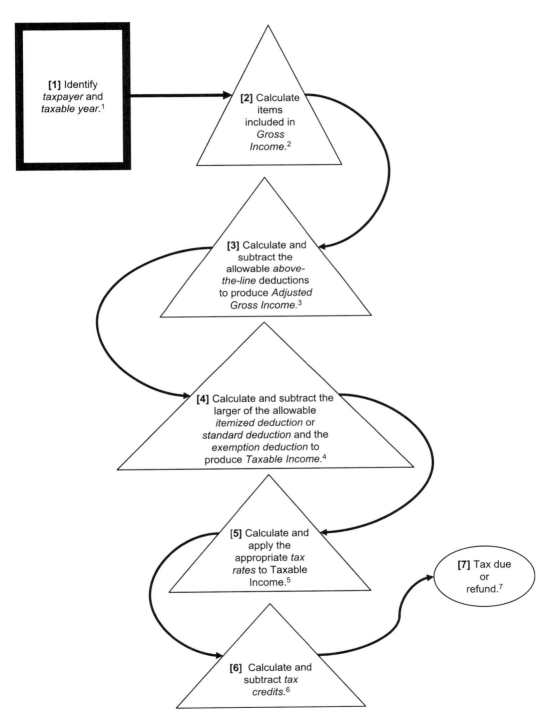

NOTES TO FIGURE 1

THE BIG PICTURE

[1] The starting place is the proper identification of the basic facts about the taxpayer in question. Because tax problems usually involve more than one taxpaying person or entity, the first task is to identify *which taxpayer's* tax consequences are relevant to the problem. See ELO, Chap. 14. The second task is to identify that taxpayer's tax characteristics that are important in the analysis of his or her income and deductions, including the taxpayer's taxable year and method of accounting. See ELO, Chap. 11; CT, pp. 89–91.

[2] Gross Income includes all income from whatever source derived, unless an exclusion applies. IRC §61. See Figure 2 (Analyzing Income) and Figure 7 (Gain/Loss on Property Dispositions). See ELO, Chaps. 2, 3, and 4.

[3] The first set of deductions available to a taxpayer are the so-called "above-the-line" deductions—i.e., those that are subtracted from Gross Income to produce Adjusted Gross Income. See ELO, Chaps. 5, 6, 7, and 8; CT, pp. 74–75. See Figures 3A–3C (Deductions) and 4A–4D (Losses), 6 (Capital Recovery), and 7 (Gain/Loss on Property Dispositions).

[4] A taxpayer must choose between claiming the standard deduction and the itemized deduction, and a rational taxpayer will choose the larger of the two. See ELO, Chaps. 5, 6, 7, and 8; CT, pp. 75–76. See Figures 3A–3C (Deductions) and 4A–4D (Losses). Almost every taxpayer may claim a personal exemption, depending on his or her family status and other factors. Subtracting these deductions from Adjusted Gross Income will produce Taxable Income.

[5] Once Taxable Income has been computed, the taxpayer must apply the appropriate rates of tax, considering the rates on ordinary income and capital gain and also the alternative minimum tax (AMT). See ELO, Chaps. 12 and 13. See Figures 10A–10C (Capital Gains) and Figure 11 (Putting It All Together).

[6] A credit is a dollar-for-dollar reduction in the amount of tax owed, and in some cases may reduce the tax liability below zero. See ELO Chap. 13; CT, pp. 97–100; and Figure 11 (Putting It All Together).

[7] The point of this exercise is to calculate the amount of tax owing or refund due the taxpayer. But in most law school tax classes, this calculation is of relatively minor importance. Instead, most professors focus on the legal questions inherent in each of the previous steps.

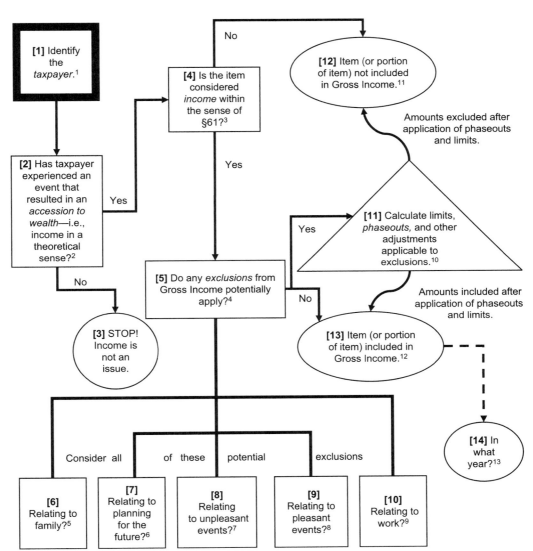

FIGURE 2

ANALYZING INCOME

Notes to Figure 2

ANALYZING INCOME

[1] In any given problem, there is usually more than one taxpayer involved in a transaction, and it is important to identify the relevant taxpayer. For income problems, the relevant taxpayer is the one who experienced the accession to wealth, regardless of what he or she did with that wealth. See ELO, Chap. 2 (III); CT, pp. 64–65. Usually, the tax consequences to each taxpayer are analyzed independently. However, situations do exist in which the tax consequences of the relevant taxpayer may be entwined with others in the problem, such as when a person makes a gift (the donee takes the donor's basis in the gifted property).

[2] An accession to wealth is an event that causes the taxpayer to be better off even if he or she doesn't end up with cash in hand. For example, if someone else pays a debt of the taxpayer, the taxpayer is better off and has had an accession to wealth. See ELO, Chap. 2 (III); CT, p. 65.

[3] IRC §61 refers to "*income* from all sources," requiring a definition of income. There are four kinds of benefits that are not considered income in the sense used in IRC §61: imputed income; loan proceeds; the capital one has invested in property; and noneconomic benefits. See ELO, Chap. 2 (IV); CT, p. 68.

[4] In order to be excluded from Gross Income, a specific statute must apply and its requirements must be strictly met. Construe exclusions narrowly. See ELO, Chap. 4; CT, pp. 69–73.

[5] Consider these potentially applicable exclusion statutes: IRC §§71 (child support, but not alimony); 102 (gifts); 1041 (transfers of property between spouses/former spouses). See ELO, Chap. 4; CT, pp. 68–71.

[6] Consider these potentially applicable exclusion statutes: IRC §§103 (interest on state/local bonds); 135 (interest on savings bonds used for education); 408 (Roth IRAs); 529/530 (distributions from certain college savings accounts); and especially 72 (defines includable portion of distribution from annuity, regular IRA distribution). See ELO, Chap. 4; CT, pp. 68–71.

[7] We might quibble about what constitutes an unpleasant event vs. "good things happening" (Box [9]), but consider these potentially applicable exclusion statutes: §§101 (life insurance received on account of death of insured); 104 (personal physical injury settlements, but not punitive damages); 108 (discharge of debt when taxpayer is insolvent or in bankruptcy, and in certain other situations). See ELO, Chap. 4; CT, pp. 69–73.

[8] Consider these potentially applicable exclusion statutes: IRC §§74 (prizes and awards); 102 (gifts); 111 (tax benefit recoveries); 117 (scholarships); 121 (sale of personal residence); 1202 (sale of qualified stock). See ELO, Chap. 4; CT, pp. 68–73.

[9] Consider these potentially applicable exclusion statutes: IRC §§79 (group term life insurance); 106 (health and disability insurance); 119 (food and lodging); 120 (group legal services); 127 (education assistance); 129 (child care assistance); 132 (other fringe benefits); 137 (adoption assistance); and 911 (foreign earned income exclusion). See ELO, Chap. 4 (IX); CT, pp. 68–73.

[10] It is common for the benefit of exclusions to be phased out, usually based on a taxpayer's Adjusted Gross Income level. See, e.g., IRC §135(b)(2). Other exclusions apply only to a certain amount of a benefit received. See, e.g., IRC §§911 (maximum $91,400 exclusion for 2009); 129 (maximum $5,000 dependent care assistance). As a result of these phaseouts and limits, some portion of the amount of the taxpayer's actual expenditure may be excluded from Gross Income and some portion may be included in Gross Income.

[11] If an item of income is excluded from Gross Income, it never enters the computation of Taxable Income, and thus is never taxed. Compare a deduction, which has the same net effect, but appears as a subtraction in the computation of tax. See ELO, Chap. 5 (II); CT, p. 73.

[12] If an item of income is included in Gross Income, it is potentially subject to tax, even though it may be offset by a deduction. The amount included is the amount of money or the fair market value of property received.

[13] Figure 2 addresses only *whether* an amount is included in Gross Income. It doesn't address *when* (in what taxable year) that should occur, which depends on the taxpayer's taxable year, method of accounting, and special rules for some kinds of income. See Figure 6 (Capital Recovery) and ELO, Chap. 11; CT, pp. 89–92.

EXAMPLE TO FIGURE 2
ANALYZING INCOME

A congressman, upon retiring from public service, becomes a consultant to a Washington lobbying firm. An old friend offers him the free use of a car and driver service for the next two years. The former congressman accepts. What are the tax consequences of this transaction to the former congressman?

Box Number in Figure	Analysis
[1]	The former congressman is the relevant taxpayer, not the friend (who may have deduction issues).
[2]	The receipt of a car/driver service increases the former congressman's wealth (otherwise he would have to make other arrangements for which he would have to pay—driving himself, paying for a car/driver service, taking a cab or (shockingly) the subway).
[4]	Although not all accessions to wealth are "income" within the sense of IRC §61, the use of a car/driver service is not one of the excluded categories of potential income.
[5]	The former congressman would very much appreciate you finding exclusion for this accession to wealth.
[9]	The former congressman probably thinks of this as a "gift" and therefore excludable under IRC §102. Is this a gift? A gift is a transfer made with "detached and disinterested generosity." We do not know sufficient facts to understand the motivation for the transfer. If any facts suggest that this transfer is business-related, or a quid pro quo for future or past activities, then the IRS will claim that it is not a gift. (And it certainly is a hefty gift. . . .)
[10]	The former congressman might try to exclude this as a working condition fringe benefit under §132(d). However, that won't apply, because it is not the employer making the car/driver service available to the former congressman, it is the friend.
[11]–[12]	If the former congressman cannot establish that the transfer is a gift, he must include the fair market value of the car/driver service in Gross Income. There are no phaseouts or limits that apply, so all of the amount must be included.
[13]	If the former congressman can establish that this is a gift, then he can exclude it from Gross Income, and there are no limits on the amount.
[14]	The proper year for inclusion is the year of receipt of the services.

FIGURE 3A

PERSONAL DEDUCTIONS

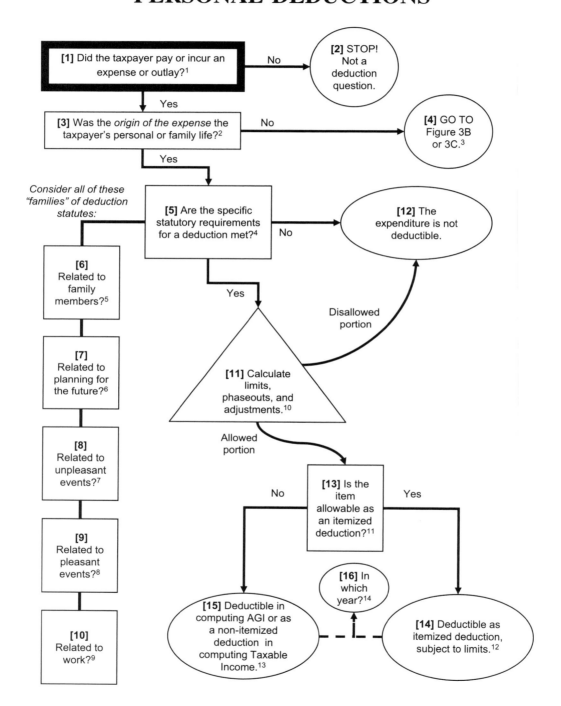

Notes to Figure 3A

PERSONAL DEDUCTIONS

[1] Look for outflows—expenses paid (for cash method taxpayers) or accrued (for accrual method taxpayers). But for losses, see Figures 4A–4C.

[2] It is the origin of an expense, not the effect of making the expenditure, that determines deductibility. See *United States v. Gilmore,* 372 U.S. 39 (1963). See EO, Chap. 5 (III); CT, p. 81.

[3] If the origin of the expense is not the personal or family life of the taxpayer, go to Figures 3B or 3C to determine if the expense is deductible as a trade or business (Figure 3B) or investment expense (Figure 3C).

[4] As a general rule, personal or family expenses are not deductible. IRC §262. However, the Code provides a deduction for certain specific kinds of personal expenses if the taxpayer meets every requirement of that statute. Construe deductions narrowly. See ELO, Chap. 6.

[5] Consider these potentially applicable deduction statutes: IRC §§71 (alimony); 151, 152 (personal and dependent exemptions). See ELO, Chap. 6 (III), (XVII); CT, pp. 74–77.

[6] Consider these potentially applicable deduction statutes: IRC §§219 (IRA contributions); 162 (health insurance for self-employed); 220, 223 (medical savings account contributions); 221 (student loan interest); 163 (home mortgage interest); 164 (investment interest), 408 (retirement planning). See ELO, Chap. 6 (VIII), (XI), (V); CT, pp. 74–77.

[7] Consider these potentially applicable deduction statutes: IRC §§1211 (capital losses—see Figures 10A–10C); 165 (losses—see Figures 4A–4C); 164 (taxes); 213 (medical expenses). See ELO, Chap. 6 (VI), (XII), and (XIV); CT, pp. 74–77.

[8] Consider these potentially applicable deduction statutes: IRC §§170 (charitable contributions); 74 (donation of prizes and awards); 151, 152 (relating to dependency exemptions). See ELO, Chap. 6 (XV), (XVII); CT, pp. 74–77.

[9] Although employment is considered a trade or business of the worker, and so expenses of working are not technically "personal" in nature, most people think of them as personal expenses. Consider these potentially applicable deduction statutes: IRC §§62 (certain educator expenses); 217 (moving expenses); 212 (unreimbursed employee business expenses). See ELO, Chap. 6 (IV), (XVI); CT, pp. 74–77.

[10] The deduction statutes are riddled with limitations and phaseouts, which can result in some or all of an otherwise deductible expenditure not being deductible. See, e.g., the AGI limitations contained in IRC §221 on the deduction for student loan interest. See ELO, Chap. 6.

[11] Some deductions are allowed only if the taxpayer itemizes—i.e., claims the itemized rather than the standard deduction. Consider: IRC §§163–165; 212; 213. See ELO, Chap 6; CT, pp. 76–77. Taxpayers generally prefer above-the-line deductions (those deductible in computing AGI) because (1) AGI is used as a limitation on many itemized deductions, (2) the taxpayer may not have sufficient deductions to make itemizing a sensible choice, and (3) certain itemized deductions are subject to potential reduction under IRC §68(f). Only certain deductions are allowable in computing AGI. Consider these potentially applicable deductions: IRC §§71; 162 (health insurance); 165; 221; 223; 1211; 172; 62; 217. See EO, Chap. 6 (X); CT, pp. 74–77.

[12] Under IRC §68(f), a taxpayer's itemized deductions (other than medical expenses, personal casualty losses, investment interest, and gambling losses) may be limited. The reduction is equal to the lesser of (i) 3% of the amount by which a taxpayer's AGI exceeds a threshold amount, which is established annually, or (ii) 80% of the itemized deductions. However, this reduction is itself reduced in 2009, so that the actual reduction is just one-third of the otherwise applicable amount, and the phaseout is eliminated for years after 2009. The threshold amount for 2009 is $166,800 for married filing jointly. See ELO, Chap. 6 (X).

[13] The standard deduction (in lieu of the itemized deduction) and personal exemptions are deductible from AGI in computing Taxable Income. Personal exemptions are subject to their own phaseout rules. The exemption amount is reduced by 2% for each $2,500 by which a taxpayer's AGI exceeds a threshold amount. For 2009, that threshold amount is $250,200 for married filing jointly. Then this otherwise applicable reduction is reduced by two-thirds, so the actual reduction is one-third of the amount that would otherwise apply. See IRC §68, ELO, Chap. 6 (X).

[14] This chart addresses only *whether* an item is deductible, not *when* it is properly deductible, which will depend on the taxpayer's taxable year, method of accounting, and special rules applicable to losses and certain deductions. See Figures 4 and 6.

EXAMPLE TO FIGURE 3A

PERSONAL DEDUCTIONS

Emily's AGI is $35,000. This year, she made the following expenditures that she would like to deduct. May she deduct them?

Medical expenses for herself:	$15,000
Contribution to §529 plan for nephew:	$500
Cash contribution to Red Cross:	$600
Vet expenses for her cat (on credit card):	$1,000
Purchase of "coffee cart" for starting new business:	$10,000

Box Number in Figure	Analysis
[1]	Emily has a number of outlays or expenditures, as listed. For the vet expense, it doesn't matter that she paid with a credit card; this is still her "expenditure."
[3], [4]	All of the expenses relate to Emily's personal life, except for the purchase of the coffee cart, which is potentially a business expenditure. Analyze that expenditure using Figure 3B.
[5]	Emily's question to you is precisely this: Does she qualify for a deduction for any of the other expenditures?
[6]–[10]	These boxes are designed to get you thinking about possible deductions Emily might claim.
[6]	*Family members:* Although Emily may think of her cat as a family member, she cannot claim a deduction for its medical expenses. The 529 plan for the nephew is possible (see below).
[7]	*Planning for the future:* Emily's contribution to the 529 plan is not deductible for federal income tax purposes, although it may be for state purposes.
[8]	*Unpleasant events:* Emily's medical expenses, assuming they are qualifying medical expenses, will be partially deductible. The cat's medical expenses will not be deductible.
[9]	*Pleasant events:* Emily's charitable contribution, assuming it is to a qualifying charity, will be deductible.
[10]	*Relating to work:* There are no expenditures relating to her Emily's employment.
[11]	There are limits potentially applicable to the charitable deduction and the medical expenses. Emily may make a charitable contribution of up to 50% of her contribution base. Emily's medical expenses are deductible to the extent that they exceed 7.5% of her AGI.
[12]	Emily's AGI is $35,000, so 7.5% of that is $2,625. This is the nondeductible portion.
[13]–[14]	The rest of the medical expense ($12,375) is deductible. The charitable contribution and medical expenses are allowed as itemized deductions, if Emily itemizes. (If she does not, they are lost.) Emily's income is not high enough to trigger a reduction in the amount of itemized deductions.

FIGURE **3B**

TRADE OR BUSINESS DEDUCTIONS

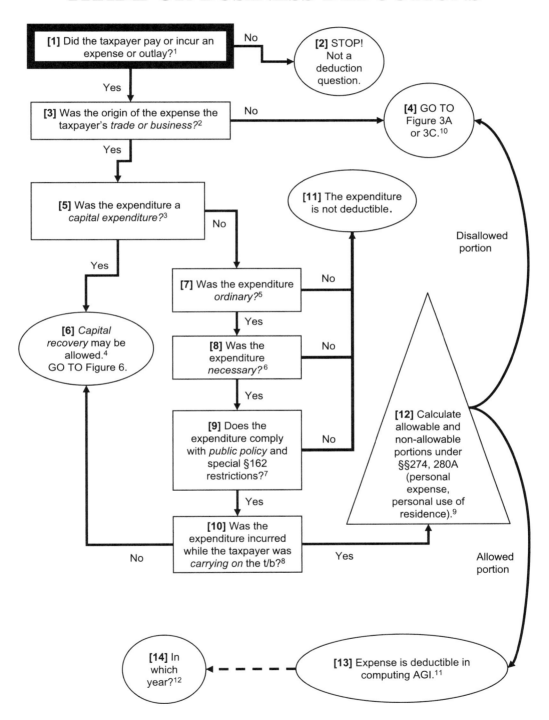

TRADE OR BUSINESS DEDUCTIONS

[1] Look for outflows—expenses paid (cash method) or accrued (accrual method). But for losses, see Figures 4A–4C.

[2] The origin of the expense, not the effect of making it or not making it, determines whether it is a trade or business expense. Although there is no specific definition of a "trade or business," it generally means holding oneself out as being in the business of selling goods and services for profit. See ELO, Chap. 7 (II); CT, p. 78. (If an activity is not for profit, a portion of the expenses—generally up to the income from the activity—will be deductible, but no loss can be generated from the activity. See ELO, Chap. 8 (III); CT, p. 82.) If the *origin* of the expense is not the taxpayer's trade or business, go to Figures 3A or 3C to determine if the expense is deductible as personal expense (Figure 3A) or investment expense (Figure 3C).

[3] A capital expenditure is an expenditure that creates a separate asset or creates a significant benefit that lasts beyond the close of the taxable year. See *Indopco v. Commissioner,* 503 U.S. 79 (1992) and ELO, Chap. 7 (III); CT, p. 79.

[4] No deduction is allowed for a capital expenditure. IRC §263. However, a taxpayer will be allowed capital recovery, either during ownership of the asset, or at disposition. See Figures 5 and 6; ELO Chap. 7 (III); CT, pp. 79–80.

[5] "Ordinary" means usual in business, even if unique in the taxpayer's experience. See ELO, Chap. 7 (II); CT, p. 78.

[6] "Necessary" means appropriate and helpful, and sufficiently connected with the trade or business. See ELO, Chap. 7 (II); CT, p. 78.

[7] See, e.g., IRC §162(c) (bribes); (f) (fines); (g) (treble damages). See ELO, Chap. 7 (II); CT, p. 79.

[8] The taxpayer must be "open for business" in order to deduct an expense. See ELO, Chap. 7 (II); CT, p. 78. If an otherwise deductible expense is incurred prior to opening, it may be amortizable under IRC §195 as a pre-opening expense. See Figure 6.

[9] IRC §§274 and 280A potentially disallow deductions for all or a portion of certain expenses that are of a mixed business/personal nature. Consider: meals (50% deductible); significant restrictions on entertainment deductions (50% deductible); home offices; and rental of personal or vacation residences. See ELO, Chap. 8 (IV); CT, pp. 82–83.

[10] If IRC §§280A or 271 disallow all or a portion of a deduction as a trade or business expense, this expense might still be deductible as a personal or investment expense. To determine this, go to Figure 3A or Figure 3C.

[11] Trade or business expenses are generally deductible from Gross Income in computing AGI. A sole proprietor computes business income and deductions on Schedule C, and the net profit is included, or the loss deducted "above the line." See ELO, Chap. 7 (I); CT, p. 77.

[12] This chart addresses only *whether* an item is deductible, not *when* it is properly deductible, which will depend on the taxpayer's taxable year, method of accounting, and special rules. See ELO, Chap. 11; CT, pp. 89–92.

<small>EXAMPLE TO FIGURE 3B</small>

TRADE OR BUSINESS DEDUCTIONS

Rocco owns a residential painting business. This year, he incurred the following expenses:

Purchase of new sprayers:	$15,000
Insurance and business fees:	$2,000
Parking fines incurred by trucks illegally parked:	$200
Pledge to contribute to local school baseball team:	$3,000

Of these expenses, which are deductible this year? Rocco is a cash-method taxpayer.

Box Number in Figure	Analysis
[1]	Rocco made an outlay or expenditure for all of the expenses except for the pledge.
[2]	The pledge is not deductible in the current year, as Rocco is a cash-method taxpayer for whom expenses are deductible when paid.
[3]	All of the remaining expenses relate to his trade or business.
[5]	The new sprayers are a capital expenditure. Go to Figure 6 to see if capital recovery will be allowed.
[7]–[11]	The other expenditures (insurance, fees, and fines) are ordinary (Box [7]), necessary (Box [8]), and are incurred in the carrying on of Rocco's trade or business (Box [10]). However, deduction of the fines would violate public policy and is prohibited by §162(f) and therefore they will not be deductible.
[12]	These are not expenditures for which a deduction is limited by IRC §274 or 280A, and therefore no limitations will be imposed by these sections.
[13]–[14]	The insurance and fees are deductible as trade or business expenses in the year that Rocco paid for them. These are deductible on Rocco's Schedule C.

FIGURE 3C

INVESTMENT DEDUCTIONS

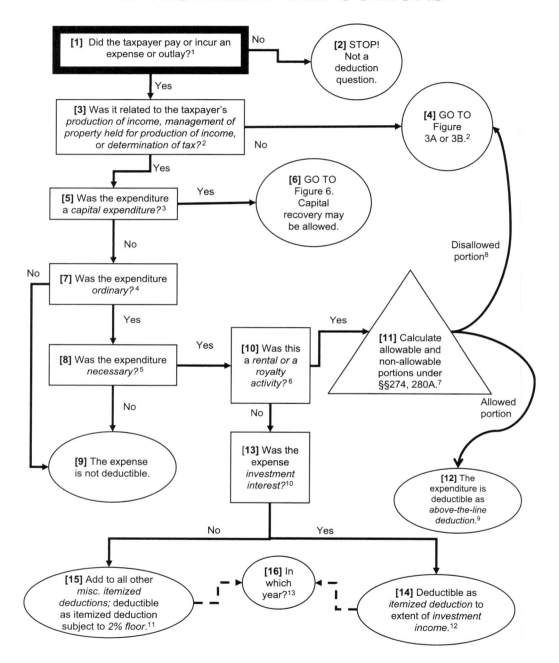

Notes to Figure 3C

INVESTMENT DEDUCTIONS

[1] Look for outflows—expenses paid (for cash method taxpayers) or accrued (for accrual method taxpayers. But for losses, see Figures 4A–4D.

[2] The origin of the expense, not the effect of making it or not making it, determines whether it is an investment expense. For these kinds of expenses, the taxpayer's activity does not rise to the level of a trade or business, but the taxpayer continues the activity in order to make a profit. Examples include investing in stocks and securities or owning a rental home. If the origin of the expense is not the taxpayer's investment activities, go to Figures 3A or 3B to determine if the expense is deductible as personal expense (Figure 3A) or a trade or business expense (Figure 3B).

[3] An expenditure that creates a separate asset or has a significant benefit that lasts beyond the close of the taxable year is a capital expenditure, which cannot be deducted. A capital recovery deduction may be available. See ELO, Chap. 7 (III); CT, p. 79; Figure 5.

[4] "Ordinary" has the same meaning in this context as it does in the context of trade or business deductions: usual in the income-producing activity, even if unique in the taxpayer's experience. See ELO, Chap. 7 (II); CT, p. 78.

[5] "Necessary" has the same meaning as in trade or business deductions: appropriate and helpful, and sufficiently connected with the income-producing activity. See ELO, Chap. 7 (II); CT, p. 78.

[6] Expenses of rental and royalty activities are generally deductible from Gross Income in computing AGI. The taxpayer computes his or her income and deductions from such activities on Schedule E and the net income is included, or the net loss is deducted, "above the line." See ELO, Chap. 7 (V).

[7] IRC §§274 and 280A disallow deductions for all or a portion of certain expenses arising from mixed personal and business activity. Consider: meals (50% deductible); entertainment deductions (50% deductible); home offices; and rental of personal or vacation residences. See ELO, Chap. 8 (IV), (V); CT, pp. 82–83.

[8] If §§274 or 280A disallows all or a portion of a deduction as an investment expense, the disallowed portion may still be deductible as a personal (itemized) expense. To determine this, go to Figure 3A, which addresses deductions for personal expenses.

[9] This figure is about whether a particular expenditure is deductible. If, together, all the expenditures result in a loss, go to Figure 4C to determine the deductibility of the loss.

[10] Investment interest is interest incurred on a debt to acquire investment assets, such as stocks or bonds. IRC §163(d)(3)(A). See ELO, Chap. 7 (IV); CT, p. 76.

[11] The 2% floor of IRC §67 allows a deduction for miscellaneous expenses only to the extent that they, in the aggregate, exceed 2% of the taxpayer's AGI. See ELO, Chap. 6 (XVI); CT, p. 77.

[12] Investment interest is deductible only to the extent of net investment income. IRC §163(d)(2). See ELO, Chap. 6 (XI); CT, p. 76. The 2% floor does not apply to investment interest. No deduction is allowed for interest incurred to carry tax-exempt investments. IRC §265.

[13] This figure addresses only *whether* an item is deductible, not *when* it is properly deductible, which will depend on the taxpayer's taxable year, method of accounting, and loss restrictions. See ELO, Chap. 11; CT, pp. 89–92.

INVESTMENT DEDUCTIONS

Shannon borrowed $10,000 at 7% interest and used the proceeds to purchase shares of XYZ stock. This year, Shannon paid $700 as interest on the loan and had the following investment income:

Dividends from XYZ:	$200
Other investment income:	$300

May Shannon deduct the interest paid on the loan?

Box Number in Figure	Analysis
[1]	Shannon made a payment for interest.
[3]	The interest related to her purchase of investment property—i.e., the XYZ stock.
[5]	Interest expense is currently deductible, although taxpayers have the option of capitalizing the interest into the basis of the property. Treas. Reg. §1.266-1(a)(1).
[7]–[8]	Interest expense is considered both ordinary (usual in the activity) and necessary (appropriately connected to the investment activity).
[10]	This is not a rental or royalty activity.
[13]	It is investment interest—i.e., interest incurred to purchase or carry investment property.
[14]	Shannon may deduct the interest to the extent of her investment income, or $500, in the year paid. The remaining $200 carries forward to future years, in which she can deduct the amount to the extent of her investment income.

FIGURE **4A**

INDIVIDUAL LOSSES—IN GENERAL

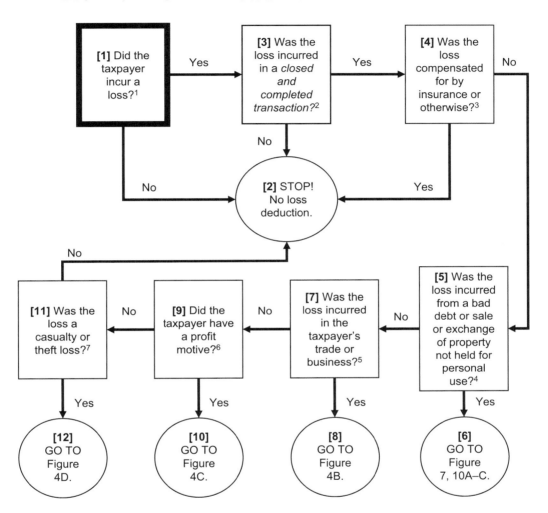

NOTES TO FIGURE 4A

INDIVIDUAL LOSSES—IN GENERAL

[1] Losses occur when a taxpayer's deductions exceed his or her income, in an activity that generates both income and deductions. Or a loss can occur when a taxpayer's property is destroyed, or is sold, or is exchanged for something less valuable. Only certain kinds of losses are potentially deductible for individuals: Losses incurred in a trade or business (see Figure 4B), or losses incurred in an activity engaged in for profit that doesn't rise to the level of a trade or business (investment losses—see Figure 4C), and personal casualty losses (see Figure 4D). See IRC §165(c); ELO, Chap. 6 (VI); CT, pp. 74–75. An individual taxpayer experiencing any other kind of loss is just plain out of luck. For example, a loss incurred on the sale of a personal residence at a loss is not deductible because the house is viewed as property held for personal use. Taxpayers bear the burden of establishing the fact and amount of the loss, as well as the proper year for claiming the loss. In a theft situation, for example, it is necessary to establish the year of the theft. For a mugging, that's easy. For an embezzlement, on the other hand, it can sometimes be quite difficult.

[2] If there is a realistic possibility that the taxpayer may recoup the loss, the transaction is not closed for purposes of assessing loss. A mere decline in value, for example, is not a realized loss for tax purposes. See ELO, Chap. 6 (XIII).

[3] Watch for situations in which the taxpayer's loss is covered by insurance or a private arrangement that substitutes for insurance, even if the taxpayer decides not to file a claim or seek indemnification. In these situations, there is no deductible loss for tax purposes. See ELO, Chap. 6 (XIII); CT, p. 74.

[4] If the loss is from the worthlessness of a debt or from the sale or exchange of property, it will generate a capital or §1231 loss. Losses from the worthlessness of a debt (a bad debt) or from the sale or exchange of property are analyzed in Figures 10A–10C.

[5] A taxpayer must be carrying on a trade or business in order to deduct a loss attributable to that activity. While the Code does not define a "trade or business," the courts have defined it as holding oneself out as selling goods or services in order to generate a profit. Cf. IRC §183 (hobby losses). See Figure 4B and ELO, Chap. 7, for an analysis of trade or business losses.

[6] A taxpayer has a profit motive if he or she has the actual and honest objective of making a profit. See *Dreicer v. Commissioner,* 78 T.C. 642 (1982). This can be contrasted with activities and transactions entered into for personal motives—i.e., not to make a profit. For losses from activities entered into for profit, but which do not rise to the level of a trade or business, see Figure 4C, and ELO, Chap. 8; CT, p. 75.

[7] A personal casualty loss (PCL) is a loss from events such as a fire, storm, flood, or earthquake. IRC §165(c)(3). It is important to identify the year of the loss, as personal casualty losses are deductible in the year they are incurred and do not generate a carryover to other years. Figure 4D analyzes personal casualty losses. See ELO, Chap. 6 (XIII); CT, p. 75.

INDIVIDUAL LOSSES—IN GENERAL

Peggy was shocked to discover this year that termites had eaten away the foundation under her home. She had to have the foundation repaired at a cost of $25,000. May she deduct this loss?

Box Number in Figure	Analysis
[1]	Peggy has definitely incurred a loss.
[3]	This is a closed and completed transaction because she is not likely to recover either the foundation or the outlay.
[4]	There is no mention of insurance or any other source for reimbursement.
[5]	This is not a bad debt or investment property.
[7]	This property was not held for use in Peggy's trade or business.
[9]	Homes are considered personal use property, not investment property.
[11]	Peggy may try to argue that this is a casualty loss, but the IRS has disagreed, saying that the "suddenness" requirement is not met. See Rev. Rul. 63-232, 1963-2 C.B. 97.
[2]	This is not a deductible loss.

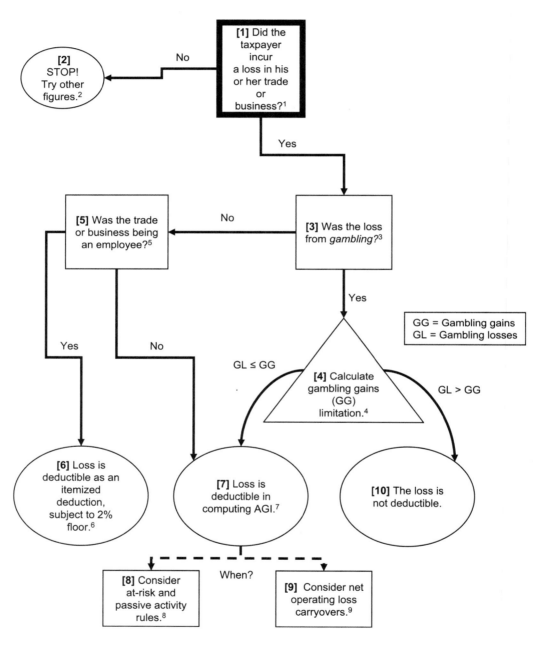

FIGURE 4B

TRADE OR BUSINESS LOSSES

[1] Did the taxpayer incur a loss in his or her trade or business?[1]

No → [2] STOP! Try other figures.[2]

Yes

[3] Was the loss from *gambling?*[3]

No → [5] Was the trade or business being an employee?[5]

Yes

GG = Gambling gains
GL = Gambling losses

Yes → [4] Calculate gambling gains (GG) limitation.[4]

GL ≤ GG

GL > GG

Yes / No

[6] Loss is deductible as an itemized deduction, subject to 2% floor.[6]

[7] Loss is deductible in computing AGI.[7]

[10] The loss is not deductible.

When?

[8] Consider at-risk and passive activity rules.[8]

[9] Consider net operating loss carryovers.[9]

Notes to Figure **4B**

TRADE OR BUSINESS LOSSES

[1] A taxpayer must be carrying on a trade or business in order to deduct a loss attributable to that activity. While the Code does not define a "trade or business," the courts have defined it as holding oneself out as selling goods or services in order to generate a profit. Cf. IRC §183 (hobby losses). See ELO, Chap. 7 (II); CT, p. 78.

[2] If the loss does not occur in connection with a taxpayer's trade or business, see if it is an investment loss (Figure 4C) or a personal casualty loss (Figure 4D).

[3] While a professional gambler is not in the business of selling goods and services, which is central to the usual definition of a "trade or business," the Supreme Court has ruled that gambling can be a trade or business. *Commissioner v. Groetzinger,* 480 U.S. 23 (1987). See ELO, Chap. 8 (VII); CT, p. 83. "Gambling" includes all the usual wagering activities and games, and also includes sweepstakes and tournaments.

[4] Special limitations apply to the trade or business of gambling, as illustrated below. See IRC §165(d). Gambling losses are deductible only to the extent of gambling gains in the year incurred. Any excess loss is not deductible and does not carry over to future years. IRC §165(d). The professional gambler's losses are allowed as a deduction from Gross Income only to the extent of gains; no excess loss is allowed as a deduction. (A nonprofessional gambler would not deduct his or her losses above the line as a trade or business loss, but would instead deduct gambling losses as an itemized deduction, subject to the limitation that losses can only be deducted to the extent of gambling gains. See Figure 4C; ELO, Chap. 8 (VII).

[5] A employee is in the trade or business of being employed. Therefore, the unreimbursed expenses of that trade or business are potentially deductible. See ELO, Chap. 6 (XVI).

[6] Some expenses, such as unreimbursed employee business expenses, are deductible as itemized deductions, but only to the extent that, in the aggregate, these expenses exceed 2% of AGI. IRC §67(a). See ELO, Chap. 6 (XVI); CT, p. 77.

[7] The taxpayer includes all the income from the business in Gross Income and claims the appropriate deductions on Schedule C. If the net effect is a loss, it is deductible from Gross Income in computing Adjusted Gross Income, subject to at-risk and passive loss restrictions.

[8] Taxpayers typically want to deduct their losses in the earliest year possible. However, a number of Code provisions limit the deduction of a loss in the current year and require the deduction of the loss to be deferred into the future. For some activities, a taxpayer's loss may be restricted to his or her amount "at risk"—i.e., the amount for which the taxpayer is personally liable. IRC §465. In addition, if the loss is a passive loss (such as a trade or business in which the taxpayer does not materially participate), IRC §469 will restrict the deduction of the loss to the taxpayer's passive income. If IRC §§465 or 469 disallow a loss for a year, it is carried forward until the taxpayer is eligible to deduct the loss. See ELO, Chap. 11 (VII); CT, p. 81.

[9] IRC §172 allows a taxpayer to carryover an operating loss to other years: 2 years back and 20 years forward (a taxpayer may carry back certain 2008 losses for more than 2 years). See ELO, Chap. 11 (VII); CT, p. 90.

TRADE OR BUSINESS LOSSES

Nathan is a retired doctor who enjoys gambling. He travels the world entering tournaments. Although in the past he has "won big" in tournaments, this year he won only $5,000 and lost $55,000 in his gambling activities. How should he treat his winnings and losses for tax purposes?

Box Number in Figure	Analysis
[1]	Nathan incurred a loss of $50,000, the excess of his losses over his winnings. The question is whether Nathan is engaged in the trade or business of gambling. If he is not, go to Figure 4C to determine how much of the loss is deductible. Let's assume that Nathan is a professional gambler.
[3]	Obviously, the losses of $55,000 are from gambling. Gambling gains were $5,000.
[4], [7]	$5,000 is deductible. (Note that Nathan must include his gambling winnings in Gross Income, so his deduction of $5,000 of loss results in the gambling activity neither increasing nor decreasing his tax.)
[4], [10]	The amount of loss in excess of $5,000 ($50,000) is not deductible, nor does it carry over to future years.

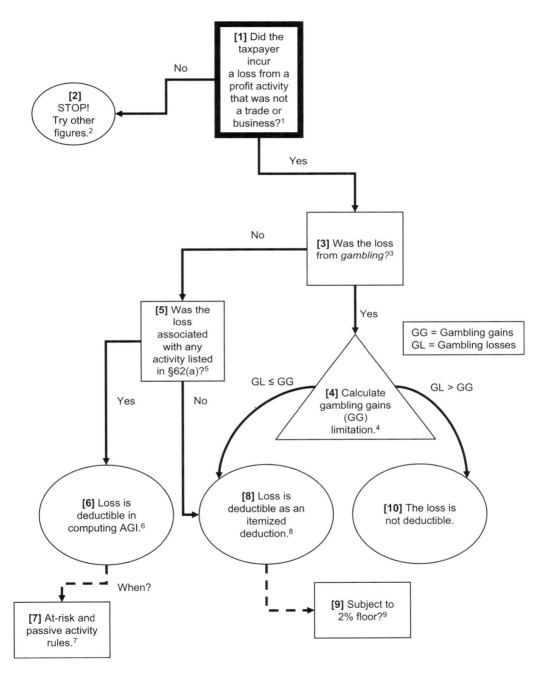

INVESTMENT LOSSES

NOTES TO FIGURE 4C
INVESTMENT LOSSES

[1] These activities are typically nonprofessional gambling, investment activities, and rental or royalty activities. The taxpayer has a profit motive, but the extent of his or her activities do not rise to the level of a trade or business. IRC §213 allows deductions for this kind of activity, and if these expenses exceed income, the taxpayer has a potentially deductible loss.

[2] If the loss doesn't arise from an investment or similar activity, see if it is a trade or business loss (Figure 4C) or a personal casualty or theft loss (Figure 4D).

[3] A nonprofessional gambler typically has a profit motive, but the activity doesn't constitute a trade or business. See ELO, Chap. 8 (VII).

[4] Gambling losses are deductible only to the extent of gambling gains. IRC §165(d). Any excess is not deductible in the year incurred, and does not carry over to any future year. Nonbusiness gambling losses are deductible as an itemized deduction, not subject to the 2% floor. See ELO, Chap. 8 (VII).

[5] Section 62(a) lists the deductions that are deductible from Gross Income in computing AGI (the so-called "above-the-line" deductions). Many of these are personal deductions (see Figure 3A) or those relating to a trade or business (see Figure 4B). Some, however, are expenses of profit-seeking activities, which do not rise to the level of a trade or business, such as rentals, royalties, or forfeitures relating to early withdrawals of savings.

[6] If a loss is deductible in computing AGI, it is subtracted from Gross Income in computing Adjusted Gross Income.

[7] For some activities, a taxpayer's loss may be restricted to his or her amount "at risk"—i.e., the amount for which the taxpayer is personally liable. In addition, if the loss is a passive loss (such as a loss from a rental of real estate), IRC §469 may restrict the deduction of the loss to the taxpayer's passive income. If IRC §§465 or 469 disallow a loss for a year, it is carried forward until the taxpayer is eligible to deduct the loss. See ELO, Chap. 11 (VII); CT, p. 92.

[8] If a loss becomes part of the itemized deduction it is available only if the taxpayer "itemizes" and is deductible from AGI in computing Taxable Income. See ELO, Chap. 5 (II).

[9] Some itemized deductions are subject to the 2% floor of IRC §67, which means that they are deductible only to the extent that, in the aggregate, they exceed 2% of the taxpayer's AGI. For investment activity, these include tax preparation fees, safety deposit box fees, and fees associated with investment accounts not properly added to the basis of the securities. See ELO, Chap. 6 (XVI); CT, p. 77.

Example to Figure 4C

INVESTMENT LOSSES

Perry became concerned about the condition of his bank. Despite his banker's assurances that FDIC insurance would protect his funds, he withdrew funds from certificates of deposit before those certificates matured. He incurred $1,200 of penalties for early withdrawal. He earned interest of $200 from the CD before he withdrew his funds. Perry believes he should report $1,000 as an itemized deduction. Is he correct?

Box Number in Figure	Analysis
[1]	Perry's investments are motivated by an intention to make a profit, but he is not in the trade or business of investing. He incurred a $1,200 loss from that activity.
[3]	This was not a gambling activity.
[5], [6]	IRC §61(a)(9) allows these penalties to be deducted in computing AGI—i.e., "above the line." (Note: Perry must include the $200 of interest in his Gross Income. Although this produces a net $1,000 loss, he must still report both transactions.)

PERSONAL CASUALTY LOSSES

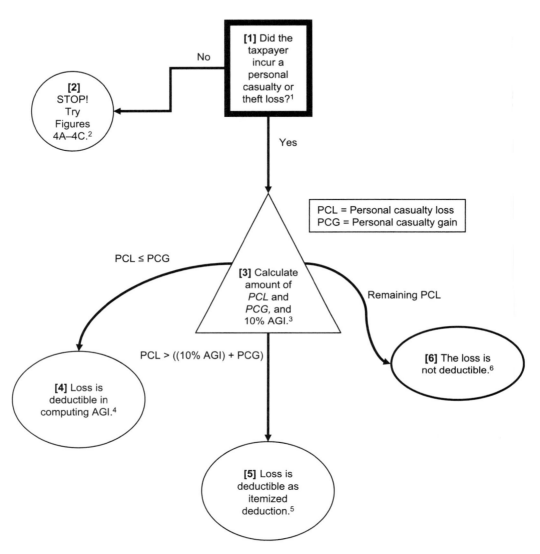

Notes to Figure **4D**

PERSONAL CASUALTY LOSSES

[1] A personal casualty loss is a loss of property held for personal use that arises from storms, earthquakes and similar disasters, or from theft. See ELO, Chap. 6 (XIII); CT, p. 77.

[2] If a loss doesn't qualify as a personal casualty loss, check to see if it qualifies as a deductible loss under other provisions of IRC §165(c): as a loss incurred in a trade or business (see Figure 4B) or a loss in an investment activity (see Figure 4C).

[3] The amount of the personal casualty loss (PCL) is limited to the lower of the fair market value (FMV) of the property immediately before the event or the taxpayer's adjusted basis in the property. Treas. Reg. §1.165-7(b)(1). In addition, each loss must be reduced by $100 ($500 in 2009)—think of it as a "deductible." A personal casualty gain (PCG) occurs when the taxpayer's property is destroyed in a casualty event, and the insurance proceeds received exceed the taxpayer's basis in the property destroyed.

[4] A taxpayer must include PCGs in Gross Income. PCLs are deductible to the extent of these gains. If PCLs are deductible against PCGs, this deduction is above the line—i.e., in computing AGI. If personal casualty gains exceed personal casualty losses in any particular year, both PCGs and PCLs are treated as capital. IRC §165(h).

[5] After allocation of PCLs against PCGs, the rest of the PCL (if any) is deductible as an itemized deduction, but only to the extent that the remaining PCLs exceed 10% of AGI. IRC §165(h). See ELO, Chap. 6 (XIII); CT, p. 77.

[6] All remaining amounts of PCLs (the amount less than 10% of AGI) are not deductible.

EXAMPLE TO FIGURE **4D**

PERSONAL CASUALTY LOSSES

Sally's sailboat was destroyed by a hurricane. It was worth $250,000 and her basis in it was $100,000. In the same year, a valuable painting was stolen from her home. It was worth $500,000 and her adjusted basis in it was $280,000. She had insurance on the boat and her insurance company paid her the FMV, or $250,000. She had allowed the insurance policy on the painting to lapse. Her AGI, without considering either of these events, was $120,000. Assume the "deductible" is $100 per event.

Box Number in Figure	Analysis
[1]	Sally has experienced one loss (the loss of the painting). Although the loss of her boat is a loss in the "real world," in the tax world she has a gain equal to the difference between what the insurance company paid her and her adjusted basis in the boat. The theft is a closed and completed transaction, unless there is some evidence to suggest that Sally's painting will be recovered. The theft of the painting was not compensated for by insurance.
[3]	PCG = $150,000. PCL = $280,000 (basis) − $100 = $279,900. 10% of AGI = $12,000.
[4]	Loss deductible in computing AGI = $150,000.The PCG and PCL included and deducted from Gross Income, respectively, are capital in nature.
[5]	Loss deductible as an itemized deduction = $279,900 − $150,000 − $12,000 = $117,900.
[6]	The amount of PCL that is not deductible is $12,100.

F<small>IGURE</small> 5

BASIS

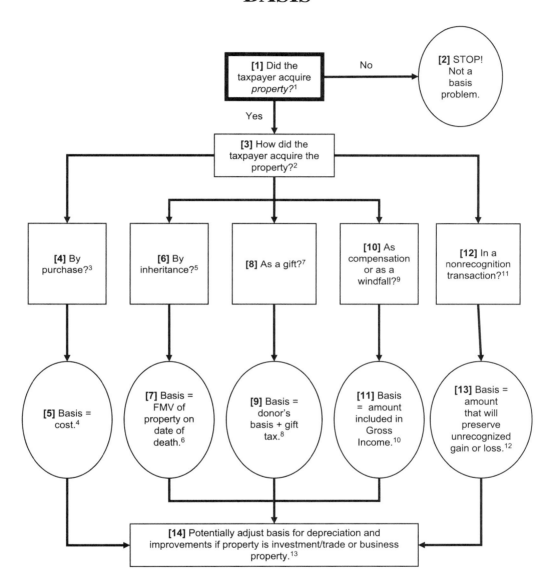

NOTES TO FIGURE 5

BASIS

[1] Basis is a concept that is only relevant to property, tangible or intangible. If a taxpayer acquires an item of property, such as land, a building, or a copyright, he or she must determine the basis of the property. Basis is relevant to capital recovery (see Figure 6) in the form of depreciation or amortization, and the determination of gain or loss on disposition. See Figure 7 (Gain/Loss on Property Dispositions). See ELO 9 (III); CT, pp. 84–86.

[2] The most important question in determining the initial basis of property is *how* the taxpayer acquired the property. In most cases, this will be by purchase (see Box [4]). Remember, however, that a taxpayer may acquire property partially by one method and partially by another, such as in a bargain sale, which is part sale and part gift.

[3] Purchase includes a purchase in the usual sense of the word, as in a purchase for money. But it also includes purchase by an exchange of one property or another (unless a nonrecognition rule applies).

[4] If a taxpayer purchases property, the initial basis of the property will be the purchase price: the amount of money, plus the fair market value of property, plus the amount of liabilities of the seller assumed by the buyer. If a taxpayer takes out a loan to purchase property, the basis will include the amount of the borrowed funds used to purchase the property.

[5] A taxpayer receives property by inheritance when he or she receives it because of someone's death—i.e., through a will, trust, or estate settlement.

[6] If a taxpayer receives property through inheritance, the initial basis of the property will be the fair market value on the date of death, or, if elected by the executor, on the alternate valuation date. This is often referred to as a "stepped-up basis," because the basis of the property in the hands of the decedent before death is often much lower than its value on the date of death. But if the property is worth less at death than the decedent's basis, then the basis to the recipient will be a "stepped-down" basis—i.e., the date-of-death value.

[7] A taxpayer receiving a gift of property does not include it in his or her Gross Income. IRC §102. A gift is a transfer made with detached and disinterested generosity.

Commissioner v. Duberstein, 363 U.S. 278 (1960). See ELO, Chap. 4 (III); CT, p. 69.

[8] The basis of the property received by gift will be the donor's basis, plus any gift tax paid by the donor. But if at the time of the gift, the donor's basis exceeded the fair market value of the property, and upon sale by the donee, this basis would generate a loss, then the basis will be the fair market value at the date of the gift. IRC §1014.

[9] Sometimes a taxpayer performs services and receives property in exchange. Or, a taxpayer may win property on a game show. Or, a taxpayer may find property, such as finding a diamond ring inside a purse purchased at a thrift store. If the taxpayer is entitled to keep the property, under state law, he or she must report the value of the property as income. See *Cesarini v. United States*, 296 F. Supp. 3 (N.D. Ohio, 1969), aff'd per curium, 428 F.2d 812 (6th Cir. 1970).

[10] In these fairly unusual cases, the basis of the property is its "tax cost basis"—i.e., the amount the person must include in Gross Income. This would be the fair market value of the property received.

[11] In a variety of transactions, Congress has determined that the time is not ripe for recognition of gain or loss. These include like-kind exchanges (§1031), involuntary conversions (§1033) and transfers of property between spouses or former spouses incident to a divorce (§1041). See Figures 8 and 9, and ELO, Chap. 10; CT, pp. 86–89.

[12] Each nonrecognition rule contains its own special basis calculation. All of these have a common thread: The basis of the "new" property must preserve, as of the moment of the exchange, the realized gain or loss that went unrecognized in the transaction. See ELO, Chap. 10; CT, pp. 86–89. Consider also IRC §267, which provides a special basis rule for the purchaser when a loss property is transferred between related parties.

[13] Once the initial basis is determined, basis is adjusted upward for improvements, and downward for depreciation or amortization. See IRC §1016 and ELO, Chap. 7 (III); CT, p. 80. Property used in a trade or business or held for investment is potentially subject to depreciation or amortization, but property held for personal purposes is not.

EXAMPLE TO FIGURE 5

BASIS

David is a broker specializing in helping people locate and purchase businesses. He usually receives as compensation for his services a commission equal to 10% of the purchase price upon the closing of a successful sale. This year, he assisted his friend Charlene in purchasing a business for a price of $1,000,000. He agreed with her that, instead of taking his usual commission, he would accept 100 shares of stock in the business. When she purchased the business, he received the shares. There are no restrictions on the shares. What is David's basis in the shares?

Box Number in Figure	Analysis
[1]	Stock is property, so David received property that must be assigned a basis.
[10]	Boxes [4]–[12] guide you through the usual ways that people acquire property, until you find the one that works best. In this case, David earned a fee. Instead of taking his fee in cash of 10% ($100,000), he agreed to take the stock. This is compensation income.
[11]	Absent other facts, his compensation amount would be $100,000. He would be required to include that amount in Gross Income, and it would become his basis in the shares. However, David might be able to prove that the stock is worth less, and that he "cut his fee" for his friend in this transaction.
[14]	Intangible property like stock is not the kind of property the basis of which is adjusted for improvements or depreciation.

FIGURE 6

CAPITAL RECOVERY

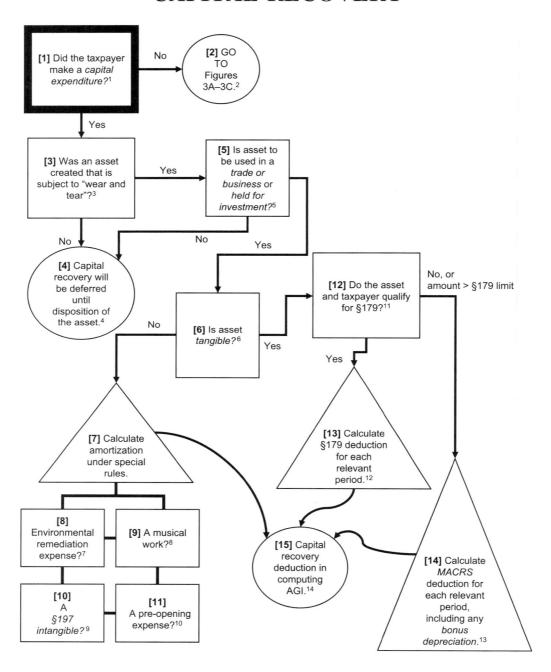

Notes to Figure 6
CAPITAL RECOVERY

[1] A capital expenditure is one that either creates a new asset or is expected to generate benefits beyond the close of the taxable year. See ELO, Chap. 7 (III); CT, p. 79.

[2] If the taxpayer has made an expenditure, but it is not a capital expenditure, it may be deductible. See Figures 3A–3C (Deductions).

[3] In order for a taxpayer to claim deductions for amortization or depreciation of an asset, it must be of a kind that is "used up" as it generates income in order to be depreciable. Example: Buildings are depreciable, but collectible art is not. Land is never depreciable. See ELO, Chap. 7 (III); CT, p. 80.

[4] If capital recovery is deferred until disposition of the asset, the gain or loss will be determined by subtracting the taxpayer's basis in the property from the amount realized. See Figure 7 (Gain/Loss on Property Dispositions).

[5] If the taxpayer holds an asset for personal use purposes, capital recovery through §179, MACRS and related provisions is not allowed. Some property partly used for business and partly for personal use is governed by §280A, so that current deductions for capital recovery may be allowed only for a portion of the property. See ELO, Chap. 8 (V); CT, pp. 82–83.

[6] Intangible assets, such as trademarks or goodwill, are "amortized," not "depreciated" under special rules that vary from asset to asset. Only four of the most commonly encountered rules are described here; there are others as well. See ELO, Chap. 7 (III).

[7] Section 198 allows a current deduction for some environmental remediation expenses.

[8] Taxpayers may elect to amortize the cost of creation or acquisition of certain musical works and copyrights over five years instead of using the income forecast method of accounting. IRC §167(g).

[9] These assets include goodwill, covenants not to compete, licenses, franchises, and permits. See ELO, Chap. 7 (III); CT, pp. 80–81. The recovery period is 15 years, and is calculated on a straight-line basis, beginning with the month the property is placed in service.

[10] Section 195 allows up to $5,000 of deduction in the year of opening, but this amount must be reduced by the amount by which the taxpayer's pre-opening expenses exceed $50,000. See ELO, Chap 7 (II); CT, pp. 78–79.

[11] IRC §179 requires that property be §1245 property held for use in a trade or business.

[12] The amount of the deduction is the cost of the property up to $250,000 (2009) but not more than the Taxable Income of the taxpayer, and the expense deduction is phased out if the taxpayer places in service more than $800,000 of assets during the year. See ELO, Chap. 7 (III); CT, pp. 79–80. IRC §280F may also impose a limit on this deduction for luxury autos or business property also used for personal purposes. The asset's basis is reduced by the capital recovery deduction. See ELO, Chap. 8 (VI); CT, p. 83.

[13] Computing the MACRS deduction requires determining the applicable recovery period for the particular asset, the applicable convention, the cost, and the date placed in service. IRC §280F may also affect the MACRS deduction for luxury autos or business property also used for personal purposes. The Code contains a wide variety of special statutes that assign cost recovery periods or methods to certain kinds of property. In addition, the taxpayer may be eligible for bonus depreciation, depending on the kind of assets, the date purchased, and the date placed in service. The asset's basis is reduced by the capital recovery deduction.

[14] The deduction for capital recovery in any year will be the sum of Boxes [7], [13], and [14], plus any basis recovered on the disposition of property.

CAPITAL RECOVERY

Sia purchases a laundry business. She pays $100,000 for equipment and $45,000 for the goodwill associated with the business. When can she deduct the cost of these purchases?

Box Number in Figure	Analysis
[1]	Sia's expenditures are capital in nature.
[3]	Both assets are potentially subject to amortization or depreciation as they are both "used up" as the taxpayer uses them to generate income.
[5]	Both assets are used in the trade or business.
[6]	Sia has purchased one tangible asset (equipment) and one intangible asset (goodwill).
[7], [10]	The goodwill is a §197 intangible. Sia will deduct $3,000 ($250/month) per year as amortization deductions attributable to the goodwill.
[12], [13]	Sia should be eligible for the §179 deduction for the purchase of the equipment, but more facts are necessary to determine how much.
[14]	Any amount that is ineligible for the §179 deduction will be eligible for MACRS deductions. How much will depend on the appropriate recovery period and the method Sia chooses. She may also be eligible for bonus depreciation.

FIGURE 7

GAIN/LOSS ON PROPERTY DISPOSITIONS

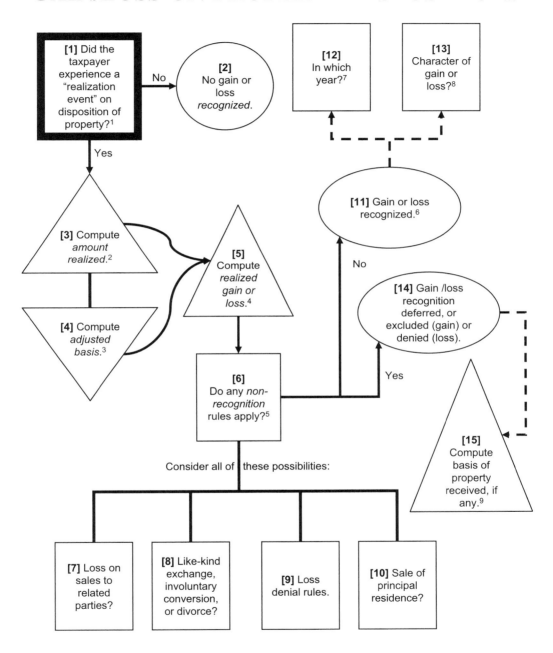

GAIN/LOSS ON PROPERTY DISPOSITIONS

[1] A realization event is a transaction in which the taxpayer gives up property and receives cash or property that is different in kind or quality from property surrendered. *Cottage Savings Ass'n v. Commissioner,* 499 U.S. 554 (1991); see ELO, Chap. 9 (III); CT, p. 84.

[2] A taxpayer's amount realized is equal to the sum of what he or she receives in the transaction—i.e., (1) the amount of money; plus (2) the fair market value of property; plus (3) liabilities that the taxpayer is relieved of as part of the transaction. See ELO, Chap. 9 (III); CT, p. 84.

[3] The taxpayer's adjusted basis in the property depends on how he or she acquired the property, as well as subsequent events affecting the property's basis. See Figure 5 (Basis), and ELO, Chap. 9 (III); CT, pp. 85–86.

[4] Realized gain or loss is equal to the difference between the taxpayer's amount realized and his or her adjusted basis in the property transferred. IRC §1001. See ELO, Chap. 9 (III); CT, pp. 84–85.

[5] Generally, realized gains and otherwise deductible losses (see Figures 4A–4C) are recognized (included in income or deducted) in the year of realization, absent a specific statutory provision deferring the gain or loss recognition. Consider whether any nonrecognition rule applies. Some nonrecognition rules are exclusion statutes (e.g., IRC §121 for excluding gain on the sale of a principal res-idence, Box [10]) or statutes limiting an otherwise deductible loss (e.g., IRC §267, Box [7]). Others are deferral statutes, such as those listed in Box [8]: IRC §1031 (like-kind exchanges, see Figure 9), IRC §1033 (involuntary conversions, see Figure 8), and IRC §1041 (transfers of property between spouses and incident to a divorce). Finally, IRC §165(a) allows the recognition of only certain types of losses by individuals. See Figures 4A–4D.

[6] The portion of the gain or loss that is recognized is either included in Gross Income, or deducted, if the loss is otherwise deductible. See Figures 4A–4D.

[7] If gain is recognized, it may nevertheless be deferred under the installment method of reporting income. See ELO, Chap. 11 (X); CT, p. 94. The installment method doesn't apply to losses.

[8] If gain or loss is recognized, it is important to characterize the gain or loss as ordinary, capital or §1231 gain or loss. See Figures 10A–10C, and ELO, Chap. 12; CT, pp. 92–95.

[9] If the taxpayer received property in an exchange that led to deferral of gain or loss, it is critical to properly compute the taxpayer's basis in the property received. Each tax deferral statute (e.g., IRC §§1031, 1033, and 1041) contains its own approach to calculating the basis of the property received in the transaction.

GAIN/LOSS ON PROPERTY DISPOSITIONS

Jack and Jill lived in identical houses on the same street. This year, both Jack and Jill sold their homes for $250,000 after living in them for some years. Jack had purchased his home several years ago for $300,000. Jill had purchased her home many years ago for $125,000. Will Jack and Jill recognize the gain or loss on their sales?

Box Number in Figure	Analysis
[1]	Both Jack and Jill have a realization event upon sale of their homes.
[3]	The amount realized for both Jack and Jill is $250,000.
[4]	The adjusted basis for Jack is $300,000. For Jill it is $125,000 (no facts suggest additional investments in the homes).
[5]	Jack's realized loss is $50,000. Jill's realized gain is $125,000.
[6], [9], [14]	Jack's loss is not deductible by reason of IRC §165, which allows only certain kinds of losses to be recognized by individuals. Because a principal residence is personal use property, a loss on its sale does not fit within any of the allowed categories.
[6], [10], [14]	Jill's gain is excluded from Gross Income under IRC §121.
[15]	Because both Jack and Jill received cash, it is not necessary to determine the basis of property received.

Figure 8

INVOLUNTARY CONVERSIONS

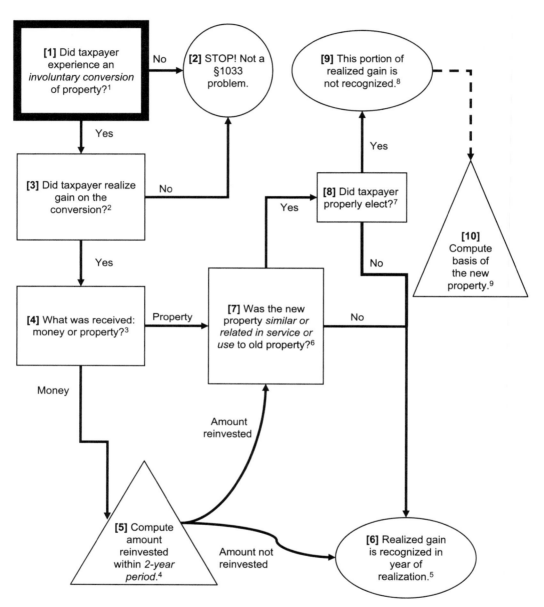

NOTES TO FIGURE 8

INVOLUNTARY CONVERSIONS

[1] An involuntary conversion occurs when property is destroyed or is condemned. Examples include natural disasters and eminent domain proceedings. When the value of what is received (usually money in the form of insurance proceeds, but sometimes property) is different from the adjusted basis of the property that is destroyed or condemned, the taxpayer realizes gain or loss on the transaction. See ELO, Chap. 10 (IV); CT, pp. 88–89.

[2] Section 1033 applies only to realized gains; for losses, see IRC §165 (personal and investment property) and §1231 (business property). For losses from casualties, see Figures 4B (Trade or Business Losses), 4C (Investment Losses), and 4D (Personal Casualty Losses).

[3] In an involuntary conversion, the taxpayer may receive other property to replace the converted property (as in some condemnation actions), but is more likely to receive insurance proceeds. See ELO, Chap. 10 (V); CT, pp. 88–89.

[4] The taxpayer must reinvest the money received in new property within two years of the close of the taxable year in which the conversion occurred. IRC §1033(a)(2)(B). Special rules apply to certain disasters, where a taxpayer is given a longer period of time in which to reinvest. IRC §1033(h). In some cases, the taxpayer will reinvest only a portion of the proceeds in new property, and in that situation, a portion of the realized gain will be recognized.

[5] Realized gain is recognized to the extent of the proceeds not reinvested in qualifying property. IRC §1033(a)(2). See ELO, Chap. 10 (V); CT, pp. 88–89.

[6] "Similarity" depends on function and use by the owner; the replacement property does not need to be identical to the converted property. Special rules apply to real property used in a trade or business and livestock. See ELO, Chap. 10 (V); CT, pp. 88–89.

[7] The taxpayer makes the election by including only the amount of the Gross Income required to be included, and providing information about the circumstances of the conversion and replacement. Treas. Reg. §1.1033-1(a)–2(c)(2).

[8] If the taxpayer receives qualifying property, or reinvests money into qualifying property, this portion of the realized gain will not be recognized in the year of conversion. IRC §1033(a)(1). See ELO, Chap. 10 (V); CT, pp. 88–89.

[9] If IRC §1033 applies to the exchange of property, the taxpayer's basis in the replacement property must be computed. The basis of the replacement property is equal to the basis of the converted property plus any gain recognized, minus any proceeds not reinvested in similar property. IRC §1033(b)(2). This usually means that the basis of the replacement property will be equal to the basis of the converted property. See ELO, Chap. 10 (V); CT, pp. 88–89.

EXAMPLE TO FIGURE **8**

INVOLUNTARY CONVERSIONS

Roxanne's property was condemned by the city in order to make way for a new freeway. She received $500,000 for the property, in which her adjusted basis had been $100,000. She immediately used those proceeds, plus $100,000 of her savings, to purchase a new property. The new property was identical in every respect to the condemned property, except that it was far away from any future freeway site. How should Roxanne report this transaction for tax purposes?

Box Number in Figure	Analysis
[1]	A condemnation is an involuntary conversion.
[3]	Roxanne realized $400,000 of gain on the conversion, which is equal to her amount realized ($500,000) minus her adjusted basis of $100,000.
[4]	Roxanne received money, not property.
[5]	She immediately invested all the money received.
[7]	The new property is identical to the old, except for location.
[8]	Assume that Roxanne will make the right election.
[9]	None of Roxanne's realized gain is recognized.
[10]	The basis of the new property is equal to the basis of the old property, plus Roxanne's additional investment of $100,000. This produces a basis of $200,000.

FIGURE 9

LIKE-KIND EXCHANGES OF PROPERTY

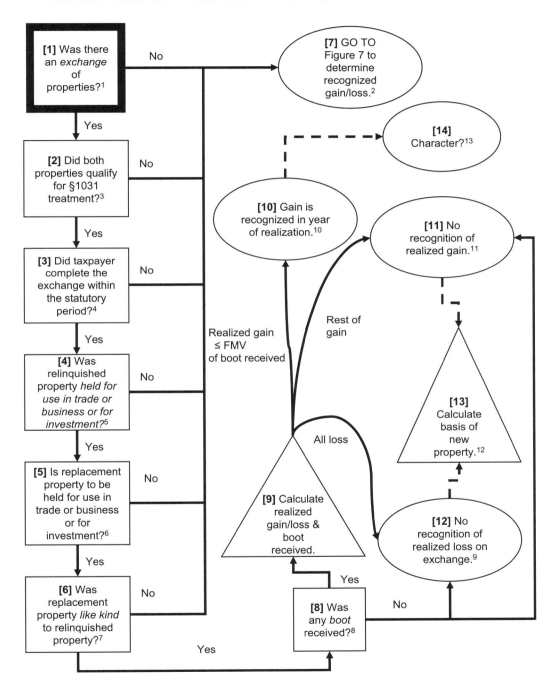

NOTES TO FIGURE 9

LIKE-KIND EXCHANGES OF PROPERTY

[1] IRC §1031 applies only to exchanges (trades) of property, not to sales. See ELO, Chap. 10 (VII); CT, pp. 87–88.

[2] If any of the requirements of §1031 are not met, the gain will be recognized in the year of realization. If loss is realized, it may be recognized, if allowed by the loss deduction rules. See Figures 4A–4D.

[3] Inventory, partnership interests, stocks, bonds, and notes are not eligible for §1031 treatment. In addition, personal use property is not eligible for §1031.

[4] Some exchanges will be made on a deferred basis, and others with three parties. There are strict statutory periods for completing deferred exchanges, and strict rules for the participation of facilitators. If a taxpayer engages in a deferred exchange, he or she must comply with the identification (45 days) and receipt (180 days) requirements of IRC §1031(a)(3) in order for the exchange to qualify.

[5-6] The taxpayer must have held the relinquished property and must intend to use the replacement property in a trade or business or for investment. Each taxpayer in the exchange is analyzed independently.

[7] Like kind means similar in character and nature. Most real estate is like kind to other real estate, but personal property is separated into classes.

[8] Boot is any nonlike-kind property, including cash, non-qualifying property and the assumption of liabilities by the other party to the exchange.

[9] No loss is recognized on the exchange of properties in a qualifying §1031 exchange.

[10] The realized gain will be recognized up to the amount of boot received. Another way to say this is that gain is recognized in the amount of the lesser or the boot received or the realized gain.

[11] The amount of realized gain in excess of the FMV of the boot received will be deferred until the taxpayer disposes of the property—if ever.

[12] The basis of the property received is equal to the basis of the property transferred, plus the gain recognized, minus the FMV of the boot received, minus the loss recognized, plus any additional investment by the taxpayer. The basis of any boot will be its FMV.

[13] If gain is recognized, its character as capital or ordinary must be determined. See Figures 10A–10C.

EXAMPLE TO FIGURE **9**

LIKE-KIND EXCHANGES OF PROPERTY

Mike owns Property A, which is farmland. Mike has a basis of $100,000 in Property A, and he holds it for investment. Mike trades Property A for Property B, which was owned by an unrelated party. Property B is a parking lot. Mike also receives $10,000 in cash. Property B is worth $80,000. Mike intends to use Property B in his business. What are the tax consequences of this transaction to Mike?

Box Number in Figure	Analysis
[1]	Mike exchanged Property A for Property B.
[2]	Property A and Property B are real property, both of which qualify for §1031 treatment.
[3]	This was a simultaneous exchange, not a deferred exchange.
[4]	Mike held Property A for investment.
[5]	Mike intends to hold Property B for use in his trade or business.
[6]	These properties are both real estate, and therefore like kind.
[8]	Mike received $10,000 of boot.
[9]	Realized gain or loss: Mike had an adjusted basis of $100,000 in Property A. His amount realized was $90,000 ($10,000 in cash and $80,000 in the form of Property B). His realized *loss* is $10,000.
[12]	No loss is recognized on the transaction, even though he received boot. Mike should have sold Property A and then purchased Property B in order to maximize his chances of recognizing the loss.
[13]	Mike's basis in Property B equals $90,000: $100,000 (is basis in Property A) + $0 (gain recognized) − $10,000 (FMV boot received) = $90,000.

FIGURE 10A

CHARACTER OF GAIN OR LOSS

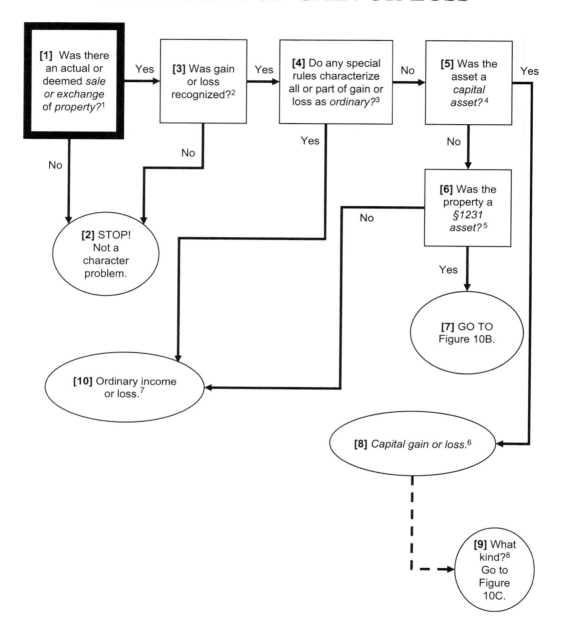

Notes to Figure 10A

CHARACTER OF GAIN OR LOSS

[1] A sale or exchange requires a giving, a receipt, and a connection between the two. The Code "deems" a sale or exchange to occur in a number of situations. For example, worthlessness of a security is a deemed sale/exchange under IRC §165(g). In addition, the transaction must involve "property," not just a substitute for ordinary income. See ELO, Chap. 12 (III); CT pp. 92–95.

[2] The character of gain or loss is only relevant if the gain or loss is recognized.

[3] Consider whether §1245 or §1250 (recapture) or §1244 (small business stock) recharacterizes as ordinary what would otherwise be capital gain or loss. See ELO, Chap. 12 (III); CT, pp. 94–95.

[4] A capital asset is *any* asset other than the nine enumerated categories listed in IRC §1221. See ELO, Chap. 12 (III); CT, pp. 93–94.

[5] A §1231 asset is real or depreciable property used in a trade or business (not property held for investment). See ELO, Chap. 12 (IV); CT, pp. 94–95.

[6] Capital gain is taxed at lower rates than ordinary income; capital losses are subject to significant restrictions on deduction. Taxpayers prefer *capital gain* to ordinary income and *ordinary loss* to capital loss. See ELO, Chap. 12 (II); CT, pp. 92–95.

[7] Ordinary income is generally taxed at higher rates than capital gain, and ordinary losses are generally more usable for taxpayers than capital losses. However, qualified dividend income is taxed at the same rates as 15% capital gain. See ELO, Chap. 13 (II); CT, pp. 92, 97.

[8] Capital gains and losses must also be categorized into four types of gain or loss. This process is illustrated in Figures 10B and 10C. See ELO, Chap. 12 (II); CT, pp. 95–96.

EXAMPLE TO FIGURE 10A

CHARACTER OF GAIN OR LOSS

Justin is an avid collector of antique automobiles. This year, he sold a 1927 Bentley for $200,000 more than he paid for it. He wants to know if he has capital gain or ordinary income from this transaction.

Box Number in Figure	Analysis
[1]	There was a sale of property.
[3]	Because he sold the car, no deferral statutes apply. Gain will be recognized.
[4], [10]	If Justin had claimed MACRS with respect to the automobile, all or a portion of the gain on the sale will be ordinary income. However, it is not clear from the facts whether he did, and in any event, collectible cars are generally not subject to wear and tear and therefore are not depreciable.
[5]	Was the car a capital asset? Assuming that it is not inventory for Justin (he is a collector, not a dealer), this would constitute a capital asset for him.
[8]	The gain should be capital in nature.
[9]	What kind of capital gain? Go to Figure 10B.

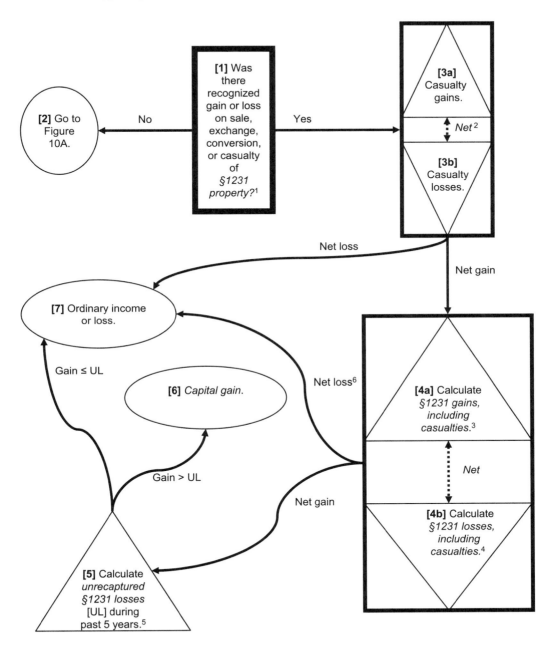

FIGURE 10B

SECTION 1231 GAIN OR LOSS

SECTION 1231 GAIN OR LOSS

[1] A §1231 asset is real or depreciable property held for more than one year and held for use in a taxpayer's trade or business (not for investment or personal use). When such assets are sold, exchanged, or involuntarily converted, the recognized gain or loss is §1231 gain or loss. See ELO, Chap. 12 (IV); CT, pp. 94–95.

[2] Net all of the taxpayer's casualty losses and casualty gains on §1231 property. If these losses exceed gains, all of the losses and gains will be considered ordinary, resulting in an ordinary loss. If losses do not exceed gains, all the casualty losses and gains or §1231 assets are put into the netting process in the next step.

[3] Add up all of the taxpayer's gains on the sale, exchange, conversion or casualty of §1231 assets. The amount taken into account here is the gain after depreciation recapture. Depreciation recapture is taken into account separately. (See Box [5] in Figure 10A.)

[4] Add up all of the taxpayer's losses on the sale, exchange, conversion or casualty of §1231 assets.

[5] If the result is a net gain, the gain is capital in nature, except to the extent of unrecaptured §1231 losses (UL) during the last five years.

[6] If the result is a net loss, it is an ordinary loss.

SECTION 1231 GAIN OR LOSS

Debi is in the business of growing and selling heritage vegetables. This year, she experienced the following events:

Sale of Equipment #1:	$5,000 Loss
Sale of Equipment #2 (net of depreciation recapture):	$2,000 Gain
Business furniture destroyed by fire (uninsured):	$6,000 Loss
Grant of easement to county under threat of condemnation:	$12,000 Gain
Sale of stock held for investment:	$10,000 Gain

Debi held all of the items described above for more than one year. Debi had $500 of unrecaptured §1231 loss in prior years. Debi did not replace the easement pursuant to §1033. What are the tax consequences of these events to Debi?

Box Number in Figure	Analysis
[1]	Debi has recognized gain or loss from the sale, conversion and casualty of §1231 property—real or depreciable property used in her trade or business (equipment, furniture, and easement).
[2]	The stock is not §1231 property. Go to Figure 10A to analyze this sale.
[3a], [3b]	Debi's casualty losses on §1231 property ($6,000) do not exceed casualty gains on such property ($12,000). Therefore, the casualty losses go into the next netting step for all §1231 gains and losses.
[4a]	Total §1231 gains: $14,000.
[4b]	Total §1231 losses: $11,000. She has a net §1231 gain of $3,000.
[5], [6], [7]	Debi's unrecaptured loss is $500. Therefore, of her net gain of $3,000, $2,500 will be capital and $500 will be ordinary.

FIGURE 10C

CALCULATING THE TAX ON CAPITAL GAINS

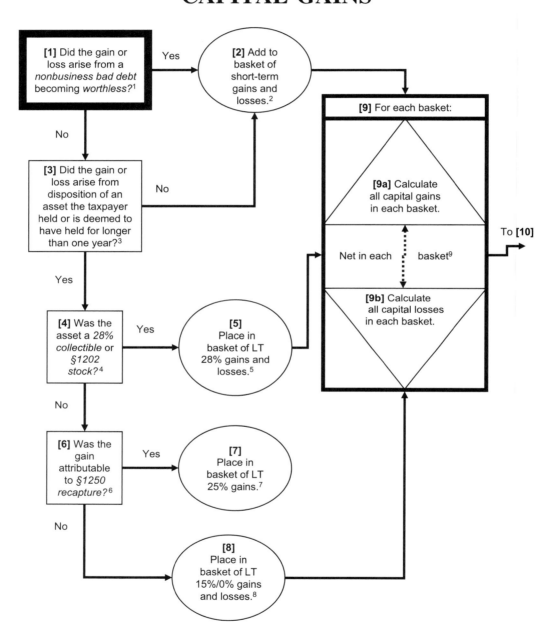

FIGURE 10C (*cont.*)

CALCULATING THE TAX ON CAPITAL GAINS

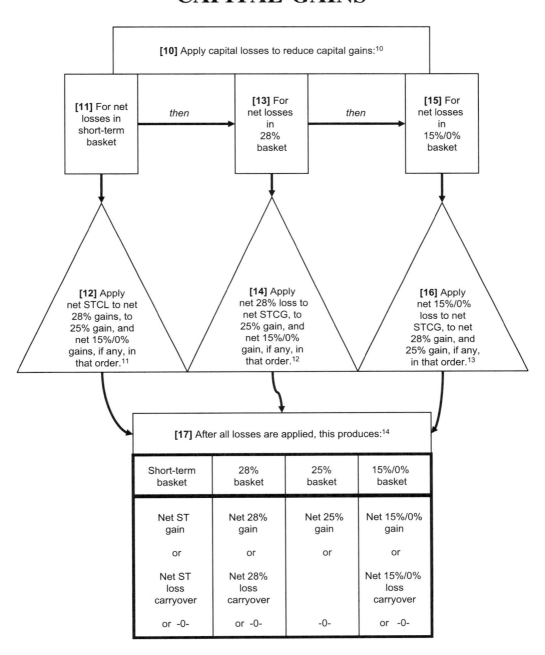

CALCULATING THE TAX ON CAPITAL GAINS

[1] A nonbusiness bad debt is treated as a short-term capital gain (STCG), regardless of the period of time the taxpayer held the debt. IRC §166(d)(1)(B).

[2] The "basket" approach requires that capital gains and losses be categorized and placed in a basket with all similar gains and losses. For example, all the short-term capital gains and losses will be placed in the "short-term basket" for the netting process and application of capital losses. There will be four baskets of capital gain/ loss: short-term; 28%; 25%; and 15%/0%. See ELO, Chap 12 (V); CT, pp. 95–96.

[3] A taxpayer's holding period is the period of time he or she actually owned the property, plus the period of time another person owned the property if that person's holding period can be "tacked" on to the taxpayer's holding period. For example, the recipient of a gift tacks the donor's holding period to his or her own. "Long-term" means that the taxpayer has held the asset for one year or longer. See ELO, Chap. 12 (V); CT, pp. 95–96.

[4] A collectible is an item such as a painting, antique, stamp collection, and so forth. IRC §1202 excludes from Gross Income a percentage of the gain on the sale of certain qualifying stock, and the included percentage is 28% gain. See ELO, Chap. 12 (V); CT, pp. 95–96.

[5] All of the gains and losses from 28% property are combined into the 28% basket.

[6] 25% long-term capital gain is gain from the sale or exchange of real property attributable to prior depreciation that has not been recaptured as ordinary income under §1250. See ELO, Chap. 12 (V); CT, pp. 95–96.

[7] The 25% basket will only have gains, not losses, so netting will not be required.

[8] 15%/0% capital gain or loss is capital gain or loss that does not fall into any other category.

[9] The netting process requires that all of the gains and losses in each "basket" be computed and compared. More losses than gains in a category will produce a net loss in that basket. More gains than losses in a basket will produce a net gain in that basket.

[10] Capital gains are deductible only to the extent of capital losses, and for individuals, $3,000 per year of ordinary income. IRC §1211(b). Therefore, the losses in each category are applied to reduce the gain in each of the other categories in the specified order. See ELO, Chap. 12 (V); CT, pp. 95–96.

[11] The amount of short-term capital loss (STCL) reduces on a dollar-for-dollar basis the net gain in the 28% basket, if any. If there is no 28% gain, or if any STCL is left over after application to the 28% basket, it is then applied to reduce gain in the 25% basket, if any. If there is no 25% gain, or if any STCL is left over after application to 25% gain, it is applied to reduce gain in the 15%/0% basket. See ELO, Chap. 12 (V).

[12] The amount of 28% capital loss (CL) reduces on a dollar-for-dollar basis the net gain in the short-term basket, if any. If there is no STCG, or if any 28% CL is left over after application to the short-term basket, it is then applied to reduce gain in the 25% basket, if any. If there is no 25% gain, or if any 28% CL is left over after application to 25% gain, it is applied to reduce gain in the 15%/0% basket. See ELO, Chap. 12 (V).

[13] The amount of 15%/0% CL reduces on a dollar-for-dollar basis the net gain in the short-term basket, if any. If there is no STCG, or if any 15%/0% CL is left over after application to the short-term basket, it is then applied to reduce gain in the 28% basket, if any. If there is no 28% gain, or if any 15%/0% CL is left over after application to 28% gain, it is applied to reduce gain in the 25% basket. See ELO, Chap. 12 (V).

[14] After the netting processes in Boxes [12], [14], and [16] are complete, the taxpayer will have the results in this figure. Keep these in mind when computing the tax. A net loss in a category carries over to future years, retaining its nature as ST, 28%, or 15%/0%, to be applied against future years' capital gain in the various categories.

EXAMPLE TO FIGURE 10C

CALCULATING THE TAX ON CAPITAL GAINS

Ron experiences the following tax events this year:

- His ZZZ stock, in which he had a basis of $100,000, became worthless.
- He sold a collectible painting, in which he had a basis of $250,000, for $50,000.
- He sold ABC stock, in which he had a basis of $120,000, for $300,000.
- His former friend, Ken, reneged on a debt to him of $60,000.

Ron had held the ZZZ stock, the painting, and the ABC stock for longer than one year. What are the tax effects of these events to Ron?

Box Number in Figure	Analysis
[1], [2]	The debt to Ken is a nonbusiness bad debt and is placed in the basket of short-term gains and losses.
[3]	All the rest of the assets were held for longer than one year, so they produce long-term capital gain or loss.
[4], [5]	The painting is a collectible. The $200,000 loss is a 28% long-term capital loss.
[6], [7]	There is no gain in the 25% category.
[8]	The sales of stock are in the 15%/0% category. The worthlessness of ZZZ stock produces a long-term capital loss of $100,000. The sale of the ABC stock produces a $180,000 long-term capital gain.
[9]	Netting: Short-term capital loss: $60,000 28% long-term capital loss: $200,000 15%/0% long-term capital gain: $80,000 ($180,000 gain on ABC stock netted against $100,000 loss on ZZZ stock)
[10]	Apply capital losses to reduce capital gains.
[11], [12]	Apply STCL of $60,000 to reduce LTCG to $20,000.
[13], [14]	Apply $20,000 of 28% long-term capital loss to reduce 15%/0% long-term capital gain to -0-.
[17]	Net result: $180,000 28% long-term capital loss to carry forward to future years, retaining its character as 28% long-term capital loss.

FIGURE 11

PUTTING IT ALL TOGETHER

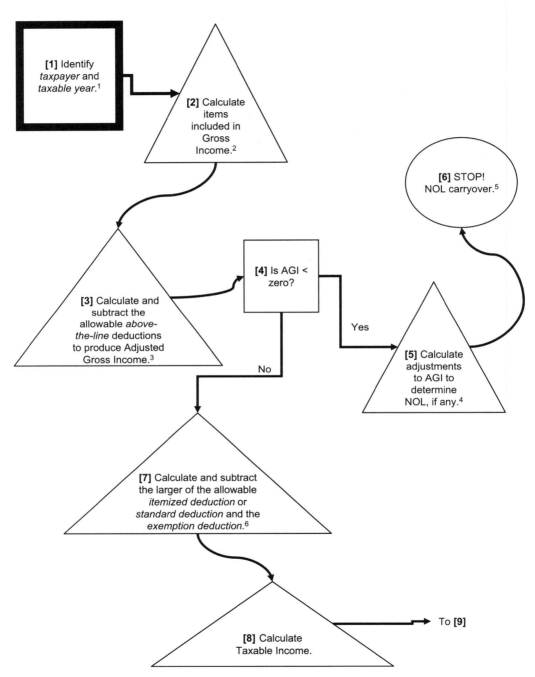

FIGURE 11 (*cont.*)

PUTTING IT ALL TOGETHER

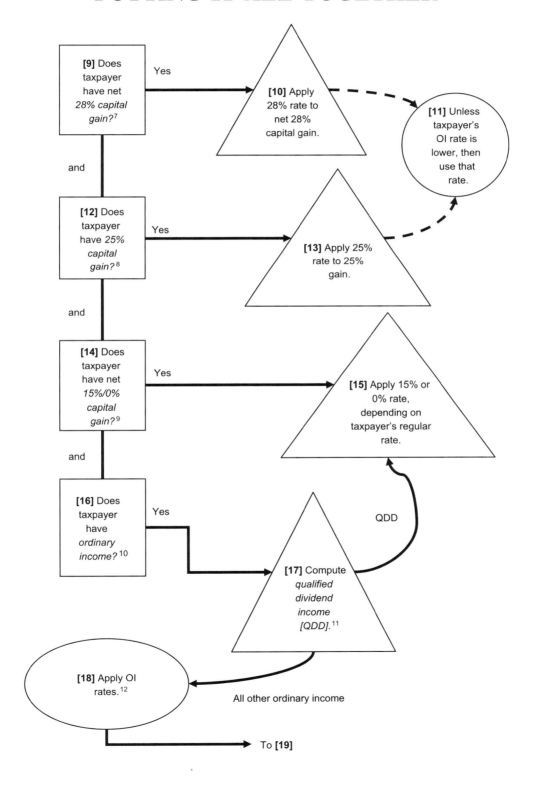

FIGURE 11 (*cont.*)

PUTTING IT ALL TOGETHER

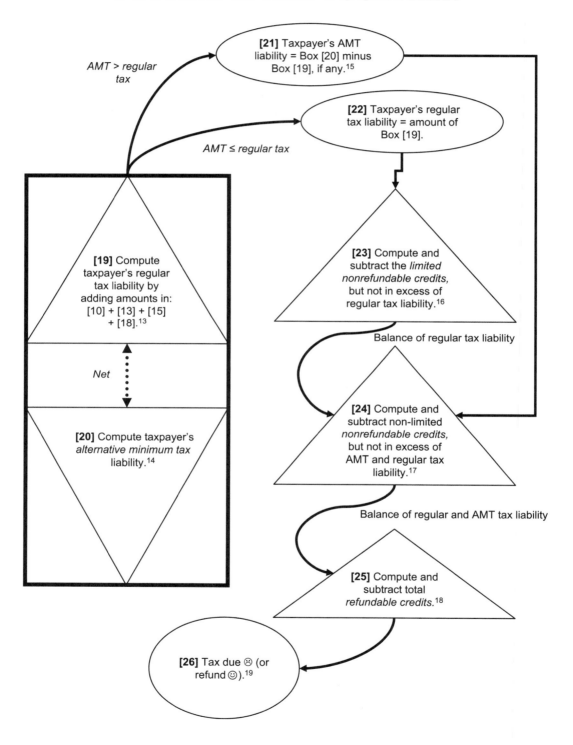

Notes to Figure 11

PUTTING IT ALL TOGETHER

1 Consider which taxpayer has income or expenditures, and consider application of assignment of income principles. See ELO, Chap. 14; CT, pp. 100–101. Every taxpayer has a taxable year, and items of income and deduction must be allocated to the proper tax year using the taxpayer's method of accounting. See ELO, Chap. 11; CT, pp. 89–90.

2 See Figures 2, 7, 8, 9, and 10A–10C.

3 See Figures 3A–3C and 4A–4D.

4 Only if the taxpayer has a negative AGI could he or she have a net operating loss (NOL). Certain adjustments must be made to a negative AGI to determine the existence of an NOL: No deduction is allowed for an NOL; capital losses are allowed only to the extent of capital gains; the 50% exclusion for gains from the sale of certain small business stock is not allowed; and deductions not attributable to a trade or business are allowed only to the extent of income not derived from the trade or business. See IRC §172(d).

5 If a NOL exists, there will be no tax in the current year. The NOL will carry forward 20 years and carry back 2 years (and for certain 2008 losses, a longer carryback is allowed). See ELO, Chap. 11; CT, p. 90.

6 See Figures 3A–3C and 4A–4D.

7 See Figure 10C.

8 See Figure 10C.

9 See Figure 10C.

10 Ordinary income is any income that is not capital gain.

11 Qualified dividend income is generally dividends received during the tax year from domestic corporations and certain qualified foreign corporations. However, if a shareholder does not hold a share of stock for more than 60 days during the 120-day period beginning 60 days before the ex-dividend date, dividends from the stock are not qualified dividend income.

12 Ordinary income is taxed at higher rates than capital gain. This is why taxpayers prefer capital gain to ordinary income. See ELO, Chaps. 12 (II), 13 (II); CT, p. 92.

13 The taxpayer's regular tax liability will be the sum of his or her tax on ordinary income plus the sum of his or her tax on capital gains.

14 The alternative minimum tax (AMT) is designed to ensure that all taxpayers pay at least some tax. The AMT system requires that certain adjustments be made to Taxable Income, eliminating or deferring some deductions in computing alternative minimum Taxable Income. Then the AMT is applied. See IRC §§55, 56; ELO, Chap. 13 (III); CT, p. 97.

15 If the taxpayer's AMT is larger than his or her regular tax, the taxpayer's tax AMT liability will be equal to the difference. See ELO, Chap. 13 (III).

16 The usefulness of certain nonrefundable credits is limited, in that they cannot offset AMT, but may offset only regular tax liability. These are: Education Credits (§25A), Foreign Tax Credit (§27), Dependent Care Credit (§21), and Elderly and Disabled Credit (§22). See ELO, Chap. 13 (IV)–(IX); CT, pp. 97–100. Because these are "nonrefundable credits," however, they can only be used up to the amount of the taxpayer's regular tax liability—i.e., they do not generate a refund.

17 Certain nonrefundable credits may be claimed up to the amount of the taxpayer's remaining regular tax liability and the taxpayer's AMT: IRA Credit (§25B), Child Credit (§24), and Adoption Credit (§23), Residential Property Energy Credit (§25D), and the credit for certain qualified plug-in vehicles (§30D).

18 The refundable credits are the Taxes Paid Credit (§31), the Earned Income Credit (§32), certain Business Credits (§38), a portion of the Child Credit (§24) and the First-Time Homebuyer's Credit (§36). See ELO, Chap. 13; CT, pp. 97–100.

19 This is the "bottom line" for the taxpayer: his or her tax liability or refund.

EXAMPLE TO FIGURE 11
PUTTING IT ALL TOGETHER

This year, David has the following items of income and expense. In addition, he paid $28,000 in federal income tax withholding.

Salary:	$100,000
Net long-term 28% capital gain:	$20,000
Net long-term 15% capital gain:	$10,000
State and local income tax:	$15,000
Charitable contributions	$10,000
Dependent care expenses for two children:	$12,000

What is David's tax liability? To make the arithmetic simple, assume that he is subject to a flat 30% tax on ordinary income and is entitled to a $3,000 personal exemption for himself, and $3,000 for each of his dependent children. Further assume he is not subject to the AMT.

Box Number in Figure	Analysis
[1]	David is the relevant taxpayer.
[2]	His Gross Income is $130,000, which is the sum of his salary and capital gain income.
[3]	In this example, he has no above-the-line deductions, so his AGI = $130,000.
[7]	David should itemize—i.e., he should claim the itemized deduction for his charitable contributions and state income taxes, for a total itemized deduction of $25,000. He can claim $9,000 in personal exemptions.
[8]	Therefore, his Taxable Income is $96,000.
[9]	David has $20,000 of 28% gain, which results in a tax of $5,600.
[14]	David has $10,000 of 15% gain, which results in a tax of $1,500.
[16]	David's other income (net of deductions) is $66,000. He is taxed (in our example) at 30%, which produces a tax of $19,800.
[19], [22]	David's regular tax = $5,600 + $1,500 + $19,800 or $26,900.
[23]	David may deduct a $1,200 Dependent Care Credit, reducing his tax liability to $25,700.
[25]	David may deduct a taxes-paid credit equal to the amount of the tax withheld during the year, or $28,000. This is a refundable credit.
[26]	David is due a refund of $2,300 (the difference between the amount paid in and his tax liability).

CAPSULE SUMMARY

SUMMARY OF CONTENTS

CHAPTER 1

GETTING STARTED IN FEDERAL INCOME TAX

See Flow Charts: Figure 1 (The Big Picture)

I. UNDERSTANDING THE BIG PICTURE

The process of computing tax liability is summarized below and can be traced in IRS Form 1040 and in Flow Charts, Figure 1: The Big Picture on page 3.

Gross Income
– Certain Deductions
   Adjusted Gross Income
– Standard Deduction *or*
   Itemized Deduction
– Personal Exemption
   Taxable Income
×Tax Rate(s)
   Tentative Tax
– Tax Credits
   Tax Due or Refund

A. Gross Income—§61: Gross income includes all income from whatever sources derived. IRC §61(a). Income from compensation, dividends, gains from dealings in property, and discharge of debt are common types of income. However, particular Code sections exclude certain types of income from gross income.

B. Deductions: Deductions are subtractions from income in computing taxable income. There are two types of deductions available in computing taxable income:

   1. Deductions from gross income in computing adjusted gross income: Certain expenditures are deducted (subtracted) from gross income in computing adjusted gross income (AGI).

   2. Deductions from adjusted gross income in computing taxable income: The taxpayer subtracts his or her personal exemptions and then takes the larger of either the standard deduction or the itemized deduction. The standard deduction is the sum of certain statutorily set amounts, and the itemized deduction is the sum of the taxpayer's allowable itemized deductions.

C. Multiply taxable income by the tax rate(s): The taxpayer's tax rate, which depends on his or her filing status, is multiplied by taxable income to produce the "tentative tax." The tax rates applicable to individuals range from 10 percent to 35 percent for ordinary income and 15 percent to 28 percent for capital gain, with some kinds of capital gain escaping tax altogether for taxpayers with relatively low amounts of other kinds of taxable income. IRC §1. The alternative minimum tax is a separate tax imposed on some taxpayers, with tax rates of 26 percent and 28 percent. IRC §55(b)(1).

D. Subtract available tax credits: A tax credit is a dollar-for-dollar reduction in the amount of tax due. Available tax credits are subtracted from the tentative tax to produce the actual tax due.

E. Six fundamental tax questions: Tax problems—and the material in this book—can be summarized in six fundamental issues.

1. **Who is the taxpayer?** Identifying the relevant taxpayer is critical. Families often try to rearrange income and deductions so as to minimize the tax on the family as a whole, while the IRS seeks to match income and deductions to the right taxpayer.

2. **Does the taxpayer have income?** To begin the analysis of a taxpayer's tax liability, it is necessary to identify his or her income in a theoretical sense and in the sense of §61. We construe income broadly.

3. **What deductions may the taxpayer claim?** The income tax is a tax on net income, not gross income. Therefore, taxpayers are entitled to reduce gross income by certain deductions, principally personal and business deductions. We construe deductions narrowly.

4. **Timing issues:** Once income and deductions are identified, the next question is when—*in which taxable year*—a taxpayer must include an item of income in gross income and when a taxpayer may claim a deduction. Taxpayers seek to defer income as far into the future as possible, and accelerate deductions to the earliest possible year.

5. **Character of income and loss:** When income or loss arises from the sale or exchange of property, it is necessary to characterize it as ordinary or capital. Taxpayers prefer capital gain to ordinary income, because capital gain is subject to preferential, lower tax rates. Taxpayers prefer ordinary loss to capital loss because the deductibility of capital losses is restricted.

6. **Rates and credits:** The final step in calculating a taxpayer's tax liability is determining the appropriate rate of tax and subtracting available tax credits. The tax rate depends on the status of the taxpayer, the amount and character of the taxpayer's income and the type of tax (AMT or regular tax).

II. SOURCES OF TAX LAW

Title 26 of the United States Code is the statutory base for all federal tax law, including the federal income tax. The Department of the Treasury, through the Internal Revenue Service (IRS), and the courts offer guidance on ambiguous provisions of the Code.

A. Administrative interpretation: The Department of the Treasury issues regulations (temporary, final, or proposed) interpreting various Code provisions as well as revenue rulings, revenue procedures, notices, announcements, private letter rulings, and technical advice memoranda on various issues.

B. **Judicial interpretation:** The U.S. Tax Court, the U.S. District Court, the U.S. Court of Federal Claims, and the U.S. Bankruptcy Courts are trial courts for tax matters. Cases are appealed to the appellate court for the circuit in which the taxpayer lives and then to the U.S. Supreme Court.

  1. **U.S. Tax Court—litigate without first paying tax:** A taxpayer may adjudicate tax matters in the U.S. Tax Court without first paying the tax, if the taxpayer files a petition within 90 days of the date of the Statutory Notice of Deficiency (90-day letter).

  2. **U.S. Bankruptcy Court:** A bankruptcy court has jurisdiction over tax matters of the debtor, and may stay proceedings in the U.S. Tax Court regarding tax matters.

  3. **Other courts—pay first, then litigate:** To litigate in the U.S. District Court or the U.S. Court of Federal Claims, the taxpayer must first pay the tax and file a claim for refund. If that claim is either denied or ignored, the taxpayer can sue for refund.

C. **Deference to IRS interpretation:** The courts interpret ambiguous statutory material in cases properly brought before them. The courts will properly give deference to an IRS-published, prelitigation interpretation of a Code provision. This means that the court will adopt the IRS's interpretation of a Code provision if it is a "reasonable" interpretation of the statute. The IRS's interpretation need not be the only reasonable interpretation or even the "best" interpretation. It need only be a reasonable interpretation. If, however, there is no published, prelitigation interpretation by the IRS, the courts need not give deference to the IRS's interpretation, and may select the interpretation that seems most reasonable.

III. TAX ETHICS

A taxpayer has a responsibility to file an accurate and non-frivolous tax return. A lawyer can advise a client to take a return position only if the lawyer abides by the applicable ethical rules imposed by the state bar association. The IRS itself regulates practice before it by imposing certain standards and the ABA has promulgated its recommended standard: A position must have a "realistic possibility of success on the merits if litigated." However, most tax lawyers observe the requirements of IRC §6694, which imposes penalties on preparers of tax returns that take "unreasonable positions." An unreasonable position is one that does not have substantial authority (if not disclosed) or which does not have a reasonable basis (if disclosed). Higher standards apply to tax shelters. Certain civil and criminal penalties attach to an inaccurate tax return.

IV. READING TAX STATUTES

Any statute is made up of two parts: its domain (the set of facts to which it applies) and its effect (the consequences of the statute applying). Consider using a five-step process—called parsing—to understand the domain and effect of an unfamiliar statute.

A. **The general rule:** Find the statute's general rule and underline it in red.

B. **Definitions:** Find the statute's terms of art and definitions and highlight these in yellow.

C. **Exceptions and special rules:** Find the statute's exceptions and special rules and mark them with a green "X."

D. **Related statutory material:** Find the statute's explicit and implicit references to related material and circle these in blue.

E. **Summarize domain and effect:** Summarize the statute's domain and effect in the margin in your own words.

V. TAX POLICY

The wisdom of a particular tax statute can be evaluated using three criteria: fairness of the system, its administrative practicality, and its economic impact.

A. **Fairness:** The U.S. income tax burden is allocated among taxpayers based on their "ability to pay." A "fair" system imposes similar taxes on those with similar abilities to pay (horizontal equity). It is impossible to measure each taxpayer's ability to pay directly, and thus taxable income is the surrogate for a taxpayer's ability to pay. If a tax statute causes the system to be more accurate in distinguishing among various taxpayers' abilities to pay, it is more "fair" than a provision that does not do so.

B. **Administrative practicality:** A good tax statute will assess and collect tax in a cost-effective manner and will not require undue governmental interference with a taxpayer's life.

C. **Economic effects:** Taxpayers change their behavior in response to tax statutes, and proponents of a taxing measure must consider the effects (both intended and unintended) that the measure likely will have on taxpayer behavior.

CHAPTER 2

IDENTIFYING GROSS INCOME

See Flow Charts: Figure 2 (Analyzing Income)

I. IRC SECTION 61—INCOME

The linchpin of the Code, §61, defines gross income as "all *income* from whatever source derived" (emphasis added). Thus it is important to define "income" in order to determine what is included in gross income (even if later it is excluded by another statute).

II. DEFINITIONS OF INCOME

A. **Haig-Simons definition—theoretical approach:** Under this approach, income is the sum of (1) the market value of rights exercised in consumption, plus (2) the change in the value of the store of property rights between the beginning and end of the period in question (usually a taxable year). The Haig-Simons definition defines a comprehensive tax base, but difficulties may arise in measuring all consumption and in valuing assets each year.

B. **"Economic benefit"—a more practical approach:** Under this approach, income is the value of any economic benefit received by the taxpayer regardless of the form of the benefit.

1. **Tangible items:** The receipt of cash or other property generates income under this approach, even if it comes from an unusual source, such as a windfall.

2. **Barter:** The exchange of services for services constitutes income to both service providers. See Rev. Rul. 79-24, 1979-2 C.B. 60.

3. **Intangible benefits:** The receipt of an intangible benefit would be included in gross income under this approach. For example, if one taxpayer satisfies another taxpayer's legal obligation, the latter has income in the amount of the satisfaction. *Old Colony Trust Co. v. Commissioner*, 279 U.S. 716 (1929). But noneconomic benefits (such as enjoyment of one's job) are not income under this principle.

III. CERTAIN ITEMS THAT ARE NOT INCOME

Certain items are not considered income by general understanding of that term in federal tax law, even though they might qualify as "income" under a theoretical definition of income.

A. **Imputed income:** The value of any services one performs for oneself or one's family and the value of any property used that one owns are imputed income, which is not considered income for purposes of federal income tax.

B. **Capital recovery:** A taxpayer's income from the sale or exchange of property is his or her profit on the transaction, not the total amount received. A taxpayer is entitled to receive his or her capital investment in the property tax-free, although the timing of this recovery is a matter for legislative determination.

C. **Loans:** Neither the creation nor the repayment of a loan is a taxable event. However, forgiveness or discharge of a loan may generate income to the debtor.

CHAPTER 3

SPECIFIC INCLUSIONS IN GROSS INCOME

See Flow Charts: Figure 2 (Analyzing Income)

I. SECTION 61

Section 61 provides that gross income includes "all income" from all sources. Courts construe §61 broadly to include most types of income in gross income, unless they are specifically excepted by statute.

II. SPECIFIC ITEMS

Section 61(a) provides a nonexclusive list of types of income specifically included in gross income.

A. Compensation income—§61(a)(1): Compensation income is the consideration transferred for the performance of services, whether in the form of salary, fees, commissions, or fringe benefits, and whether in the form of cash, property, or other services.

   1. **Amount included:** The amount of compensation income is the amount of cash received or the fair market value of the property or services received.

   2. **Timing issues:** The taxable year in which a taxpayer will include an amount of compensation income will depend on the taxpayer's method of accounting, and if compensation is paid in the form of property, the rules of §83.

   3. **Character:** Compensation income is ordinary income, potentially taxable at the highest tax rate.

B. Gross income from business—§61(a)(2): A taxpayer engaged in business as a sole proprietor will include his or her gross income from business and will subtract available deductions from that amount, reporting the net result (income or loss) on the tax return.

C. Gains derived from dealings in property—§61(a)(3): When a taxpayer sells property, his or her gain is the excess of the amount realized over the taxpayer's adjusted basis in the property. Sales can take many forms, some of which result in tax deferral.

D. Investment income—§61(a)(4)–(7): Various types of investment income are included in gross income, including dividends, interest (both explicit and imputed), rents, royalties, and income from annuities.

   1. **Imputed interest—OID rules, §§483, 7872:** Most loans explicitly provide for interest to be paid. Some, however, provide for no interest or a below-market rate of interest, and the Code often will recharacterize these loans or investments to impute interest to the transactions.

   2. **Annuities—§§61(a)(9), 72:** A taxpayer receiving a regular annuity payment is receiving a partial return of his or her invested capital, and the balance of the payment is income. To determine the amount of a payment that is excluded from gross income, multiply the payment by the exclusion ratio. The exclusion ratio is the following fraction:

$$\frac{\text{Investment in the contract}}{\text{Total expected return under the contract}}$$

The amount of the payment in excess of the excluded amount is included in gross income of the taxpayer, subject to certain limitations.

E. Alimony—§§61(a)(8), 71: A taxpayer receiving alimony must include it in his or her gross income. The federal definition of alimony governs the tax consequences of alimony payments, regardless of the label used under state law for the payment.

1. **Definition of alimony:** For a payment to qualify as alimony, it must meet six requirements: (1) it must be paid in cash, not in property or services; (2) the payment must be received by or on behalf of the spouse or former spouse pursuant to a divorce decree or separation instrument; (3) the decree must not designate the payment as nondeductible and nonincludable; (4) the payor and recipient must not be members of the same household at the time of the payment; (5) there must be no obligation to make a payment after the death of the recipient spouse; and (6) the payment must not be, in substance, support for the child of the payor (there is an incentive to characterize child support as alimony because alimony is deductible to the payor, and child support is not deductible).

2. **Front-end loaded alimony:** If alimony payments vary by more than $15,000 in the first three years, and the payments are greater in the beginning than at the end of the three-year period, they will be "front-end loaded." In that case, the "excess alimony amount" is included in the gross income of the payor spouse and is deducted from the income of the recipient spouse in the third post-separation year.

3. **Property settlements:** If an amount payable in divorce is not alimony or child support, it is likely a property settlement, governed by §1041.

F. **Discharge of indebtedness income—§61(a)(12):** Creation of a loan is not a taxable event to either the creditor or the debtor, for neither has a net economic benefit. If, however, the creditor forgoes collection under the debt, the debtor will have a benefit equal in amount of the debt forgone. This is discharge of indebtedness income and must be included in the debtor's gross income.

1. **Enforceable debt:** To have discharge of indebtedness income, there must be an enforceable debt in the first place. See *Zarin v. Commissioner*, 916 F.2d 110 (3d Cir. 1990).

2. **Identifying discharge:** A discharge occurs when the creditor agrees to accept something less than he or she originally agreed to take, in satisfaction of the loan. Payment of a debt is not discharge, nor is payment of a debt by another, or payment deferral. If the creditor receives what he or she bargained for, even if that amount is different from the amount loaned, there is no discharge.

3. **Contested liability doctrine:** If a taxpayer in good faith disputes the amount of the debt, a subsequent settlement of the debt is treated as the amount of the debt for tax purposes.

4. **Possible exclusion—§108:** Certain types of discharge of indebtedness income are excluded from the gross income of the taxpayer. The newest of these—ripe for testing—is the exclusion of gain on certain residential foreclosures. In general, if a taxpayer excludes discharge of indebtedness income, he or she may also be required to reduce his or her "tax attributes."

III. PRIZES, AWARDS, HELPFUL PAYMENTS, AND EMBEZZLEMENTS

Code sections other than §61 provide for specific inclusions in gross income, and judicial doctrines also include some amounts in gross income.

A. Prizes and awards—§74: Prizes and awards are included in gross income unless the recipient did nothing to be selected, the recipient is not required to render substantial future services as a condition of receiving the prize, and immediately transfers the prize to charity.

B. Helpful payments—§§82, 85, 86: Various types of helpful payments are included in gross income. Unemployment compensation is generally includable, although $2,400 is excludable in 2009. A portion of Social Security benefits received is also potentially includable, depending on the income of the recipient.

C. Embezzled funds: Embezzlers must include the proceeds of their embezzlements in their gross income unless they can show that the transaction is akin to a loan. See *Gilbert v. Commissioner*, 552 F.2d 478 (2d Cir. 1977).

D. Income in respect of a decedent: When a taxpayer dies with the right to income, it must be allocated to someone: the estate of the decedent, an heir, or someone else. Section 691 provides the rules of the road for this kind of income.

CHAPTER 4

SPECIFIC EXCLUSIONS FROM GROSS INCOME

See Flow Charts: Figure 2 (Analyzing Income)

I. EXCLUSIONS—IN GENERAL

When an item is excluded from gross income, even though it may be income in the sense of §61, a specific statute provides that it will not be included in gross income. Exclusions are construed narrowly; an item must fit within the precise domain of an exclusion statute in order to be excluded from gross income.

II. DEATH BENEFITS—§101

Amounts received under a life insurance policy by reason of the death of the insured are excluded from gross income.

A. Transfer for valuable consideration: The exclusion does not apply to payments made under policies that were transferred for valuable consideration; in that case, the exclusion is limited to the purchaser's purchase price under the contract.

B. Chronic or terminal illness: The exclusion extends to amounts paid to or for the care of chronically or terminally ill insureds.

III. GIFTS—§102

The recipient of a gift or an inheritance may exclude the cash or value of the property received from gross income, regardless of amount.

A. Definition: A gift is a transfer made with detached and disinterested generosity. See *Duberstein v. Commissioner*, 363 U.S. 278 (1960).

B. Exceptions

  1. Income from property: The exclusion does not apply to the income derived from property received by gift.

  2. Employee gifts: The exclusion does not apply to any transfer made by an employer to an employee; these amounts are considered compensation income, not gifts.

C. Basis—§1015: A recipient of property by gift or inheritance must determine the basis he or she has in the property.

  1. Property received by gift: The recipient of property by gift takes the donor's basis in the gift, plus a portion of any gift tax paid on the transfer. However, if at the time of the gift the fair market value of the property was less than its basis, for purposes of determining loss on subsequent sale or disposition, the basis is the fair market value of the gift on the date of the gift. IRC §1015(a).

  2. Property received by inheritance—§1014: The recipient of property through inheritance takes as his or her basis in the property the fair market value of the property on the date of the decedent's death or the alternate valuation date if that date is elected.

IV. INTEREST ON STATE AND LOCAL BONDS—§103

A taxpayer may exclude the interest on qualifying state and local bonds.

V. COMPENSATION FOR PERSONAL INJURY OR SICKNESS—§104

Section 104 excludes from gross income amounts received as a result of personal physical injury or sickness. This excludes compensatory damages from suit or settlement of personal *physical* injury actions (in lump sums or in structured settlements), but does not exclude punitive damages (except in very limited situations), previously deducted medical expenses, and pre- or postjudgment interest.

VI. DISCHARGE OF INDEBTEDNESS INCOME—§108

Certain types of discharge of indebtedness income may be excluded from gross income. The exclusion is generally conditioned on the taxpayer giving up certain tax benefits.

A. Types of discharge of indebtedness income excluded: Only certain types of discharge of indebtedness income are excluded under §108. Of these, the principal types are the following:

1. **Bankruptcy—§108(a)(1)(A):** If the discharge occurs in a Title 11 (bankruptcy) case, the discharge of indebtedness income is excluded from gross income.

2. **Insolvency—§108(a)(1)(B):** If the discharge occurs at a time the taxpayer is insolvent, the discharge of indebtedness income is excluded from gross income to the extent of the insolvency. Insolvency is the amount of the taxpayer's debts over the fair market value of his or her property.

3. **Certain farm debt—§108(a)(1)(C):** If the discharge is of "qualified farm indebtedness" the discharge of indebtedness income will be excluded from gross income.

4. **Certain real property debt—§108(a)(1)(D):** If the discharge is qualified real property business indebtedness, and the taxpayer is not a C corporation, the discharge of indebtedness will be excluded from gross income. Qualified real property business indebtedness is generally debt incurred in connection with real property used in a trade or business, and which is secured by that property.

5. **Qualified principal residence indebtedness:** If the discharge is of acquisition indebtedness for a taxpayer's principal residence, the discharge will generally be excluded from gross income if the discharge occurs before January 1, 2013. The limit on this exclusion is $2,000,000. IRC §108(a)(1)(E).

B. **"Paying the piper"—§108(b):** Each dollar of exclusion generally requires a reduction in the taxpayer's tax benefits—i.e., net operating losses, tax credits, capital loss carryovers, and other carryovers. The taxpayer may elect in some circumstances to apply the exclusion amount to reduce the basis of depreciable property. For example, the exclusion for qualified principal residence indebtedness requires the reduction of the taxpayer's basis in the property by the amount of the excluded discharge of indebtedness income. The result of this reduction is that the taxpayer will have a greater amount of income in the future.

VII. QUALIFIED SCHOLARSHIPS—§117

Amounts received as a "qualified scholarship," which generally means amounts received by degree candidates at regularly operated educational institutions for tuition, books, fees, and supplies, are excluded from gross income. A qualified scholarship does not include room and board or amounts paid for services.

VIII. EXCLUSION FOR GAIN ON SALE OF PRINCIPAL RESIDENCE—§121

Section 121 allows a taxpayer to exclude from gross income $250,000 ($500,000 for joint returns) of gain on the sale of a principal residence, if the taxpayer has owned and used the dwelling as a principal residence for at least two of the past five years.

IX. EMPLOYMENT-RELATED EXCLUSIONS

The Code provides a variety of employment-related exclusions.

A. **Meals and lodging—§119:** An employee may exclude from gross income the value of meals and lodging provided by an employer if the meals or lodging are provided for the convenience of the employer, are provided on the business premises of the employer, and in the case of lodging, the employee is required to accept the lodging as a condition of employment.

    1. **Convenience of the employer:** "Convenience of the employer" means that the employer has a "substantial noncompensatory business reason" for supplying the meals and lodging, considering all the facts and circumstances of the situation.

    2. **Business premises:** The business premises of an employer are the grounds of the employer's place of business. The circuits have split on whether the business premises for state police include all public roads and contiguous restaurants.

    3. **Condition of employment:** The condition of employment requirement is generally satisfied by showing that the employee is on call for the business of the employer.

B. **Statutory fringe benefits—§132:** The value of any fringe benefit that qualifies under §132 is excluded from the gross income of the employee. In some cases, the provision of the benefit must meet antidiscrimination rules.

    1. **No additional cost service—§132(b):** If the employer regularly provides the service to the public and provides it to the employee without incurring any significant additional cost, it will be excluded from the gross income of the employee who receives the service.

    2. **Qualified employee discounts—§132(c):** If employees enjoy a discount on property or services provided to the public by the employer, and the discount does not exceed a stated percentage, the value of the discount will be excluded from the gross income of the employees taking advantage of the discount.

    3. **Working condition fringe—§132(d):** An employee receiving a benefit that would have generated a deduction as a trade or business expense or as depreciation to the employee had he or she purchased the benefit individually may exclude the benefit from gross income.

    4. **De minimis fringe—§132(e):** If the benefit provided to the employees is so small that accounting for it would be unreasonable or administratively impractical, it will be excluded from the gross income of the employees receiving it.

    5. **Qualified transportation fringe—§132(f):** An employee who receives transit passes, van transportation, or parking may exclude the benefit from gross income, within specified dollar limitations.

    6. **Qualified moving expense reimbursement—§132(g):** If an employee receives reimbursement for amounts that would be deductible as moving expenses under §217, he or she may exclude these amounts from gross income.

7. **Athletic facility—§132(j)(4):** The value of an on-premises athletic facility may be excluded from the gross income of an employee if it is operated by the employer and is used mostly by employees.

8. **Qualified retirement planning services—§132(m):** An employer may provide financial planning services, if certain conditions are met.

C. **Insurance premiums and payments—§§79, 105, 106:** The cost of employer-provided health insurance premiums is excluded from the gross income of the employee. When an employee receives benefits, these are excluded from gross income up to the amount of the employee's medical expenses. The employee may also exclude the cost of employer-provided term life insurance attributable to coverage up to $50,000; premiums attributable to excess coverage are includable in the employee's gross income.

D. **Dependent care assistance—§129:** The employee may exclude up to $5,000 of employer-provided dependent care assistance in the form of actual care provided or as reimbursement.

E. **Educational assistance—§127:** The employee may exclude up to $5,250 of qualifying educational assistance provided by the employer.

F. **Adoption expenses—§137:** An employer may provide up to $12,150 (in 2009) of adoption assistance to employees, which may be excluded from their gross incomes, subject to certain income limitations.

G. **Unemployment Compensation—§85(c):** In 2009, a taxpayer may exclude up to $2,400 of unemployment compensation received.

X. EDUCATIONAL INCENTIVES

A. **Interest on U.S. savings bonds—§135:** To the extent the redemption proceeds of U.S. savings bonds are used for qualified education expenses, the income element of such redemption (interest) is excluded from gross income. Income level restrictions apply. IRC §135.

B. **Section 529 plans—§529:** Distributions from §529 plans, which are state-sponsored plans for education savings, are excluded from gross income to the extent they are used for qualified education expenses. Unlike many education incentives, these funds can be used for K–12 as well as postsecondary education.

C. **Education savings accounts—§530:** Distributions from education savings accounts (formerly known as Education IRAs) are excluded from gross income to the extent they are used for qualified education expenses. Unlike many education incentives, these funds can be used for K–12 as well as postsecondary education.

XI. CHILD SUPPORT—§71

A custodial parent may exclude child support received from his or her gross income.

XII. VOLUNTEER FIREFIGHTERS

Volunteer firefighters can exclude up to $360 per year in stipends and certain state tax breaks. IRC §139B.

CHAPTER 5

DEDUCTIONS—IN GENERAL

See Flow Charts: Figures 3A (Personal Deductions), 3B (Trade or Business Deductions), and 3C (Investment Deductions)

I. DEFINITION OF DEDUCTION

A deduction is a subtraction from income in computing adjusted gross income or taxable income.

A. Compare exclusion: By contrast, an exclusion causes an item of income not to be included in gross income. An exclusion and a deduction will have the same tax effect for taxpayers, but will reach this result by very different paths.

B. Compare tax credit: A tax credit is a dollar-for-dollar reduction in the amount of tax due.

II. ROLE OF DEDUCTIONS

Deductions figure prominently in two phases of computation of taxable income. One group of deductions is subtracted from gross income in computing adjusted gross income (AGI). Another group is subtracted from AGI in computing taxable income.

III. COMMON THEMES OF DEDUCTION CONTROVERSIES

Three common themes arise in deduction controversies.

A. An event: A taxpayer must experience an outlay, an outflow, or a loss in which there is no realistic possibility of recovery of the item. Deductions are narrowly construed, and each and every requirement of a deduction statute must be met.

B. Personal versus business expenses: A common theme in the analysis of deductions is the question whether an expense is "personal" or "business." This distinction is important because, as a general rule, personal expenses are not deductible unless a specific statute provides otherwise. Business expenses are generally deductible. Taxpayers seek to characterize deductions as business related, rather than personal, in order to deduct them.

C. Expense or capital expenditure? An expense may be deducted currently, but if an expenditure is for a capital item (a capital expenditure), its cost must be added to basis and be recovered in accordance with the statutory scheme governing capital recovery. Taxpayers prefer to characterize expenditures as expenses rather than capital expenditures in order to accelerate capital recovery.

CHAPTER 6

PERSONAL DEDUCTIONS

See Flow Charts: Figures 3A (Personal Deductions) and 4D (Personal Casualty Losses)

I. IN GENERAL—§262

While personal expenditures are not generally deductible, specific Code provisions allow a taxpayer to deduct certain personal expenses if the statutory requirements are met.

II. TWO KINDS OF PERSONAL DEDUCTIONS

A. "Above-the-line" deductions: This group of deductions is subtracted from gross income in computing AGI. Taxpayers seek to increase "above-the-line" deductions because AGI serves as a measure for certain itemized deductions, and lowering AGI will potentially increase the deductible portion of these itemized deductions.

B. "Below-the-line" deductions: This group of deductions is subtracted from AGI in computing taxable income and includes the personal exemption and either the standard or the itemized deduction. The itemized deduction is the sum of a number of deductions including home mortgage interest, taxes, casualty losses, medical expenses, charitable contributions, bad debts, and miscellaneous expenses.

III. "ABOVE-THE-LINE" PERSONAL DEDUCTIONS

A. Alimony—§215: A taxpayer may deduct the amount of alimony or separate maintenance paid during the year. Alimony has a special definition under federal tax law. §62(a)(10).

B. Moving expenses—§217: A taxpayer may deduct qualifying moving expenses associated with a move to a new place of employment 50 or more miles from the taxpayer's former employment. §62(a)(15).

C. Contributions to regular IRAs—§219: A taxpayer may claim a deduction for certain retirement savings. In general, an individual may deduct the lesser of $5,000 (2009) or his or her earned income to an individual retirement account (IRA). Taxpayers 50 years of age and older can make an additional contribution. If the taxpayer participates in a qualified plan and has income in excess of a certain amount, the contribution may be made, but no deduction is allowed. §62(a)(7).

D. Losses—§165: A taxpayer may deduct losses incurred during a taxable year that are not compensated for by insurance or otherwise. However, an individual taxpayer may deduct only three types of loss.

1. **Trade or business losses—§165(c)(1):** A taxpayer may deduct losses incurred in a trade or business.

2. **Investment losses—§165(c)(2):** A taxpayer may deduct losses incurred in an activity engaged in for profit, which does not constitute a trade or business. For example, losses on the sale of stock would be investment losses, but losses on the sale of a principal residence would not be, as a principal residence is held for personal, rather than investment, purposes. The IRS has taken the position that theft losses from Ponzi schemes, which a taxpayer incurs in an activity engaged in for profit, but not in a trade or business, properly belong in this category. See Rev. Rul. 2009-9, 2009-14 I.R.B. 735.

3. **Personal casualty losses—§165(c)(3):** A taxpayer may deduct certain casualty losses associated with property not held for investment or in a trade or business, such as losses from theft, fire, storm, and flood. Casualty losses up to the amount of casualty gains are deducted from gross income in computing AGI. The remaining deductible losses constitute an itemized deduction to the extent that they exceed a "deductible" and 10 percent of the taxpayer's AGI.

E. **Interest on education loans—§221:** Up to $2,500 of the interest paid on certain student loans is potentially deductible, as an above-the-line deduction. The deduction is phased out as income rises. §62(a)(17).

F. **Qualified tuition and related expenses—§222:** A taxpayer may claim a deduction for tuition and related expenses paid before January 1, 2010. The maximum deduction is $4,000 (for taxpayers whose AGI does not exceed $65,000 (single) or $130,000 (joint)) or $2,000 (for taxpayers whose AGI does not exceed $80,000 (single) or $160,000 (joint)). For taxpayers with higher incomes, the deduction is zero. §62(a)(18).

G. **Health savings accounts—§223:** A taxpayer subject to a high-deductible health plan can deduct certain contributions to a health savings account (HSA). §62(a)(19).

H. **Costs incurred in civil rights actions and whistleblower actions:** A taxpayer who incurs attorneys' fees or other costs in certain civil rights actions and tax whistleblower actions may deduct such expenses. There are only a limited number of actions that qualify, and otherwise the taxpayer would likely be required to deduct these amounts as miscellaneous itemized deductions. §62(a)(20).

I. **Certain other personal "above-the-line" deductions:** Taxpayers potentially may deduct certain other expenses, including up to $250 of classroom expenses for teachers, certain expenses of the armed forces reserves, certain costs of clean fuel vehicles, and various other expenses.

IV. THE CHOICE: STANDARD OR ITEMIZED DEDUCTION

A taxpayer may deduct either the standard or the itemized deduction, but not both. The rational taxpayer will choose the larger of the two. The standard deduction is the sum of various deductions: the basic standard amount, the aged/blind amount, the real property tax standard deduction (for 2009), and the motor vehicle sales tax deduction (for 2009).

§63(c)(1). The itemized deduction is the sum of the taxpayer's itemized deductions, which are discussed below.

A. Basic standard deduction: The basic standard deduction is $5,700 (single) or $11,500 (married filing jointly) (2009).

B. Real property tax standard deduction: The real property tax standard deduction is the lesser of the amount that the taxpayer pays in state or local real property taxes or $500 (single) or $1,000 (married filing jointly) (2009).

C. Motor vehicle sales tax standard deduction: In 2009, a taxpayer who purchases a new vehicle may claim as part of the standard deduction an amount equal to the sales tax on a maximum of $49,500 of the vehicle's purchase price.

V. ITEMIZED DEDUCTIONS

A number of deductions are available to the taxpayer only if he or she claims the itemized deduction. The principal itemized deductions are discussed below.

A. Interest—§163: Personal interest is not deductible. Personal interest is interest other than (1) trade or business interest, (2) investment interest, (3) qualified residence interest, or (4) passive activity interest.

    1. Investment interest—§163(d): A taxpayer may deduct interest to finance the purchase of investments, but only to the extent of net income from those investments.

    2. Qualified residence interest—§163(h): Qualified residence interest is deductible by individuals. There are three types of qualified residence interest attributable to loans on the taxpayer's principal residence and one other qualifying residence (which the taxpayer uses at least 14 days per year for personal purposes).

        a. Acquisition indebtedness: Interest is deductible on loans up to $1 million, the proceeds of which are used to acquire or construct a qualifying residence and which are secured by that residence.

        b. Home equity indebtedness: Interest is deductible on loans up to $100,000 that are secured by a principal residence and do not exceed the taxpayer's "equity" in the residence—i.e., the difference between the fair market value and any indebtedness secured by that residence.

        c. Qualified mortgage insurance premiums: Sometimes, a debtor purchases "mortgage insurance," which repays the mortgage if the borrower cannot. The premiums are prepaid or built into the monthly payment. If the mortgage insurance is provided by qualifying institutions, a portion of the premiums is treated as interest on home acquisition indebtedness, and thus deductible. A phaseout of this deduction occurs as AGI rises above $100,000. See IRC §163(h)(3)(E)(i).

B. Taxes—§164: A taxpayer may deduct state, local, and foreign real property, personal property, and sales or income taxes. A taxpayer may elect to deduct state/local sales taxes in lieu of income taxes. In addition, for 2009, there is a special motor vehicle sales tax deduction for the taxes attributable to the first $49,500 of the purchase price of a new vehicle. This deduction is phased out as AGI reaches $135,260. §164(b)(5).

C. **Personal casualty losses—§165(c)(3), (h):** A casualty loss is a loss through complete or partial destruction of property from a sudden, unexpected, and unusual cause such as fire or storm. A taxpayer may deduct personal casualty losses to the extent that they exceed (1) $100 per event ($500 in 2009) and (2) 10 percent of the taxpayer's adjusted gross income.

D. **Medical expenses—§213:** A taxpayer may deduct medical expenses, but only to the extent that they exceed 7.5 percent of his or her AGI. Medical expenses are expenses for the cure, treatment, or management of a disease or accident and include health insurance premiums paid by the taxpayer but do not include certain other items such as nonprescription drugs and certain elective cosmetic surgery.

E. **Charitable contributions—§170:** A taxpayer may deduct contributions to qualifying charitable organizations. The amount of the deduction is the amount of cash or the fair market value of any property contributed. Limitations based on a taxpayer's AGI are imposed; usually, this is 50 percent of AGI. The taxpayer must not receive a personal benefit as a result of the contribution.

F. **Miscellaneous expenses—§67:** A number of expenses are deductible only to the extent that they, in the aggregate, exceed 2 percent of the taxpayer's AGI. These include employee's unreimbursed business expenses and certain investment expenses.

VI. PERSONAL EXEMPTION—§151

A taxpayer is entitled to deduct a personal exemption for him or herself and for any dependent of the taxpayer. The amount is $3,650 for 2009. The personal exemption is phased out in pre-2010 years as income rises.

CHAPTER 7

BUSINESS AND INVESTMENT DEDUCTIONS

See Flow Charts: Figures 3B and 3C (Deductions), Figures 4B and 4C (Losses), Figure 5 (Basis), and Figure 6 (Capital Recovery)

I. IN GENERAL

Net business income is included in a taxpayer's gross income, and net loss from a business constitutes a deduction, subject to certain limitations. To compute net income or loss from business, a taxpayer begins with gross income from the business and subtracts available deductions. A taxpayer doing business as a sole proprietor reports this income and the available deductions on Schedule C and the net result (income or loss) is then reported on his or her own tax return, subject to certain limits on losses. A taxpayer who owns rental or royalty property will compute the income and deductions associated with this activity on Schedule E and report the net result (profit or loss) on his or her own tax return, subject to certain limitations. In both situations, it is critical to identify available deductions.

II. ORDINARY AND NECESSARY BUSINESS EXPENSES—§162

A taxpayer may claim a deduction for all the ordinary and necessary expenses paid or incurred in carrying on a trade or business, or while away from home, and rental payments for business property.

A. Five requirements: There are five distinct requirements for deduction of an expenditure under §162.

   1. **Ordinary:** Ordinary means "usual in the course of general and accepted business practice," arising from a transaction commonly encountered in the type of business in question, even if the expenditure is unique for the particular taxpayers. See *Deputy v. DuPont*, 308 U.S. 488 (1940). In addition, the expenditure must be reasonable in amount, and this particular issue often arises in the area of compensation.

   2. **Necessary:** There must be a reasonable connection between the expense and the furtherance of the business. Necessary means "appropriate and helpful" to the business, but the courts are reluctant to second-guess the judgment of business people, except in extreme cases.

   3. **Expense:** The expense requirement distinguishes between expenses (which may be deductible) and capital expenditures, which must be capitalized.

   4. **Trade or business:** To be deductible, the expense must be incurred in connection with a taxpayer's trade or business. The principal function of the trade or business requirement is to distinguish between personal activities and business activities.

      a. **Definition:** To be engaged in a trade or business, a taxpayer must be involved in an activity with continuity and regularity and must have the primary purpose of creating income or profit rather than merely engaging in a hobby. See *Commissioner v. Groetzinger*, 480 U.S. 23 (1987).

      b. **Hobbies:** A trade or business requires a profit motive, which is not characteristic of hobbies. Hobbies may generate income, and certain deductions attributable to them may be available under §183.

   5. **Carrying on:** The expense must be incurred during the time the taxpayer is actually engaged in carrying on a trade or business.

      a. **Going concern:** A taxpayer is carrying on a trade or business from the date that it is a going concern—i.e., has regular activity in the areas in which the business is organized.

      b. **Pre-opening expenses—§195:** Expenses incurred prior to opening must be capitalized. Up to $5,000 of expenses that would have been deductible if the taxpayer had been engaged in a trade or business when they were incurred can be deducted in the year of opening, but this amount is reduced by the amount by which pre-opening expenses exceed $50,000. Any remaining amount is amortized over 15 years.

B. Limits on deduction: Section 162 is riddled with exceptions and special rules; only the principal exceptions are discussed here.

    1. Public policy: No deduction is allowed for illegal bribes and kickbacks, for fines or similar penalties paid to the government, or for the two-thirds portion of the treble damages of antitrust damages.

    2. Excessive CEO compensation: There is no deduction for compensation of a chief executive officer of a publicly traded company in excess of $1 million unless it is performance based. Financial institutions that received subsidies in 2008 and 2009 are also subject to special restrictions on compensation.

III. CAPITAL RECOVERY FOR BUSINESS ASSETS

A. In general—§263: A taxpayer may not claim a current deduction for capital expenditures, generally defined as "permanent improvements or betterments made to increase the value of any property or estate."

    1. Capital recovery: When a capital expenditure is made, the cost is said to be "capitalized." The taxpayer will be entitled to recover that capitalized amount at some point during his or her ownership of the asset (capital recovery). "Recovery" means that the taxpayer's economic investment in the asset will constitute a tax benefit, either as a deduction during the ownership of the asset, or at sale when the taxpayer reports as gain the amount received in excess of his or her investment in the property.

    2. Timing: The timing of capital recovery is completely within the discretion of Congress. Taxpayers prefer to recover capital as soon as possible, preferring accelerated depreciation systems to systems that defer capital recovery until sale or other disposition of the asset.

B. Definition of capital expenditure: Neither the Code nor the regulations offer a precise definition of a capital expenditure.

    1. Separate asset test: If an expenditure creates a separate, identifiable asset with a useful life that will extend substantially beyond the taxable year, the expenditure is probably a capital expenditure. See *Commissioner v. Lincoln Savings & Loan Assn.*, 403 U.S. 345 (1971) and Reg. §1.263-2(a).

    2. Future benefits test: Even if a separate asset is not created, if an expenditure creates more than an insignificant future benefit, it is a capital expenditure. See *Indopco, Inc. v. Commissioner*, 503 U.S. 79 (1992).

C. Section 179 deduction: Section 179 allows a taxpayer to deduct up to a specified amount attributable to capital expenditures for equipment and tools purchased for the business. This deduction also reduces the basis of the asset(s) by the amount of the deduction claimed. In 2009, the §179 amount is $250,000, reduced by the cost of

§179 property the taxpayer places in service that exceeds $800,000, or the taxable income of the taxpayer, whichever is less.

D. Modified accelerated cost recovery system (MACRS) deduction for tangible business assets—§§167, 168: MACRS is the method by which taxpayers claim capital recovery for tangible business assets.

1. **Dual function of deduction:** The MACRS deduction is a deduction from gross income in computing net business income or loss. Each time the taxpayer claims an MACRS deduction, the basis of the asset is reduced by the same amount (producing the "adjusted basis" of the asset).

2. **Calculation of MACRS deduction:** The MACRS deduction is computed by applying the "applicable recovery method" to the "basis" of the asset over the "applicable recovery period," taking into account "applicable conventions."

    a. **Applicable recovery method:** Three different recovery methods are available under MACRS: straight-line and two accelerated methods.

    b. **Basis:** The basis of an asset is generally its cost, unless it is acquired by some other means.

    c. **Applicable recovery period:** The recovery period for an asset is the period of years over which the taxpayer claims capital recovery for the item. The recovery period for assets is defined by statute or by the IRS.

        i.   **Real property:** Residential real property has a recovery period of 27.5 years. Nonresidential real property has a recovery period of 39 years.

        ii. **Personal property:** Personal property can be 3-, 5-, 7-, 10-, 15-, or 20-year property. For example, office furniture is 10-year property.

    d. **Applicable conventions:** The applicable convention expresses the beginning date of capital recovery. Recovery generally begins when property is placed in service, and the conventions provide that regardless of when the property is actually placed in service, it will be deemed placed in service on a particular date. Real property uses a midmonth convention, and personal property a midyear convention.

E. Bonus depreciation: From time to time Congress enacts special depreciation rules designed to jump start investment in assets such as equipment, vehicles, etc. The typical approach is to allow a large percentage of the cost of the asset to be deducted in the year it is first used. In 2009, for example, 50 percent of the cost of certain new equipment can be deducted in the year it is placed in service. §168(k). Of course, this reduces the adjusted basis of the asset, but provides the taxpayer a significant tax benefit for making the purchase.

F. Section 197 intangibles: Section 197 allows a taxpayer to amortize the cost of "section 197 intangibles" ratably over 15 years. A §197 intangible includes purchased goodwill, going-concern value, covenants not to compete, patents, copyrights, secret formulas or processes, and various other intangibles.

IV. OTHER BUSINESS DEDUCTIONS

A taxpayer engaged in business may deduct taxes, interest, losses, bad debts, travel and entertainment expenses (within limits), and charitable contributions incurred in his or her business endeavors. The deduction for business automobile travel is measured on a per-mile basis (55 cents per mile in 2009) unless the taxpayer elects to calculate exact expenditures. See Rev. Proc. 2008-72, 2008-50 I.R.B. 1286.

V. RENTAL AND ROYALTY ACTIVITIES

A taxpayer who owns rental property, or property that generates royalties, probably is not engaged in a "trade or business." Nevertheless, the taxpayer may deduct the ordinary and necessary expenses incurred to generate this income and may depreciate or amortize assets that are subject to periodic capital recovery.

VI. SPECIAL RULES FOR LOSSES

Net loss from a trade or business, or from rental or royalty activities may be limited if the taxpayer does not materially participate or does not have sufficient amounts "at risk." See IRC §§465, 469.

CHAPTER **8**

MIXED BUSINESS AND PERSONAL EXPENSES

See Flow Charts: Figures 3A (Personal Deductions) and 3B (Trade or Business Deductions)

I. IN GENERAL

Business expenses are usually deductible, while personal expenses are not. Some expenses, however, have a mixed character. They are connected to the taxpayer's business, but also have a connection to his or her personal life. This mixed character raises questions about their deductibility. The Code takes a variety of approaches to these types of expenses.

II. ORIGIN TEST

For an expense to be deductible as a business expense, it must have its origin in the taxpayer's business, not his or her personal life. In making this determination, the courts will inquire into the so-called origin of the expense—the reason the expense was incurred—considering all the facts and circumstances of the situation. See *United States v. Gilmore*, 372 U.S. 39 (1963).

III. HOBBY LOSSES—§183

A taxpayer who has no profit motive for an activity may deduct only the expenses associated with the activity to the extent that such expenses are deductible under Code sections that do not require a profit motive (nonbusiness expenses) plus expenses in the amount equal to the gross income from the activity minus the nonbusiness expenses.

A. Existence of profit motive—Reg. §1.183-2: Whether a taxpayer has engaged in an activity for profit is to be determined from all of the facts and circumstances of the situation. The regulations offer nine factors indicative of a profit motive.

B. Exception—§183(d): If an activity produces income in three out of the five consecutive years ending in the year in question, it is rebuttably presumed to be engaged in for profit.

IV. SECTION 274 RESTRICTIONS

Section 274 imposes significant limitations on the deduction of certain business expenses.

A. Meals: A taxpayer must be physically present at meals, and the expense for the meal must not be lavish or extravagant. Only 50 percent of the cost of meals is deductible.

B. Entertainment: The taxpayer must be present at the entertainment, and the expense for the entertainment must not be lavish or extravagant. Only 50 percent is deductible.

    1. Directly related standard: For entertainment that does not occur in connection with a business meeting, the taxpayer must establish that the expense was directly related to the active conduct of the trade or business.

    2. Associated with standard: If the entertainment occurs immediately before or after a substantial and bona fide business meeting, the taxpayer must establish that the expense was associated with the active conduct of the trade or business.

C. Foreign travel: A taxpayer who engages in substantial personal activity while traveling outside the United States for more than one week is subject to significant restrictions on the deduction of travel expenses. In addition, significant restrictions are placed on expenses of travel on cruise ships outside the United States.

D. Business gifts: Regardless of the cost of a gift, a business-related gift can generate a deduction of only $25.

E. Substantiation requirements: A taxpayer must be able to prove his or her expenses by adequate substantiation. This is the requirement for all deductible or creditable expenditures, not just those for meals and entertainment.

V. HOME OFFICES AND VACATION HOMES—§280A

When a taxpayer uses a portion of his or her residence as an office or rents out a vacation home while still using it for part of the year for personal purposes, an allocation must be made between deductible (business) and nondeductible (personal) expenses associated with use of the residence.

A. Home offices: In order to deduct any expenses attributable to a home office, the taxpayer must use the office as the principal place of business, or as a place where the taxpayer regularly meets with patients, clients, or customers.

    1. Restriction on deductions: If the taxpayer meets this test, a portion of the expenses allocable to the business activity may be deducted, but not in excess of the gross income from the business minus the sum of the nonbusiness deductions plus business deductions not related to the use of the property.

    2. Remember §121: Section 121 allows a taxpayer to exclude from gross income some or all of the gain on the sale of a principal residence. This exclusion does not apply to deductions previously claimed for depreciation on a home. Thus, taxpayers must carefully consider whether it is worthwhile it to claim such a deduction.

B. Vacation homes: Deductions attributable to rental use of a home cannot exceed the percentage of those expenses equal to the total expenses multiplied by a fraction. The numerator of the fraction is the total number of days the unit is rented at fair rental value, and the denominator is the total number of days during the year in which the unit is used. This limitation does not apply to deductions that are allowable regardless of rental use, such as qualified residence interest.

VI. "LUXURY" AUTOMOBILES AND LISTED PROPERTY—§280F

A. Automobiles: Section 280F limits the amount of MACRS deductions that may be claimed each year for passenger automobiles, thus essentially disallowing depreciation for "luxury" automobiles.

B. Listed property: For certain types of property, the taxpayer will be required to use the straight-line method of depreciation unless the predominant use of the property is for business.

VII. GAMBLING LOSSES

Gambling losses are deductible only to the extent of gains from gambling.

CHAPTER **9**

TRANSACTIONS IN PROPERTY

See Flow Charts: Figures 5 (Basis), 6 (Capital Recovery), and 7 (Gain/Loss on Property Dispositions)

I. IN GENERAL

A six-step approach to sales or exchanges of property will ensure that all issues are addressed: (1) identifying transactions in "property," (2) identifying a realization event, (3) computing realized gain or loss, (4) determining the amount of recognized gain or loss, (5) determining the basis of property (not cash) received in the transaction, and (6) determining the character of any recognized gain or loss.

II. TRANSACTIONS IN PROPERTY

While most transactions in property are easy to identify—sales or trades of real estate, personal property, or stocks—in some situations it can be difficult to distinguish between sales of property and acceleration of streams of ordinary income. Only the former potentially generates gain or loss.

III. REALIZATION EVENT—§1001

A realization event occurs when a taxpayer exchanges property, receiving some materially different item. A "materially different" item of property is one that bestows on a taxpayer a different legal interest than what he or she had before. See *Cottage Savings Association v. Commissioner*, 499 U.S. 554 (1991). Thus, all sales and most exchanges will be realization events.

IV. REALIZED GAIN OR LOSS—§1001(a)

Realized gain or loss is equal to the difference between the amount realized on a sale or other disposition of property and the adjusted basis of the property transferred.

A. **Amount realized—§1001(b):** A taxpayer's amount realized on the sale or other disposition of property is equal to the sum of the cash and fair market value of property or services received, plus the amount of liabilities assumed by the other party to the transaction.

B. **Adjusted basis:** The adjusted basis of property is equal to its initial basis adjusted upward for improvements and downward for capital recovery (depreciation) deductions.

   1. **Basis—purchases—§1012:** The basis of property is usually equal to its cost. If a taxpayer performs services and receives property in payment, the amount the taxpayer includes in gross income as payment will constitute the basis of the property.

   2. **Basis—other transactions:** The basis of property received other than by purchase is determined under specific Code sections.

      a. **Property received from a decedent—§1014:** Property received from a decedent takes a basis equal to its fair market value on the date of death.

> **b. Property received by gift—§1015:** If property is received by gift, the donee generally takes the property with the same basis as the donor had in the property, increased by a portion of any gift tax paid. If, at the time of the gift, the adjusted basis of the property in the donor's hands is greater than its fair market value, for purposes of determining loss on sale or other disposition by the donee, the donee's basis is the fair market value of the property on the date of the gift.
>
> **c. Property received in divorce—§1041(d):** Property received incident to a divorce has the same basis that it had immediately prior to the transfer.

V. RECOGNIZED GAIN OR LOSS—§1001(c)

Realized gain or loss is generally recognized unless a specific Code section prohibits or limits recognition.

VI. BASIS OF PROPERTY RECEIVED IN THE SALE OR DISPOSITION

If the taxpayer sells property for cash, there is no need to determine the basis of the property received (since cash neither appreciates nor depreciates in value, there is no need to assign cash a basis for tax purposes). If, however, the taxpayer receives property in an exchange, the basis of that property must be determined, for later the taxpayer may sell or otherwise dispose of the property.

A. Full-recognition transactions: In a transaction in which the selling taxpayer recognizes all realized gain or loss, the property received will have a basis equal to its fair market value.

B. Nonrecognition transactions: In transactions in which the selling taxpayer does not recognize all or part of the realized gain or loss, the property received will have a basis different than its fair market value, determined under specific Code sections.

VII. CHARACTER

The character of the gain or loss recognized will depend on the nature of the asset in the hands of the transferor.

VIII. TRANSFERS OF ENCUMBERED PROPERTIES

In most sales or other dispositions of property, the selling taxpayer satisfies all mortgages or other encumbrances prior to sale. The repayment of a mortgage or other debt is not, in itself, a taxable event. In some situations, however, the taxpayer transfers the property subject to the debt; in other words, the buyer assumes the mortgage as part of the purchase price. In this situation, the consequences to the seller and purchaser must be considered.

A. **Mortgage amount less than fair market value:** If the mortgage on the seller's property is less than the fair market value of that property, the seller's amount realized includes the assumption of debt regardless of the nature of the debt as recourse or nonrecourse. The seller will compute realized gain in the usual fashion: amount realized (including the debt assumption) minus the adjusted basis of the property transferred. The buyer will include the debt assumption in basis as part of the cost of the property.

B. **Mortgage amount greater than fair market value:** If the mortgage on the seller's property exceeds the fair market value of that property, the nature of the mortgage as recourse or nonrecourse becomes important in determining the tax consequences of sale.

1. **Nonrecourse debt:** If the mortgage is nonrecourse, the seller's amount realized will include the full amount of the assumption, and the seller will compute realized gain in the usual fashion: amount realized (including the mortgage assumption) minus the adjusted basis of the property. Whether the buyer can include the total debt assumed as part of the purchase price is unclear; the buyer may be limited to the fair market value of the property as basis.

2. **Recourse debt:** If the mortgage is recourse, the buyer will not assume it because to do so would place the buyer's other assets at risk. Instead, a number of different transactions may occur with different consequences to the seller/debtor.

3. **Foreclosure or deed in lieu of foreclosure:** This is treated as two transactions. The foreclosure is a sale of the property for the price received at foreclosure (or the fair market value of the property if the debtor gives a deed in lieu of foreclosure). The gain or loss on the sale of property is equal to the difference between the amount realized and the adjusted basis of the home. For a principal residence, gain can be excluded under §121, but loss cannot be recognized. For investment properties, loss could be recognized. Then, the second part of the transaction is the discharge of the debt, if any. This can lead to discharge of indebtedness income, which may be excluded under §108 if any of the exclusions apply (such as the insolvency or qualified real property indebtedness exclusions). *Aizawa v. Commissioner*, 99 T.C. 197, aff'd 29 F.3d 630 (9th Cir. 1994).

CHAPTER 10

NONRECOGNITION TRANSACTIONS

See Flow Charts: Figures 8 (Involuntary Conversions) and 9 (Like-Kind Exchanges)

I. IN GENERAL

In some property transactions, realized gain or loss is not recognized in whole or in part at the time of the transaction. These transactions are called nonrecognition transactions and include like-kind exchanges, involuntary conversions, divorce transactions, and other transactions. When realized gain or loss is deferred rather than recognized, the property received in the transaction takes a basis that preserves that realized gain or loss for later recognition.

II. LIKE-KIND EXCHANGES—§1031

A. Requirements: There are five requirements for a qualifying like-kind exchange.

1. **Exchange of property:** The taxpayer must exchange property for property, rather than selling property or engaging in some other transaction. See *Jordan Marsh Co. v. Commissioner*, 269 F.2d 453 (2d Cir. 1959).

2. **Nature of property transferred:** The property transferred must not be inventory, stocks, bonds, notes, other evidences of indebtedness, interests in a partnership, certificates of trust or beneficial interest, or choses in action.

3. **Property transferred—use:** The taxpayer must have held the property transferred for use in a trade or business, or for investment. The IRS has recently issued guidance on the application of §1031 to vacation or second homes rented for part of the year.

4. **Property received—use:** The taxpayer must intend to hold the property received for use in a trade or business, or for investment. The IRS has recently issued guidance on the application of §1031 to vacation or second homes rented for part of the year.

5. **Like kind:** The property received must be like kind to the property transferred in the exchange. *Like kind* refers to the nature and character of the property rather than to its grade or quality.

   a. **Real property:** An exchange of real property for real property is a like-kind exchange regardless of the development status of the two properties. *Koch v. Commissioner*, 71 T.C. 54 (1978).

   b. **Depreciable personal property—Reg. §1.1031(a)-1(b):** The regulations offer a safe harbor for determining whether depreciable personal properties are like kind, in which properties of the same "class" are considered like kind. Properties outside the same class must be examined under the general like-kind test.

   c. **Other personal property:** Intangible and nondepreciable personal property and personal property held for investment must be examined under the general like-kind test.

B. Effect of qualifying like-kind exchange: If a taxpayer engages in a qualifying like-kind exchange of property for property, he or she will not recognize any of the realized gain or loss on the transaction.

1. **Effect of boot—§1031(b):** If the taxpayer receives boot (nonlike-kind property), the taxpayer will recognize gain, but not loss, in the amount of the lesser of the fair market value of the boot or the realized gain.

2. **Basis of property received—§1031(d):** The basis of like-kind property received in a like-kind exchange is equal to the basis of the property transferred, plus the gain recognized, minus the fair market value of the boot received, minus any loss recognized, plus any boot paid (additional investment in the property). The basis of any boot (nonlike-kind property) received is its fair market value.

C. **Deferred and three-party exchanges—§1031(a)(3):** A potential problem arises when the taxpayer wishes to transfer property in a like-kind exchange, but the potential buyer who wants the taxpayer's property does not have suitable property to exchange. This problem can be overcome by creating a deferred exchange, but the property to be received by the taxpayer must be identified within 45 days after the taxpayer relinquishes his or her property and must be received before the earlier of the 180th day after the date the taxpayer relinquishes his or her property or the due date of the taxpayer's return for the year of transfer of the relinquished property. Any intermediary used must meet specific identity requirements to avoid agent status.

D. **Effect of mortgages in like-kind exchanges**

1. **One mortgage:** If the property transferred in a like-kind exchange is subject to a mortgage, the transferee's assumption of that mortgage as a part of the transaction is treated as boot to the transferor. The mortgage assumption is also treated as boot for purposes of computing the taxpayer's basis in the property received.

2. **Two mortgages:** If both the property transferred and the property received are subject to mortgages assumed in the like-kind exchange, the regulations allow the "netting" of the mortgages. The party with the net relief from liabilities (i.e., whose property was subject to the higher mortgage at the outset) is treated as having received boot in the amount of the net relief from liability. The mortgage netting rule applies only to the computation of gain recognition; the full amounts of the mortgages are considered in the computation of basis of the properties received by each party.

3. **Two mortgages plus boot:** The mortgage netting rule allows the party with net assumption of debt to avoid recognition of gain. But this applies only to the mortgage portion of the transaction. If the person with net assumption of debt receives boot, the usual recognition rules will apply so that realized gain will be recognized to the extent of the fair market value of the boot received.

III. INVOLUNTARY CONVERSIONS—§1033

A taxpayer may be able to defer, in whole or in part, recognition of gain on the "involuntary conversion" of property.

A. **Conversion into similar property:** If a taxpayer's property is involuntarily converted into property that is similar or related in service or use, the taxpayer will not recognize any of the realized gain on the conversion.

B. **Conversion into money:** If the taxpayer's property is involuntarily converted into money, the taxpayer may elect to recognize gain in the amount of proceeds that are not reinvested in property similar or related in service or use to the converted property.

C. Similar property: Real property used in a trade or business or held for investment must be like kind to the property converted, invoking the same standard as in §1031. All other property must meet the "similar" standard, which is a stricter standard than "like kind." The similar standard requires that the properties have the same physical characteristics and that the taxpayer use the properties in the same way.

D. Statutory replacement period: The taxpayer must reinvest within two years after the close of the taxable year in which the taxpayer realizes any portion of the gain on conversion.

E. Basis of replacement property: The basis of the replacement property will be the basis of the property converted, plus the gain recognized, minus the unreinvested proceeds of conversion, minus any loss recognized on the conversion.

F. Inapplicable to loss: Section 1033 does not apply to loss realized on the involuntary conversion of property; those losses would be casualty losses, potentially deductible under §165(c)(2) and (3).

IV. SPOUSAL AND DIVORCE TRANSFERS—§1041

A. Nonrecognition: Section 1041 provides that no gain or loss will be recognized on transfers of property between spouses or on transfers incident to a divorce.

    1. Incident to a divorce: A transfer of property is incident to a divorce if it occurs within one year of the date the marriage is terminated, or if it is contemplated by the divorce decree and occurs within six years of the date of termination of the marriage (or later if there is a good reason for the delay).

    2. Indirect transfers: A transfer usually occurs directly from one spouse to the other. However, a qualifying transfer also can be made to a third person if made by direction or ratification of the other spouse or provided for in the divorce decree.

B. Effect of qualifying transfer to spouse or former spouse: The transferor in a §1041 transfer will not recognize gain or loss on the transfer. In addition, the recipient of property will not include any amount in gross income, and will take the property with the same basis as the property had immediately prior to the transfer.

C. Related material: Consider in connection with §1041 the rules relating to alimony and child support.

CHAPTER 11

TIMING OF INCOME AND EXPENSES

I. THE ANNUAL ACCOUNTING CONCEPT

Federal income tax returns are filed on an annual basis in which taxpayers tote up their income, deductions, and allowable credits for their taxable year, and apply the tax rates for that year to their taxable income.

A. **Calendar and fiscal years:** A taxpayer may use a calendar year or a fiscal year (which is a year other than a calendar year). Most individuals use a calendar year.

B. **Problems with annual accounting:** While annual accounting is administratively easy, it can inaccurately measure a taxpayer's ability to pay, particularly for transactions that span more than one taxable year. Several Code sections have evolved to address these difficulties.

1. **The net operating loss deduction—§172:** A taxpayer's excess of deductions over expenses constitutes a net operating loss that the taxpayer may carry back 2 years and forward 20 years. This allows the taxpayer to more accurately reflect income over a period of years. For losses incurred in 2008 by a qualifying small business, however, a special rule allows the taxpayer to elect to carry these losses back three, four, or five years (or to carry them forward).

2. **Claim of right doctrine and §1341:** A taxpayer must include amounts in gross income over which he or she has a claim of right and unfettered use, even if the taxpayer may be required to return all or a portion of the amount to another person. Section 1341 calculates the tax due if the taxpayer is required to return items previously included in gross income, in a taxpayer-friendly way.

3. **Tax benefit rule—§111:** The recovery of an item that constituted a deduction or credit in a prior year will be income to the taxpayer to the extent of the prior tax benefit. A "recovery" is an event that is fundamentally inconsistent with the previous deduction or credit.

II. METHODS OF ACCOUNTING

A. **Cash method of accounting:** A taxpayer using the cash method of accounting will report income when it is received, actually or constructively, and will claim deductions when amounts are actually paid (regardless of when they are due).

1. **Constructive receipt:** A taxpayer will be considered to have received items to which he or she had a right and had the ability to claim but did not do so.

2. **Restrictions on use of the cash method:** Some taxpayers may not use the cash method of accounting, as Congress has determined that it would unreasonably accelerate deductions for these taxpayers.

B. **Accrual method of accounting:** A taxpayer using the accrual method of accounting will report income when all events that fix the taxpayer's right to the income have occurred, and the amount thereof can be determined with reasonable accuracy. Accrual-method taxpayers will deduct expenses when all events that fix the liability have occurred and its amount can be determined with reasonable accuracy, subject to special rules that defer deductions until "economic performance."

III. ACCOUNTING FOR INVENTORIES

Taxpayers engaged in manufacturing and retail activities are required to account for inventories. Under an inventory approach, the taxpayer deducts from gross sales the cost of goods sold to determine the profit from sales for the year. Included in inventory are amounts attributable to the cost of manufacturing or purchasing the product, and certain taxpayers also must include in inventory an amount attributable to indirect costs (administrative costs, for example) under the UNICAP rules. Taxpayers identify inventory that is deemed sold in the cost of goods sold by adopting the LIFO (last-in, first-out) or FIFO (first-in, first-out) inventory methods.

IV. INSTALLMENT METHOD OF REPORTING INCOME—§453

When a taxpayer sells property other than inventory in a sale in which at least one payment will be received after the close of the taxable year, the taxpayer may report the gain realized on the sale over the period of time payments are received by using the installment method.

A. **Applicable to gain, not loss:** The installment method is applicable to gain, not loss. It is also not applicable to the interest portion of the transaction; interest is determined and accounted for separately.

B. **Amount includable in gross income:** The amount of gain to be reported each year is the payment for the year multiplied by the gross profit ratio, which is a fraction the numerator of which is the gross profit (sales price minus adjusted basis) and the denominator of which is the total contract price (amount to be received under the contract). The remaining amount of any payment is excluded from gross income as capital recovery.

V. RESTRICTED PROPERTY—§83

In many deferred compensation situations, the taxpayer receives property in exchange for the performance of services that is restricted in some fashion as to transfer or enjoyment. Section 83 defines (1) whether the taxpayer has income, (2) when the taxpayer has income, and (3) how much income the taxpayer has in these situations.

A. **Income?** A taxpayer potentially has income if there is a "transfer" of property to the taxpayer. An employer's setting aside of funds or property for the taxpayer's benefit is not income if the property can be reached by the employer's general creditors. But if the taxpayer has rights in the property that are not subject to the employer's creditors' claims, the taxpayer may have income.

B. **When?** A taxpayer must include the value of the property in gross income in the earlier of the first year in which the taxpayer owns the property without a requirement that he or she perform significant future services (i.e., the property is not subject to a "substantial risk of forfeiture") or the first year in which the property is transferable.

C. **How much?** The taxpayer includes in gross income the value of the property minus the amount the taxpayer paid for it. A taxpayer who receives restricted property may make what is known as a §83(b) election, in which the taxpayer elects, within 30 days of receiving the property, to include its value in gross income (minus amounts paid for it), even though it is restricted. This would be appropriate for restricted property that is expected to increase in value.

VI. SPECIAL LIMITATIONS ON LOSS DEDUCTIONS

In addition to the restrictions on deductible losses of §165(c), discussed above, the Code imposes additional loss restrictions on certain types of losses. These are properly viewed as timing rules because they potentially cause losses incurred in a particular taxable year to be deferred to future taxable years.

A. Passive losses—§469: Passive losses are losses from passive activities—i.e., activities that qualify as trades or businesses but in which the taxpayer does not materially participate. Passive losses incurred during a taxable year may be deducted only to the extent of the taxpayer's passive income for that year, and losses that are disallowed under this rule carry forward to future years when the taxpayer has passive income or disposes of the investment generating the passive loss.

B. Amounts at risk—§465: A taxpayer's losses from certain activities are limited to a taxpayer's amount "at risk"—i.e., the amount by which the taxpayer can be held liable to third parties upon failure of the venture. Losses disallowed by the at-risk rules carry forward to future years in which the taxpayer has amounts at risk.

CHAPTER 12

CHARACTER OF INCOME AND LOSS

See Flow Charts: Figures 10A–10C (Capital Gains and Losses)

I. IN GENERAL

When a taxpayer sells or exchanges property and recognizes gain or loss, the character of that gain or loss—as capital or ordinary—must be determined.

II. CAPITAL/ORDINARY DISTINCTION

The capital/ordinary distinction has implications for both income and loss.

A. Income—§1(h): Tax is imposed on an individual's ordinary income at rates up to 35 percent. However, the maximum rate on "net capital gain" is potentially much lower, ranging generally from 0 percent to 28 percent, with some capital gain escaping tax entirely for taxpayers with relatively small amounts of other kinds of income. Thus, taxpayers prefer to characterize income as capital gain subject to the preferential rate.

B. Loss—§1211: Section 1211 imposes a significant restriction on the deductibility of capital losses. Corporations may deduct capital losses only to the extent of their capital gains. IRC §1211(a). Individuals may deduct capital losses to the extent of their capital gain income, plus $3,000 of ordinary income. IRC §1211(b). Unused capital losses carry forward (and for corporations, carry back) to other taxable years.

III. AN APPROACH TO CHARACTERIZING GAIN OR LOSS

A. An approach to characterization problems—See Figure 10A: To characterize gain or loss as capital or ordinary, apply these five steps:

1. Was there an actual or deemed sale or exchange of property?

2. Was gain or loss recognized from that sale or exchange?

3. Was the property sold or exchanged a "capital asset"?

4. Does §1231 apply to treat gains as capital or losses as ordinary?

5. Do any special recharacterization rules apply to transform capital gain or loss into ordinary income or loss?

B. Did that event constitute a "sale or exchange" of "property"? For the taxpayer to have a capital gain or loss, the recognized gain or loss must arise from the "sale or exchange" of "property." This generally requires a "giving, a receipt, and a causal connection between the two." See *Yarbro v. Commissioner*, 737 F.2d 479 (5th Cir. 1984). Some events that might not otherwise meet this standard are deemed to be sales or exchanges by statute, such as losses from the worthlessness of stock or securities. Moreover, the item in question must constitute a sale or exchange of property, not the prepayment of income. See *Hort v. Commissioner*, 313 U.S. 28 (1941) (lease cancellation payment).

C. Was gain or loss recognized from that sale or exchange? For a taxpayer to have a capital gain or loss, there must be a realization event, and any gains or losses from that event must be recognized.

D. Was the property sold or exchanged a "capital asset"? For the taxpayer to have a capital gain or loss, the recognized gain or loss must be from sale or exchange of a property that qualifies as a "capital asset."

1. **Excluded categories:** Section 1221 defines a capital asset as "property held by the taxpayer (whether or not in connection with his trade or business)" except for eight enumerated categories of property, of which only five are usually important in the basic tax class. Thus, an item is a capital asset *unless* it falls within any of these five categories.

   a. **Inventory/stock in trade—§1221(a)(1):** A taxpayer's stock in trade or inventory held primarily for sale to customers in the ordinary course of business is not a capital asset.

      i. **Definition:** "Primarily" means "of first importance" or "principal." See *Malat v. Riddell*, 383 U.S. 569 (1966).

      ii. **Dealers:** To have inventory, the taxpayer must hold the property primarily for sale to customers in the ordinary course of business. It is the relationship of the taxpayer to the assets, not the taxpayer's status generally, that determines whether assets constitute inventory. See *Van Suetendael v. Commissioner*, 3 T.C.M. 987 (1944), aff'd, 152 F.2d 654 (2d Cir. 1945).

   iii. Real estate: Whether a taxpayer holds real estate as an investor or as a dealer depends on the analysis of seven factors discussed in *United States v. Winthrop*, 417 F.2d 905 (5th Cir. 1969).

b. Real and depreciable property—§1221(a)(2): Real property used in a trade or business or property used in a trade or business that is subject to depreciation under §167 is not a capital asset. This type of property is §1231 property, discussed below.

c. Creative works—§1221(a)(3): Creative works generated by the taxpayer, such as material subject to copyright, letters, and memoranda are not capital assets. There is an exception for certain musical works, for which the taxpayer may elect capital asset treatment.

d. Accounts/notes receivable—§1221(a)(4): A taxpayer's accounts or notes receivable from the sale of inventory are not capital assets.

e. Supplies—§1221(a)(8): Supplies and similar items used in a taxpayer's business are not capital assets.

2. "Related to" the trade or business: Relying on the case of *Corn Products Refining Co. v. Commissioner*, 350 U.S. 46 (1955), taxpayers asserted that items that were integrally connected with their trade or business should be treated as noncapital assets. In *Arkansas Best Corp. v. Commissioner*, 485 U.S. 212 (1988), the U.S. Supreme Court reexamined *Corn Products*, concluding that the relation of an asset to a taxpayer's business was irrelevant in determining its status as a capital or noncapital asset. In determining whether an item was included in the noncapital category of inventory, certain "inventory substitutes" could be included in that category. The Court limited the holding of *Corn Products* to an application of the inventory substitute idea.

E. Does §1231 apply to characterize gains as capital? See Figure 10B: Section 1221(2) excludes from the definition of a capital asset real and depreciable property used in a trade or business or held for investment—known as §1231 property. But all is not lost. Section 1231 may apply to treat net gains from this kind of property as capital and losses as ordinary.

   1. An approach to §1231: The first question is whether there was a sale or exchange, conversion or casualty of "§1231 property." If the property is not §1231 property, its character is determined under the usual rules set forth in Section III (A)–(D), above, and Figure 10A. Then, the taxpayer determines all of the recognized gains and losses from §1231 assets involving casualties, and if such losses exceed such gains, all are removed from the calculation. If such losses do not exceed gains, all are included, along with all other §1231 gains and losses, and the losses and gains are netted against one another. If the final result is a net loss, all §1231 gains and losses are ordinary. If the final result is a net gain, all gains and losses are capital, except to the extent of unrecaptured §1231 losses during the previous five years.

2. **Section 1231 property:** Section 1231 gains and losses arise from the sale of property used in the trade or business of the taxpayer, or from the involuntary or compulsory conversion of property used in the trade or business, or any capital asset held for more than a year and held in connection with the taxpayer's trade or business.

3. **Recapture rule:** The recapture rule may limit the recharacterization of gains as capital under §1231. If the taxpayer has had, within the previous five years, §1231 losses that were characterized as ordinary, the current year's gain must be characterized as ordinary to the extent of the previous loss.

F. **Do any special recharacterization rules apply?** Recognized gain or loss on the sale or exchange of a capital asset will usually be capital. However, the Code may, in certain circumstances, require all or a part of the gain or loss to be characterized as ordinary.

1. **Recapture for personal and real property:** The recapture provisions require that upon sale or exchange of property that would otherwise generate capital gain, a portion of the recognized gain be characterized as ordinary. Recapture thus seeks to account for the previous benefit of depreciation deductions taken with respect to the property.

   a. **Personal tangible property—§1245:** On the sale or exchange of depreciable personal property that otherwise qualifies as a capital asset or a §1231 asset generating capital gain, the portion of the gain equal to the lower of the realized gain or depreciation previously claimed with respect to the property will be characterized as ordinary. Any remaining balance will be capital.

   b. **Real property—§1250:** Section 1250 requires recapture of the accelerated portion of depreciation taken with respect to real property to be recaptured upon sale. However, because real property acquired since 1987 has been depreciated using the straight-line method, the practical impact of this provision is minimal today.

2. **Small business stock—§1244:** Individual taxpayers and partnerships may claim a portion of the loss on the sale or worthlessness of small business stock as ordinary rather than capital. The maximum amount considered ordinary is $50,000 for a single taxpayer or $100,000 for a married couple filing a joint return. A small business corporation is a corporation that issues the stock to the taxpayer in exchange for property and must have derived more than 50 percent of its income from active business sources during the five-year period ending on the date of the loss.

IV. CALCULATING CAPITAL GAIN AND LOSS—See Figure 10C

The final step in addressing character issues is determining the taxpayer's net capital gain (which is included in the taxpayer's gross income and is taxed at preferential rates) or deductible capital loss, and the net capital loss carryforward.

A. **Definitions:** Section 1222 sets forth a number of definitions relating to capital gains and losses that are relevant in calculating capital gain and loss. There are three baskets of capital gain/loss: the 28 percent group (collectibles); the 25 percent group (unrecaptured §1250 gain); and the 15/0 percent group (everything else). If a taxpayer is in the 10 or 15 percent bracket for ordinary income, he or she will enjoy the 0 percent rate on capital gains, but only to the extent theses gains exceed his or her ordinary income.

B. Holding period: Capital gains and losses must be characterized as long term or short term. Long-term gain or loss is gain or loss from the sale of an asset held for more than one year. Short-term gain or loss is gain or loss from the sale of an asset held for one year or less. The period of time during which a taxpayer owns (or is deemed to own) an asset is his or her holding period for the asset. The calculation of a taxpayer's capital gain and loss depends on the taxpayer's holding period of the assets generating capital gain and loss. The holding period usually begins with the taxpayer's acquisition of the asset, but in some cases, the taxpayer's holding period will include another person's holding period for the asset or the taxpayer's holding period for another asset.

    1. Exchanged basis property—§1223(1): For exchange transactions involving the transfer of capital or §1231 assets in which a taxpayer's gain is deferred in whole or in part, the taxpayer's holding period for the property received in the transaction will include the period the taxpayer held the property he or she transferred in the transaction. An example of this is the holding period for property received in a qualifying like-kind exchange.

    2. Transferred basis property—§1223(2): If a taxpayer receives property in a transaction in which the taxpayer's basis is determined by reference to another person's basis in the same property, the taxpayer's holding period includes the period of time that other person held the property. An example of this is the holding period for a gift.

C. An approach to calculating net capital gain and net capital loss: Figure 10C provides a systematic approach for calculating net capital gain and net capital loss. First, the taxpayer's long- and short-term capital gains and losses are categorized into each group (28 percent; 25 percent; and 15/0 percent). Then, the gains and losses in each group are netted against one another to produce gain or loss in each category. Then, any losses in the short-term, 28 percent, or 15/0 percent groups are applied to reduce gains in the other categories. This produces a net gain or a net loss in each category. The maximum rate of tax is the tax rate applicable to the group (such as 28 percent), but if the taxpayer's regular rate is lower, that rate will apply.

CHAPTER **13**

TAX RATES AND CREDITS

See Flow Charts: Figure 11 (Putting It All Together)

I. IN GENERAL

The applicable tax rate is applied to taxable income to produce the tentative tax. Available tax credits are subtracted from the tentative tax to produce the actual tax due.

II. TAX RATES

The current tax rate on ordinary income is progressive within a limited range, with tax rates for individuals ranging from 10 percent to 35 percent (in 2009). The specific rate applicable to an individual depends on his or her taxable income and filing status.

A. **Phaseouts:** As income rises, certain tax benefits are phased out, including the full benefit of the itemized deduction and the personal exemption.

B. **Children:** Children with sufficient income to owe tax file their own tax returns reporting their gross income and available deductions and credits. In some circumstances a child's parents may claim the child's investment income on the parents' return pursuant to the "kiddie tax."

C. **Preferential rates on capital gains:** Net capital gain is taxed at a maximum rate of 28 percent (collectibles), 25 percent (net unrecaptured §1250 gain), or 15 percent or 0 percent (everything else). If the taxpayer's rate on ordinary income is lower, the taxpayer gets the benefit of that rate.

D. **Qualified dividend income:** Qualified dividend income is subject to the 15/0 percent tax rate regime applicable to capital gains in the 15/0 percent category, removing the distinction between capital gain and ordinary income for many corporate distributions.

III. THE ALTERNATIVE MINIMUM TAX

A. **In general:** The alternative minimum tax (AMT) is a surtax imposed on taxpayers with certain kinds of income or deductions. The purpose of the AMT is to ensure that every taxpayer, even those with the kinds of activities that reduce tax through tax-exempt income or significant deductions, pay some amount of tax.

B. **AMTI:** The AMT is imposed on "alternative minimum taxable income" (AMTI). AMTI is computed by taking regular taxable income and adding back in certain items that were excluded and certain items that were deducted in the computation of regular taxable income. Important adjustments include the deduction for state taxes, the deduction for personal exemptions, the inclusion of certain tax-exempt interest, and a longer, slower depreciation period for certain assets.

C. **Exemption/tax rates:** The AMT is imposed on AMTI in excess of an exemption amount, which is $46,700 (single) and $70,950 (married filing jointly) (2009 amounts). The benefit of the exemption is phased out as income rises. The first $175,000 of AMTI is taxed at 26 percent and the balance of AMTI is taxed at 28 percent.

IV. TAX CREDITS

A tax credit is a dollar-for-dollar reduction in the amount of tax due. A refundable credit can reduce tax below zero, generating a refund. A nonrefundable credit can only reduce tax to zero and will not generate a refund. Increasingly Congress uses tax credits instead of deductions or exclusions to carry out its tax policy and other policy initiatives.

A. **Contrast deductions and exclusions:** While a tax credit is a dollar-for-dollar reduction in the amount of tax due, a deduction is a subtraction from either gross income or adjusted gross income in computing taxable income. Moreover, if an amount is excluded from gross income, it is never included in the computation of gross income.

B. **Credit for tax withheld—§31:** Perhaps the most familiar tax credit is the credit for the amount of tax withheld from wages, salaries, bonuses, and similar payments.

C. **Dependent Care Credit—§21:** Expenses for care of a dependent are not deductible, because they are personal expenses. Section 21 allows a taxpayer who maintains a household with at least one qualifying individual to claim a nonrefundable tax credit for certain expenses, equal to the taxpayer's "applicable percentage" multiplied by the "employment-related expenses."

   1. **Qualifying individual:** A qualifying individual is a dependent under the age of 13 for whom the taxpayer is entitled to a deduction as a dependent, or any other dependent or a spouse of a taxpayer who is physically or mentally unable to care for him- or herself.

   2. **Applicable percentage:** The taxpayer's applicable percentage ranges from 35 percent for taxpayers with AGI of $15,000 or less, to 20 percent for taxpayers with AGI above $43,000.

   3. **Employment-related expenses:** Employment-related expenses are those incurred for care of a qualifying individual while the taxpayer works, subject to two limitations.

      a. **Dollar limitation:** Employment-related expenses are limited to $3,000 for one qualifying individual and $6,000 for two or more qualifying individuals.

      b. **Earned income limitation:** Employment-related expenses are limited to the earned income of a single taxpayer, or if a married couple files a joint return, to the earned income of the lesser-earning spouse. Special rules impute an amount of income to students and disabled taxpayers for purposes of this limitation.

   4. **Coordination with §129:** Section 129 allows a taxpayer to exclude from gross income up to $5,000 of dependent care assistance provided by an employer. A taxpayer may not claim both the exclusion and the tax credit for the same dollar of dependent care assistance.

D. **Earned income tax credit:** A low-income "eligible individual" may claim a refundable tax credit. To compute the amount of the credit, the "credit percentage" is multiplied by the taxpayer's earned income, up to a certain amount known as the "earned income amount." Then, from that figure is subtracted the taxpayer's "phase-out percentage" multiplied by the taxpayer's AGI, reduced (but not below zero) by the phaseout amount. These percentages and amounts vary depending on the income and family status of the taxpayer. See chart.

1. Eligible individual: An eligible individual is an individual with a dependent child under the age of 19 or a taxpayer who is a U.S. resident between the ages of 25 and 65 and who cannot be claimed as a dependent on another person's tax return.

2. Earned income amount: Earned income includes wages, salary, and self-employment income.

3. The chart below gives the 2009 amounts for computing the earned income credit.

Qualifying Children	Credit Percentage	Earned Income Amount	Threshold Phaseout Amount—Single	Threshold Phaseout Amount—Joint
0	7.65%	$5,970	$7,470	$10,590
1	34%	$8,950	$16,240	$19,540
2	40%	$12,570	$16,240	$19,540
3 or more	45%	$12,570	$16,230	$19,540

E. **Higher education credits:** Section 25A allows taxpayers to claim tax credits for certain education expenses. The American Opportunity Tax Credit (formerly known as the HOPE scholarship credit) is a credit of up to $2,500 per student of qualified education expenses for the first four years of undergraduate work. It is partially refundable. The Lifetime Learning Credit is a credit equal to 20 percent of up to $2,000 of certain qualifying educational expenses. Income level restrictions apply. It is a nonrefundable credit.

F. **First-Time Homebuyer Credit:** Section 36(h) allows a first-time homebuyer to claim a refundable credit of up to 10 percent of the purchase price of a principal residence purchased before December 1, 2009, with a maximum credit of $8,000. If the taxpayer sells the home within 36 months, or ceases to use it as his or her principal residence, the credit is recaptured upon sale. Otherwise, this credit is a significant subsidy to the purchase of a residence.

G. **Making Work Pay Credit:** Section 36A allows a taxpayer to claim a refundable credit equal to the lesser of 6.2 percent of the taxpayer's modified AGI or $400 ($800 for married taxpayers filing jointly). The credit is phased out by reducing the available credit by 2 percent of the amount by which the taxpayer's modified AGI exceeds $75,000 ($150,000 for married taxpayers filing jointly). The credit is available in 2009 and 2010.

H. **Other tax credits:** The Code contains a variety of other tax credits usually given less attention in the basic federal income tax course.

1. **Child tax credit—§24:** A taxpayer may claim a credit for $1,000 per child, with income limitations starting at $75,000 for single taxpayers, and $110,000 for married taxpayers. This is a partially refundable credit.

2. **Blind/elderly/disabled tax credit—§22:** A taxpayer who qualifies as blind, elderly, or disabled is entitled to an additional tax credit.

3. **Adoption expense credit—§23:** A taxpayer who incurs certain qualifying adoption expenses may claim a credit for these expenses, but this credit is phased out as AGI rises.

4. **Foreign tax credit—§901:** A taxpayer may claim a deduction for certain foreign income and other taxes paid or may choose to claim a credit for these taxes. A credit is usually more valuable than a deduction for foreign taxes paid or accrued.

CHAPTER 14

IDENTIFYING THE TAXPAYER

I. IN GENERAL

The identification of the proper taxpayer to report income and claim deductions is crucial in maintaining a tax system that fairly allocates income among various taxpayers.

II. "PERSONS" SUBJECT TO TAX

Both natural persons and legal entities may be subject to tax.

A. Individuals—§1: Individuals are subject to tax at rates ranging from 10 percent to 35 percent (in 2009). Single individuals, including children, file a tax return reporting only their income. Married couples can, and usually do, file a joint return reporting their combined income and deductions. Married couples have the option of filing separately, but usually do not, as this can produce a higher joint tax liability.

1. **Child's services income—§73:** Income from a child's services is reported on the child's tax return, even if the parent is entitled to the income under state law.

2. **The kiddie tax—§1(g):** A child's investment income may be subject to tax at the parental rate, and parents may elect to report a child's investment income on the parents' tax return. A "child" is a person under age 19, or under age 24 if a full-time student.

B. Legal entities: A legal entity—such as a corporation, partnership, estate, or trust— may be required to file a tax return reporting its items of income, deduction, and credit. These are usually beyond the scope of the basic tax class.

III. ASSIGNMENT OF INCOME

In a progressive tax system, an incentive exists for those in high tax brackets to direct income to related persons in lower tax brackets in order to reduce the overall tax imposed on the group. This strategy is known as "assignment of income." Because assignment of income threatens to undermine the integrity of the progressive tax structure, a variety of judicial and legislative responses have arisen over the years to combat it.

A. Judicial views on services income: A common scenario involves the taxpayer who performs services for compensation but attempts to direct the compensation to another person (usually a relative in a lower tax bracket) prior to receiving it.

   1. Diversion by private agreement: If a taxpayer who performs services attempts to direct the compensation to another person by private agreement, the taxpayer (not the transferee) will be required to include the amount in gross income. See *Lucas v. Earl*, 281 U.S. 111 (1930).

   2. Diversion by operation of law: By contrast, if the law governing the legal relationships provides that both the taxpayer and another person have legal rights to the income, the tax consequences will follow from these legal relationships. As a result, the taxpayer and the other party will include their proportionate shares of the income in gross income. See *Poe v. Seaborn*, 282 U.S. 101 (1930).

B. Judicial views on income from property: If an owner of income-producing property gives some interest in the property to another person, the issue arises of which person (the donor or donee) should be taxable on the income from the property.

   1. Transfers of property: If the donor transfers the property itself, the donee will properly report the income from the property.

   2. Transfers of income only: The general rule is that attempts to transfer only the income from the property to another, without a transfer of the property itself, will be respected only if the income interest is transferred for its entire duration. Otherwise, the donor will be taxed on the income and will be deemed to have made a gift of the income to the donee. See *Blair v. Commissioner*, 300 U.S. 5 (1937); *Helvering v. Horst*, 311 U.S. 112 (1940).

C. Statutory responses to assignment of income and related problems

   1. The kiddie tax—§1(g): Certain investment income of a child under the age of 14 must be taxed at his or her parents' tax rate. The special tax rate applies only to "unearned income" in excess of $1,800. The parents have the option of including the child's investment income on their own returns.

   2. Reallocation of income and deductions—§482: Under the broad statutory authority granted in §482, the IRS may reallocate among related entities items of gross income, deduction, and credit if necessary to prevent the evasion of tax or clearly to reflect income. This statute goes far beyond assignment of income principles, giving the IRS a powerful tool with which to combat the misallocation of tax items among related entities.

CHAPTER 15

TIME VALUE OF MONEY: PRINCIPLES AND APPLICATIONS

I. IN GENERAL

While the concept of the time value of money is not specifically invoked in any tax statute, its principles permeate much tax-planning activity. Taxpayers invoke basic time value of money concepts when they attempt to defer income and accelerate deductions. The IRS and ultimately Congress may seek to block these strategies by accelerating income and precluding the early deduction of expenses.

II. INTEREST

Interest is the cost of using money. A lender charges the borrower interest for the privilege of using the lender's funds during the period of the loan, and thus the lender is said to "earn interest" on the loan. Interest is what creates the concept of the "time value of money." A specified sum of money will earn interest at the market rate over a period of time; thus, the value of that sum a year in the future will be the sum plus the interest earned during the year.

A. **Simple interest:** Simple interest is calculated as a percentage of the principal sum only.

B. **Compound interest:** Compound interest is computed by applying the interest rate to both the principal sum and the accrued but unpaid interest. Compounding generally occurs daily, monthly, half-yearly, or annually.

III. VALUING AMOUNTS

A. **Future value:** Future value is the value of a sum of money invested for a specified period at a specified interest rate. The future value of a sum will be the amount that an investor will have at the maturity of the investment, given the number of years to maturity and the rate of return (i.e., the interest rate) of the investment. Future value can be calculated using present and future value tables or by using the following formula:

$$FV = PV(1 + i)^n$$

B. **Present value:** Present value is the current value, given an assumed interest rate, of the right to a stated amount in the future. Another way to express this is that present value is the sum that must be invested today at a given interest rate to produce a stated sum in the future. Present value can be calculated using present and future value tables [see Figure 15A, in ELO] or by using the following formula:

$$PV = \frac{FV}{(1 + i)^n}$$

IV. SPECIFIC TIME VALUE OF MONEY APPLICATIONS

The Code recognizes time value of money principles in specific applications, even though it does not import the concept on a global basis.

A. Applicable federal rates: The IRS publishes interest rates monthly for calculations under various Code provisions such as imputed interest and interest on tax over- and underpayments.

B. Tax under- and overpayments—§6621: The U.S. government pays interest on tax overpayments and taxpayers must pay interest on tax underpayments. The interest rate is published from time to time by the IRS.

C. Original issue discount (OID): While most debt instruments provide for a market rate of interest payable currently or otherwise, some debt instruments may not specifically provide for market interest. Yet, these instruments do pay interest in an economic sense, for no creditor would lend money without compensation. Without the OID rules, such instruments might create two misstatements of tax reality. First, repayment of the principal plus an additional sum might be considered a return of capital and capital gain rather than interest, which is ordinary income. Second, the creditor might defer the inclusion of any income until maturity even though presumably the interest is accruing during the entire outstanding period of the loan. The OID rules, while complicated in the extreme, seek to address these character and timing issues.

1. **General approach:** The holder of a debt instrument must include in gross income an amount equal to the daily portions of the original issue discount for each day during the year on which the instrument is held. IRC §1272(a)(1). Thus, the original issue discount is considered ordinary income and is included during the outstanding period of the loan, rather than deferred until maturity.

2. **Exceptions to OID treatment:** The OID rules do not apply to certain types of transactions that are not considered abusive, including sales of farms by certain taxpayers for $1 million or less, sales of principal residences, and sales involving total payments of $250,000 or less. IRC §1274(c).

D. Imputed interest—§483: Section 483 imputes to the creditor interest on certain loans made in connection with sales or exchanges of property to which the OID rules do not apply.

1. **General approach:** The creditor must include in gross income the total unstated interest ratably over the term of the contract. IRC §483(a).

   a. **Which loans?** Section 483 applies to contracts for the sale or exchange of property for which at least one payment is due more than one year after the date of the contract. IRC §483(c).

   b. **Total unstated interest:** Total unstated interest is the excess of the total payments due under the contract, over the sum of the present values of those payments and the present value of any payment provided for in the contract, using a discount rate equal to the applicable federal rate. IRC §483(b).

2. **Correlative effects of imputed interest:** The imputation of interest under §483 reduces the amount characterized as the amount realized (principal) by the parties to the transaction. This reduces the gain (usually capital) reported by the seller of the property and, in turn, reduces the basis of the purchaser in the property. Moreover, the purchaser of the property, who is deemed to pay interest, may be able to deduct that interest, if the deduction requirements of §163 are met.

3. **Exceptions to §483:** Section 483 does not apply to sales not exceeding $3,000 and to any debt instrument to which the OID rules apply.

E. **Below-market loans—§7872:** If a taxpayer makes a loan to another that does not provide for market interest, the transaction may be recharacterized to ensure that the creditor includes market interest in his or her gross income and that any other aspects of the transaction (such as compensation or gifts, for example) are properly taken into account. IRC §7872(a).

1. **General approach:** Below-market "demand," "term," and "gift" loans are recharacterized so that the creditor includes the appropriate amount of interest in gross income. IRC §7872(a)(1).

   a. **Demand and gift loans:** For demand and gift loans, the forgone interest is treated as transferred from the lender to the borrower and retransferred from the borrower to the lender on the last day of the taxable year. IRC §7872(a)(1). Each leg of the transaction is characterized in accordance with its substance. For a gift loan, for example, the first leg (lender to borrower) is treated as a gift, and the second leg (borrower to lender) is treated as interest.

   b. **Other types of loans:** For other types of loans, first compute the excess of the amount loaned over the present value of all payments to be received under the loan. The lender is deemed to have transferred this amount to the borrower on the date the loan is made, and the below-market loan is treated as having OID in that same amount. The transfer from the lender to the borrower is characterized in accordance with its substance (e.g., compensation), and the characterization of the loan as having OID means that the lender must include the OID in gross income over the period of the loan.

      i. **Demand loan:** A demand loan is a loan payable on demand of the creditor.

      ii. **Term loan:** A term loan is a loan payable on a certain date that is fixed or determinable. IRC §7872(f)(6).

      iii. **Gift loan:** A gift loan is a loan in the context of which the creditor's forbearance of interest is most appropriately viewed as a gift. IRC §7872(f)(3).

      iv. **Below-market loan:** A demand loan is below market if its stated interest rate is less than the applicable federal rate at the time the loan is made. IRC §7872(e)(1)(A). A term loan is below market if the amount loaned is greater than the present value of the payments due under the loan, using the applicable federal rate as the discount rate. IRC §7872(e)(1)(B).

2. **Exceptions to §7872:** Section 7872 doesn't apply to gift loans between individuals, to compensation-related loans, and to shareholder loans if the total outstanding principal amount of such loans does not exceed $10,000. IRC §7872(c)(2), (3). Section 7872 also does not apply to any loan to which either the OID rules or §483 applies. IRC §7872(f)(8).

V. BASIC TAX STRATEGIES: INCOME DEFERRAL, ACCELERATION OF DEDUCTIONS, AND CLAIMING TAX CREDITS

Time value of money principles inspire the most basic tax strategies. The best of all tax strategies from the taxpayer's point of view is the exclusion of amounts from gross income entirely (so that tax will never be due on these amounts) or a deduction for the full amount of an expenditure (that shelters the same amount of income from tax). However, exclusions are relatively rare in the Code, and deductions are limited. Most strategies rely on a delay in tax; the taxpayer invests the amount that would otherwise be paid in tax and earns interest on that amount. The tax ultimately will be due, but the taxpayer who has invested the saved tax will usually come out ahead.

A. **Income deferral:** A taxpayer may seek to defer the inclusion of an amount of gross income to a future year. This requires that the taxpayer have a sufficient ownership interest in the funds so that they are invested for his or her benefit but have an interest that will not require the taxpayer to include the amounts in gross income currently. Many income deferral strategies also assume that the taxpayer will be in a lower tax bracket when amounts will be included in his or her gross income (e.g., at retirement). Examples of income deferral strategies include the following:

1. **Method of accounting:** A taxpayer may attempt to take advantage of the rules of his or her particular method of accounting to defer income to future years. Consider in this context the limitations on the use of the cash method of accounting and the doctrine of constructive receipt as limitations on the cash-method taxpayer's ability to defer items of gross income.

2. **Realization principle:** Because income from the sale or exchange of property must be realized before it can be recognized, taxpayers may invest in property to defer the recognition of income until sale. Consider also in this context the effect of §1014, which by giving an heir a fair market value basis in property received from a decedent, encourages taxpayers to hold property until death and thus to exclude from the income tax the appreciation in the property prior to death.

3. **Nonrecognition provisions:** Certain nonrecognition provisions may allow the taxpayer to defer the recognition of gain on the disposition of property. These include like-kind exchanges, spousal and divorce transactions, and involuntary conversions.

4. **Retirement planning:** Most of retirement planning is based on the income deferral strategy. Employers' contributions to retirement plans are not included in the gross income of the employee until retirement, and the fund earns interest for the benefit of the employee during the employee's working years.

5. **Education savings incentives:** Section 529 plans and education savings accounts allow taxpayers to invest money but not be taxed on the earnings until distribution, and then only if the distributions are not used for qualified education expenses.

B. **Deduction acceleration strategies:** Taxpayers prefer to accelerate and maximize deductions because a deduction "shelters" an amount of income from tax. The tax benefit from a deduction is equal to the amount of the deduction multiplied by the taxpayer's tax rate. Examples of deduction strategies include the following:

1. **Method of accounting:** A taxpayer may attempt to take advantage of the particular rules of his or her method of accounting to accelerate deductions. Consider in this context the limitations placed on deductions of prepayments for cash-method taxpayers and the economic performance rules for accrual-method taxpayers.

2. **Capital recovery:** A taxpayer prefers accelerated capital recovery for investment in assets. For example, a taxpayer usually will claim double-declining balance depreciation rather than straight-line depreciation for an asset for which the double-declining balance method is available. Consider in this context §179 deductions, the MACRS method of capital recovery, §195 (amortization of pre-opening expenses), and §197 (amortization of intangibles), and, if available, bonus depreciation. But consider the effect of recapture and the AMT on the claiming of capital recovery deductions.

3. **Loss limitations:** Various loss limitations restrict taxpayers' ability to claim a deduction for certain losses. Consider in this context the capital loss restrictions (§1211), the passive loss restrictions (§469), the at-risk limitations (§465), and the rules against the recognition of losses in certain transactions (§165 and various nonrecognition rules).

CHAPTER 16

RECOGNIZING RELATED TAX STATUTES: A TRANSACTIONAL APPROACH TO TAX

I. AN APPROACH: STUDY TAX FIRST!

One approach to ensuring a complete analysis of a tax question is to take the approach of STUDY TAX FIRST!

A. **STUDY the transaction:** The first step in any tax problem is to study the facts of a transaction carefully. Be sure you understand who did what with whom, when, why, and how. It may be helpful to draw the transaction to ensure that you understand its various components.

B. **What is the TAX problem?** A specific tax question may accompany a set of facts. More commonly, however, the facts end with a general question such as "What are the tax consequences of these transactions?" or "Advise the taxpayer." These raise two different kinds of tax problems.

1. **Reactive problem:** In a reactive problem, events have occurred already, and the problem is to determine their tax consequences. Consider the alternative characterizations of the transaction, and conclude as to which one is most appropriate.

2. **Proactive (planning) problem:** In a proactive problem, the taxpayer is typically considering a transaction and seeks advice on how best to structure it. Consider alternative means to achieve the taxpayer's goals, and choose the one that produces the best overall tax and nontax consequences.

C. **FIRST! analysis: Facts, Issues, Rules, So what? and Taxpayer advice:** This involves in-depth analysis of the tax issues.

1. **Facts:** Characterize the transaction as one of the common transactions. Consider whether it is, for example, a sale or exchange of property or a compensation transaction.

2. **Issues:** There are six fundamental issues in tax, all or some of which may be relevant to a particular transaction.

   a. Who is the relevant taxpayer?

   b. Does the taxpayer have income?

   c. What deductions may the taxpayer claim?

   d. What is the character of income or loss?

   e. Timing issues—when must a taxpayer include an item in gross income, and when may a taxpayer claim a deduction?

   f. What is the taxpayer's rate of tax and is the taxpayer entitled to any credits?

3. **Rules—what tax concepts and Code provisions apply?** This step of the FIRST! analysis identifies the concepts and Code provisions potentially applicable to the transaction at hand. The characterization of the transaction as a type (in the Facts step) is very helpful in identifying potentially applicable statutes and concepts. Once potentially applicable rules are identified, the domain of each is examined with the facts in mind to determine if the concept or statute actually applies.

4. **So what? Applying the rules:** The applicable rules identified in the previous step must be applied—i.e., their consequences in the particular transaction must be determined.

5. **Taxpayer advice:** In the final step, recall that the point of the exercise is tax advice. Whether advising the taxpayer or the government, the tax problem posed must be addressed. Consider in this context what would be an appropriate return position or structure for a transaction, advice with respect to a tax controversy, or an appropriate government position. Basic tax strategies such as income deferral, deduction acceleration, and the claiming of credits should be considered, along with congressional and judicial responses to these techniques.

II. COMMONLY ENCOUNTERED TRANSACTIONS

Commonly encountered transactions can be analyzed using the STUDY TAX FIRST! approach.

A. Compensation transactions

1. **Recognizing this transaction:** To recognize the basic transaction, look for a person performing services in exchange for value or a promise to transfer value.

2. **FIRST! analysis:** For the payor, the essential question is whether a deduction is available for amounts paid for services. For the service provider, the essential question is whether he or she has income, and if so, how much and when it will be included in gross income. The expenses of performing services may be deductible, and compensation income will be ordinary income, potentially taxable at the highest tax rate. Advice to taxpayers in compensation transactions generally focuses on strategies to accelerate the deduction to the payor and defer the inclusion of income to the service provider.

B. Transactions in property: A second major category of commonly encountered transactions is the sale or other disposition of property, including sales and various types of exchanges. (Gifts are treated as intrafamilial transfers, discussed below.)

1. **Recognizing this transaction:** Transactions in property involve a taxpayer transferring an item of property that he or she owns, usually in exchange for value. In a gift transaction, the donor will not receive value for the property, but in nongift contexts, we assume that the seller will dispose of the property at fair market value.

2. **FIRST! analysis:** The tax problem may be posed for the buyer, the seller, or both. For the seller, the essential questions are the amount of gain or loss to be recognized on the transaction and the character of that gain or loss. Sales or exchanges of property may generate capital gain or loss, subject to the preferential rate for net capital gain and the capital loss restrictions of §1211. If the seller has received something other than cash in the transactions, the basis of that property must be computed. For the buyer, the essential question is the basis of the property acquired. Advice to taxpayers in this situation centers on the computation of realized and recognized gain or loss and strategies to exclude or defer income and accelerate loss.

C. Personal expenditure transactions

1. **Recognizing this transaction:** In a personal expenditure transaction, the taxpayer is making expenditures for essentially personal items that would not be deductible but for specific Code sections that allow deduction.

2. **FIRST! analysis:** The crucial questions for the taxpayer are whether he or she is entitled to claim a deduction for these amounts, and when. Income issues may arise if the taxpayer has been compensated for personal losses or physical injuries. Advice to taxpayers in personal expenditure transactions involves identification of allowable deductions and acceleration of these deductions to the earliest possible year.

D. Education incentives

1. **Testing:** The number and relative newness of many education incentives suggests that this area of personal expenditure is fertile ground for testing.

2. **Exclusions:** The following provisions potentially allow exclusions for education-ally related savings and expenses:

   a. Scholarships—§117

   b. Employer assistance—§127

   c. Interest on U.S. savings bonds—§135

   d. Section 529 plans

   e. Education savings accounts—§530

3. **Deductions:** Student loan interest is deductible for certain taxpayers—§221—and certain qualifying tuition and related expenses are deductible—§222.

4. **Credits:** Two provisions potentially allow a credit for educational expenses:

   a. American Opportunity Tax Credit (formerly the HOPE scholarship credit)—§25A

   b. Lifetime Learning Credit—§25A

E. Business transactions

1. **Recognizing this transaction:** Business transactions generally involve a tax-payer's sale of inventory or services for profit. Look for a taxpayer potentially engaged in business—the regular undertaking of an activity for profit.

2. **FIRST! analysis:** For the business taxpayer, the essential question is the net income from the business, which requires a determination of the taxpayer's gross business income and available deductions. Timing issues (including inventory issues) generally figure prominently in the computation of income and deductions. The character of the business income generally will be ordinary, potentially subject to the highest rate of tax. Advice in business transactions involves calculation of gross income from business and identification of available deductions and credits.

F. Intrafamilial transfers

1. **Recognizing this transaction:** In this type of transaction, members of a family are transferring money or property among themselves, and the typical transactions include gifts, divorce transfers, and inheritances.

2. **FIRST! analysis:** The tax consequences to the transferor and transferee of any intrafamilial transfer must be considered.

   a. **Gifts—§§102, 1015:** The making of a gift is not a taxable event to the trans-feror, and thus the transferor realizes and recognizes no gain or loss on the transfer (unless it is a partial sale, which is properly treated as a sale transac-tion). The transferee generally receives property tax-free—i.e., without being required to include its value in gross income. The recipient of a gift takes the property with the same basis the property had in the hands of the donor, unless the property's fair market value was less than its basis at the time of the gift. In that situation, for purposes of determining loss only, the donee takes the fair market value of the property on the date of the gift as his or her basis.

b. **Inheritances—§§102, 1014:** The recipient of property by bequest or inheritance need not include its value in gross income, and takes the property with a basis equal to fair market value on the date of death or at the alternate valuation date six months later, if elected.

c. **Divorce transfers—§§71, 215, 1041:** The payment of alimony (federally defined) constitutes a deduction to the payor and is includable in the gross income of the recipient. The payment of child support, by contrast, generates no deduction to the payor and no income to the recipient. The transferor of property "incident to a divorce" recognizes no gain or loss on the transfer, and the recipient of the property need not include its value in gross income. The recipient takes the property with the same basis it had immediately before the transfer.

d. **Assignment of income and the "kiddie tax"—§1(g):** Taxpayers in high tax brackets may attempt to allocate income from services or property to related taxpayers in lower tax brackets. Attempted assignments of services income or income from property that constitutes a "carved-out interest" will not be respected by the IRS or courts, and the transferor will be taxed on the income purportedly assigned. Taxpayers may, however, transfer property to another so that the income from that property is properly taxed to the transferee. The "kiddie tax," however, serves as a check on this strategy by requiring certain unearned income of children to be taxed at their parents' tax rate rather than their lower individual rates.

e. **Advice:** Advice in intrafamilial transfers centers around ensuring that the transfer is tax-free to both the transferor and transferee, computing the basis of the property transferred, and identifying proper (and improper) assignments of income.

EXAM TIPS

SUMMARY OF CONTENTS

Exam Tips on
GETTING STARTED IN FEDERAL INCOME TAX

☛ Make sure you understand the "big picture" of how the federal income tax is imposed:

Gross Income
− Certain Deductions
= Adjusted Gross Income (AGI)
− Either Standard or Itemized Deduction
− Personal Exemptions
= Taxable Income
× Tax Rate
= Tentative Tax
− Tax Credits
= **Tax Due or Refund Owing**

☛ The most valuable thing you can do at the beginning of the course is to become comfortable reading the Code and applying it. When you read a tax case, read the statute that the case is based on. Analyze how the taxpayer interpreted the statute and how the IRS interpreted it—and ultimately how the court interpreted it.

☛ Tax professors almost universally allow students to take the Code book into the exam. By that time, you will have "parsed" the important statutes for later reference. When discussing a tax problem on an exam, it never hurts to cite the statutes involved, but if pressed for time, don't cite to particular subsections, paragraphs, etc.

☛ An ingenious tax professor will offer up a "new" tax statute that you've never seen before and pose problems from it. This tests your ability to read statutes. Use the parsing approach, and you'll be fine. (*The good news:* It's usually a relatively simple statute.)

☛ Given the recent important changes in the standards of tax practice, be ready to discuss the propriety of various return positions, and the different standards involved in penalty assessment, tax preparer assessment and—most important—lawyers' ethical duties in giving tax advice.

☛ Tax procedure, including how cases get to court, is usually tested *indirectly* on tax exams.

    ☞ *Look for:* A taxpayer who has filed a return with a problematic return position.

    ☞ *Analyze:* The likelihood of success if challenged on the merits, and the taxpayer's options for resolving this controversy.

☛ Policy questions place you in the position of a legislator, an aide, or even an advocate faced with a statute that arguably produces unfair, impractical, or even absurd results. Be sure to present both sides of the issues. There is no "right" answer to these questions; you're being tested on your understanding of tax fairness, how tax statutes are administered, and your ability to predict expected and unexpected consequences of tax statutes. These questions can be paired with the "new" statute described above.

If you don't remember anything else, remember this: The U.S. income tax system imposes tax on a taxpayer's "taxable income," which is a surrogate for his or her ability to pay.

Exam Tips on
IDENTIFYING GROSS INCOME

☛ If the question is whether the taxpayer has "income," determine what theory is being used to define gross income. Is this a theoretical question of comparing a broad tax base (Haig-Simons) with the more practical statutory scheme? Or is this a question based solely on a single theory, or on the statutory system of the Code?

☛ Questions requiring identification of gross income focus on a taxpayer receiving *"anything"* of value, including:

  ☞ Cash

  ☞ Property

  ☞ Services

  ☞ The use of the taxpayer's own property, or the value of the taxpayer's own services (imputed income)

  ☞ Discharge of debt

☛ Questions requiring identification of gross income also focus on the few things that are *not* income in our system:

  ☞ Loan proceeds are not income, because of the offsetting obligation to repay.

  ☞ Capital recovery is not income; a taxpayer is entitled to recover his or her invested capital without tax.

  ☞ Imputed income is not income in our system, but is income under certain theories of taxation.

  ☞ Noneconomic benefits, such as living in a beautiful place or the enjoyment of one's job, are not income.

☛ Some questions combine a nontaxable receipt and a later development that might change the result.

  ☞ Example: In Year 1, Kelly borrows $45,000 from Alex. That isn't income, because Kelly is required to pay Alex back. But later, Alex forgives the debt. This is income to Kelly in the year of forgiveness, because she has been discharged of the obligation. (It might, however, be excludable under a specific statutory rule, but that's for a later chapter.)

☛ Questions involving barter are common—on exams and in the real world. A barter transaction involves the exchange of goods or services, and is distinguishable from imputed income, which involves the use of property or services for oneself.

If you don't remember anything else, remember this: Gross income includes all income from whatever source derived, really!

Exam Tips *on*
SPECIFIC INCLUSIONS IN GROSS INCOME

☛ Make sure you read the call of the question. Tax questions typically involve transactions between two or more people. *Which* person's tax consequences are you asked to address in the question? Usually a taxpayer's tax consequences are independent of others' tax consequences, but sometimes they are tied together (such as a donee of a gift of property taking the donor's basis in that property).

☛ Some receipts aren't income, by definition. If these rules apply, you do not reach the specific statutory inclusions in gross income. These excluded amounts are:

☞ Loan proceeds

☞ Capital recovery

☞ Imputed income

☛ Questions about income inclusion involve the taxpayer's receipt of something of value. Identify the transfer of things of value, such as:

☞ Cash or check

☞ Services

☞ Property

☛ Compensation for services is a common transaction.

☞ *Look for:* Someone providing services to another in exchange for something of value.

☞ *Analyze:* Focus on the service provider—what he or she did, and what is received. The fair market value of services or property received is gross income to the service provider.

☛ Most, if not all, kinds of investment income are includable in gross income. Dividends, rents, royalties, and interest are all includable.

☛ In a divorce setting, one party may pay alimony to the other. Be sure to analyze the transaction from both sides, and include any alimony in the gross income of the recipient.

☞ *Look for:* The payment of cash from one party to the other in a divorce setting.

☞ *Analyze:* Are the requirements for alimony met? Are the payments front-end loaded?

☛ Understand loan transactions. A loan isn't a taxable event, nor is the repayment of the loan principal. When a taxpayer takes out a loan, what he or she does with the proceeds (buys a house, for example) is an independent transaction, even if the seller of the property is the one making the loan (seller financing).

☛ Be able to identify discharge of debt situations.

☞ *Look for:* A loan from one party to the other, and then the lender doing something that reduces or eliminates the debt, or a discharge by operation of law.

☞ *Analyze:* How much discharge income does the taxpayer have? In later chapters we will consider possible exclusions.

☛ Some payments are partially includable in gross income, such as:

☞ Some annuity payments

☞ Some Social Security payments

☛ Most receipts are includable in gross income. If in doubt, include an item in gross income, because gross income is a concept that is construed *broadly*.

If you don't remember anything else, remember this: Compensation income is included in gross income, regardless of the form in which it is paid.

Exam Tips *on*
SPECIFIC EXCLUSIONS FROM GROSS INCOME

☛ Questions about exclusions focus on the taxpayer's receipt of something of value that would otherwise be included in the taxpayer's gross income.

☞ *Look for:* Receipt of property, money, or some other benefit to the taxpayer that would be considered gross income under §61.

☞ *Analyze:* Is there a specific statutory exclusion that exempts it from gross income?

☛ Interpret exclusions *narrowly*.

☞ Make sure the purported exclusions precisely fit within the domain of the statute. If in doubt, don't exclude an item; include it in gross income.

☞ Many exclusions (and deductions) have complex limitations based on income. In a test situation, the limitation phaseout figures would usually be given to you and the goal would be to demonstrate your ability to understand how these limitations work and show that you comprehend the structure of the statute. However, professors have differing perspectives on the importance of knowing and applying these limitations. *Ask* your professor about his/her approach.

☞ Understand the difference between the exclusion for gifts for income tax purposes, and the so-called annual exclusion for gift tax purposes.

   ☞ A person can receive an unlimited amount of gifts, in terms of value, without including them in gross income.

   ☞ The gift tax exclusion is limited to a dollar amount ($13,000 in 2009); this is the amount any person may give to another person without counting against the donor's lifetime exclusion amount.

☞ **Remember:** Damages for nonphysical injuries are includable in gross income; damages for physical injuries are excludable; punitive and delay damages are included in the gross income.

☞ Section 108 provides a number of potential exclusions from gross income for discharge of indebtedness income.

   ☞ *Look for:* A discharge of debt situation that generates gross income to the taxpayer, but surrounding circumstances that make it seem somewhat "unfair" to tax the income.

   ☞ *Analyze:* Does some subsection of §108 apply? If so, are there corresponding reductions in tax benefits? Or, is there a gift that would protect otherwise includable discharge of indebtedness income from being taxed?

☞ Consider the employment situation carefully:

   ☞ *Look for:* Compensation income in the form of noncash items, such as medical insurance, fringe benefits, dependent care assistance, or other benefits.

   ☞ *Analyze:* Is there a benefit to the taxpayer that would otherwise be included in his or her gross income? If so, is there a specific statutory exclusion that would prevent it from being included in the taxpayer's gross income?

If you don't remember anything else, remember this: True gifts are excluded from the recipient's gross income.

Exam Tips on *DEDUCTIONS—IN GENERAL*

☞ Deduction questions involve an outflow of value from the taxpayer in question to another person.

   ☞ *Look for:* The taxpayer paying someone else for something, in cash or property, or experiencing some other outflow, as in a loss.

   ☞ *Analyze:* Is this item deductible? If so, how much is deductible?

☛ If something is deductible, is it a deduction from gross income in computing adjusted gross income (an above-the-line deduction)? Or, is it deductible from AGI in computing taxable income (a below-the-line deduction)? Make sure you understand why the distinction is important.

☛ Deductions are construed narrowly. If in doubt, deny the deduction.

☛ The allowance of a deduction is not the whole story. *When* will it be deductible?

☛ Some outlays involve either deductions or credits—or both.

  ☞ Be ready to explain which is more valuable to the taxpayer. A credit is a dollar-for-dollar reduction in tax, so it is usually more valuable, while a deduction is potentially worth the marginal tax rate of the taxpayer multiplied by the amount of the deduction.

  ☞ *Remember:* A taxpayer cannot claim a credit and a deduction for the same dollar of outlay.

If you don't remember anything else, remember this: *If in doubt, deny the deduction.*

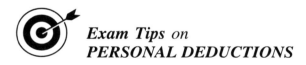

Exam Tips on
PERSONAL DEDUCTIONS

☛ Questions involving personal deductions deal with expenditures associated with a taxpayer's personal life. Address these separately from business deductions.

  ☞ *Look for:* Outlays by taxpayers for charity, health, etc.

  ☞ *Analyze:* Deduction by deduction—is this a deductible expense, and if so, how much is deductible?

☛ Know which deductions belong where: "above the line" or "below the line"—i.e., deductible from gross income in computing AGI (above the line) or deductible from AGI in computing taxable income (below the line).

☛ Most taxpayers described on law exams are "itemizers"—i.e., they do not take the standard deduction, but instead take the deductions listed on Schedule A as itemized deductions.

☛ Many deductions have specific limitations tied to AGI.

  ☞ *Look for:* Charitable donations, medical expenses, casualty losses, educational loans, miscellaneous expenses, retirement savings.

  ☞ *Analyze:* Determine if the outlay is deductible at all; if it is, apply the limitations to determine the deductible percentage.

☛ *Don't* allow a taxpayer to claim *both* the standard and itemized deduction.

☛ Personal deductions are usually deductible in the year the outlay is made, if at all, not later. Timing issues are usually not a large feature of these questions. Nevertheless, as a precaution, think about *when* an amount is deductible.

If you don't remember anything else, remember this: Try as they might, taxpayers can't deduct their usual living expenses.

Exam Tips *on* BUSINESS AND INVESTMENT DEDUCTIONS

☛ Questions dealing with pure business deductions obviously involve a taxpayer's activities with respect to trade or business.

   ☞ *Look for:* Usually a sole proprietorship is illustrated in the basic income tax course, but a trade or business can be carried on by a corporation or partnership.

   ☞ *Analyze:* Identify each outlay. Analyze them expenditure by expenditure. Is an expenditure deductible, and if so, how much is deductible?

☛ What is a trade or business?

   ☞ *Look for:* Regular, continuous activity; sales of goods or services; a profit motive.

   ☞ *Analyze:* If a taxpayer is not engaged in a trade or business, can a deduction be claimed under another theory—e.g., investment activity or §280A?

☛ Work through the four requirements to test deductibility under IRC §162: ordinary, necessary, incurred in carrying on (not pre-opening), and a trade or business. If an expense flunks any of these requirements, it is not currently deductible.

☛ Timing questions often arise in these questions.

   ☞ *Look for:* The taxpayer's method of accounting—cash or accrual.

   ☞ *Analyze:* If an expenditure is deductible, *when* is it deductible?

☛ Watch for expenses that have benefits for a longer period than the taxable year. Usually, these must be capitalized. If so, when will the taxpayer be allowed to recover the invested capital? Over time (as in MACRS) or upon disposition of the investment?

☛ MACRS questions involve some arithmetic skills. Intimidated or pressed for time? Explain how MACRS would be applied to the particular situation, and come back later to do the math if you have time.

☛ There are some business deductions, such as interest and taxes, which do not have to meet the ordinary and necessary business expense test.

☞ Some expenditures have both personal and business connections. In that case, usually some or all of the expenditure will be nondeductible.

If you don't remember anything else, remember this: Taxpayers carrying on a business can deduct all the usual expenses of business.

 ***Exam Tips*** *on*
MIXED BUSINESS AND PERSONAL EXPENSES

☞ Mixed business and personal expenses are often a major focus of deduction questions; they offer ample opportunities to test tax skills.

  ☞ *Look for:* A taxpayer making an expenditure that benefits his or her business yet is integrally tied to personal enjoyment or lifestyle (food, entertainment, vacations, home life, cars, or trucks).

  ☞ *Analyze:* Find the applicable statute (e.g., §§183, 280A). Which approach does the statute take: nondeductible, partially deductible, deductible in full if requirements are met? Make sure the taxpayer's situation meets the applicable requirements in order to qualify for a deduction.

☞ **Remember:** It is not enough to have expended funds and met the statutory requirements for a deduction. The taxpayer has the duty of substantiating the deduction with adequate records.

☞ Most of the statutes contain objective tests. But §183 is an "intent" test.

  ☞ *Look for:* Facts relevant to the nine factors evidencing profit motive.

  ☞ *Analyze:* Analyze each factor as to its particular impact on the taxpayer. Does the question ask you to be an advocate? Or an advisor?

☞ Use the origin of the expense test when there is no statute on point: if the origin is personal—nondeductible; if the origin is business—deductible.

☞ Section 280F offers ample opportunity for policy questions.

  ☞ Do the limitations make sense in an era of Humvees and big SUVs?

  ☞ Do you think this section is effective in achieving its goals? How do taxpayers likely change their behavior in response to the limitations on listed property, for example? Or are gas prices more effective in changing behavior?

☞ Construe deductions narrowly. If in doubt, deny the deduction.

If you don't remember anything else, remember this: An expense with a significant connection to both the personal and business activities of a taxpayer is likely to be only partially deductible—if at all.

Exam Tips on
TRANSACTIONS IN PROPERTY

☛ Questions involving transactions in property involve sales, exchanges, trades, and other dispositions of property.

   ☞ *Look for:* A taxpayer giving up a property in exchange for something else—cash, other property, promises, services, assumption of liabilities.

   ☞ *Analyze:* Which taxpayer's tax consequences are you asked to analyze? Both, or just one of them? If both taxpayers are at issue, analyze them separately.

☛ **Careful:** Don't jump right to the question of gain included in income, or loss deductible from income. Make sure there is a realization event, and that there is realized gain or loss, before asking what gain or loss is recognized.

☛ If in doubt, consider a transaction a realization event. Most transactions are realization events.

☛ Compute realized gain by subtracting the adjusted basis of the property given up from the value of what the taxpayer receives. If the property received is difficult to value, refer to the value of the property given up.

☛ **Remember:** Rational, unrelated taxpayers will trade value for value and will adjust differences in value by paying or receiving additional property. If taxpayers are related, there may be a gift involved.

☛ Most realized gain is recognized. If in doubt, include it in income.

☛ Realized loss is recognizable only if there is a statute that allows it. Deductions are a matter of legislative grace and are interpreted narrowly. If in doubt, deny the deduction of the loss.

If you don't remember anything else, remember this: A taxpayer's realized gain or loss is the difference between the amount he or she receives on sale and the taxpayer's adjusted basis in the property.

Exam Tips on
NONRECOGNITION TRANSACTIONS

☛ Be able to articulate Congress's reasons for granting nonrecognition treatment for some—but not all—transactions.

☛ The nonrecognition statutes are relevant only if there is realized gain or loss on the disposition of property.

☞ *Look for:* An exchange of one property for another in which the taxpayer realizes gain or loss; usually in a situation in which the taxpayer hasn't fundamentally changed the nature of the investment.

☞ *Analyze:* Which taxpayer's tax consequences are relevant? One or both? Compute the realized gain or loss, and then ask if the requirements of a nonrecognition statute are met.

☛ Section 1031 is probably the most popular statute for testing, not only because it is important in tax law in general, but also because it offers fertile ground for testing the student's knowledge of the requirements and consequences of the statute.

☞ *Look for:* Situations that raise questions about the taxpayer's use of the properties, or the like-kind nature of the properties.

☞ *Analyze:* Each requirement; make sure you analyze realized gain or loss, recognized gain or loss, adjusted basis in the property received in the exchange.

☛ **Remember:** Section 1031 is not optional. A taxpayer may not recognize loss on a transaction that qualifies as a §1031 exchange. A better way to recognize loss: Sell the old property and buy the new property with cash.

☛ Involuntary conversions can generate realized gain or loss.

☞ *Look for:* A disaster, or some event outside the control of the taxpayer that leads to the loss of property.

☞ *Analyze:* If realized gain (receipt of insurance proceeds, or exchange of properties), do the requirements of §1033 apply?

☛ If loss is realized, §1033 doesn't apply to that loss. Does §165 allow a deduction for a casualty loss? Are there both casualty losses and recognized casualty gains? Offset them.

☛ Divorces also offer fertile ground for testing.

☞ *Look for:* Divorce or separation and the transfer of money or property pursuant to the divorce.

☞ *Analyze:* Is this a transfer of property, or is it alimony or child support? If a transfer of property, the nonrecognition rules of §1041 will usually apply, but watch for special circumstances that would disqualify the transaction. Be sure to determine the basis of property received in the divorce. Is there alimony or child support? If so, who gets the deduction, and who must include payments in gross income?

If you don't remember anything else, remember this: The basis that a taxpayer receives for property received in a nonrecognition transaction will preserve, as of the date of the exchange, the taxpayer's realized gain or loss that went unrecognized in the transaction.

Exam Tips on
TIMING OF INCOME AND EXPENSES

☛ Questions of timing arise only *after* you have determined that there is an item of income or an expense that may be deducted. Don't get ahead of yourself by jumping straight to timing issues. (But don't forget them, either!)

☞ *Look for:* Is there an item of income, and if so, how much? Is there an expense or loss that is deductible, and if so, how much?

☞ *Analyze:* Then, and only then, ask *when* the income is includable in the taxpayer's gross income, and when is the expense or loss deductible?

☛ Know what taxpayers try to do: Defer income and accelerate deductions. So, what does the IRS try to do? (Accelerate income and defer deductions, when taxpayers try to play games!)

☞ *Look for:* Taxpayers accelerating deductions and postponing income. Look for situations in which taxpayers have access to income but don't include it in gross income, or haven't yet made an economic outlay of some sort but still claim deductions.

☞ *Analyze:* Do the rules of a taxpayer's method of accounting prevent the taxpayer from achieving his or her goals? The tax benefit rule? Or even the basic principles of matching income and deductions or taxable year?

☛ When the facts describe a transaction occurring over two or more years, timing issues are likely to be important. If a result seems "unfair" to a taxpayer because of multiple-year transactions, timing issues are likely to be a big issue.

☞ *Look for:* Income in one year, and deductions in another; profit in one year, and losses in another; recovery of previous deductions; repayment of amounts received in previous years.

☞ *Analyze:* Chronologically—address the first year first, then later years, in order. Explain how the years affect each other, if they do. Think about claim of right, the tax benefit rule, and NOL issues.

☛ Some kinds of property transactions raise important timing issues.

☞ *Look for:* Sales of property with deferred payment; stock or other property given to employees or others for services.

☞ *Analyze:* Over what period of time will income be recognized, or in what year will there be a sudden influx of income from property received in exchange for services?

☛ If a question describes the taxpayer's method of accounting, it may have important timing issues. Scan for the words "cash method" or "accrual method."

☞ *Look for:* When is an amount paid or received? When is the obligation due? Is there uncertainty about the amount?

☞ *If in doubt:* Include an amount in income and defer the expense, particularly for accrual method taxpayers.

☛ If a question describes the taxpayer's accounting year, it may have important timing issues. Scan for the words "calendar year" or "fiscal year."

  ☞ *Look for:* Transactions occurring at the end of one year and the beginning of the next.

  ☞ *Analyze:* Chronologically—analyze the first year first, and then move to the next year. Explain how the two years affect each other, if they do.

If you don't remember anything else, remember this: *Cash-method taxpayers include income when they receive it (actually or constructively) and claim deductions when they make expenditures.*

Exam Tips on
CHARACTER OF INCOME AND LOSS

☛ **Warning:** Professors have varying degrees of interest in the technical aspects of calculating net capital gain or loss. Some are happy if you know the different categories of capital gain and are content to leave the rest to a computer program. Others insist that you know the exact process—and can explain it as well as apply it. *In doubt? Just ask your professor about his or her approach.*

☛ Questions of character arise only after there is a determination that gain or loss has been recognized. If there is no recognized income or loss, there is no question of character.

☛ Be able to recognize when a taxpayer is trying to characterize income as capital or a loss as ordinary—and know why. Make sure the requirements for capital gain or loss are met.

☛ If there is a sale or exchange of an asset, determine what kind of asset it is: capital, noncapital, or §1231 asset.

  ☞ *Look for:* Is the taxpayer engaged in a trade or business?

  ☞ *Analyze:* Business assets are likely to be inventory (noncapital) and §1231 assets. Nonbusiness assets are likely to be capital assets. But the connection with the business isn't the determinative factor. Study §1221 carefully for the definition of capital assets.

☛ Is there a "deemed" sale or exchange? Even if there is no direct sale, there still may be a sale or exchange leading to capital gain/loss.

☛ Know the different kinds of capital gain: 28, 25, and 15/0 percent.

☛ To get ready for any capital gain/loss calculation problem, have your friends pose various scenarios to you (and you to them).

If you don't remember anything else, remember this: Capital gain or loss arises from the sale or exchange of a capital asset.

Exam Tips *on* TAX RATES AND CREDITS

☛ The computation of tax is the *last* step in analyzing a taxpayer's tax consequences. Professors don't usually ask law students to actually compute the tax. Law students are required to understand the concepts involved in tax computation.

☛ Know the differential in tax rates on ordinary income and capital gain and qualified dividend income.

    ☞ *Look for:* A taxpayer with gain from dealings in property (not inventory) and other kinds of income, such as salary income.

    ☞ *Analyze:* Differentiate between the types of income and note the different tax rates that apply.

    ☞ *Note:* Most taxpayers one meets on exams have relatively high ordinary income levels, so that the preferential rates for capital gains will make a difference. However, when a taxpayer has low levels of ordinary income, and significant amounts of net capital gain in the 28 percent or 25 percent categories, the regular rates of tax will usually produce a lower rate than the capital gains rates. The capital gains rates are maximum rates; if the tax produced by the regular tax rates is lower, those rates will apply.

☛ Be able to compute Alternative Minimum Taxable Income (AMTI) using taxable income as the starting place.

    ☞ Know the adjustments to taxable income. Look for taxpayers who have relatively high itemized deductions or tax-exempt income, or can take advantage of significant income deferrals

    ☞ Be ready to explain the rationale for the Alternative Minimum Tax (AMT) and comment on its effectiveness.

☛ Understand the difference between a credit, a deduction, and an exclusion, and the impact of each on a taxpayer.

☛ Be familiar with the numerous credits available to taxpayers.

    ☞ *Look for:* Adoptive parents, parents who use day care, low-income taxpayers, first-time homebuyers, energy-saving expenditures.

☞ *Analyze:* Have the taxpayers met the specific requirements for claiming the credit? If so, is it limited by the taxpayers' income level?

☛ The bundle of education incentives available to taxpayers creates opportunities for testing.

☞ *Look for:* A taxpayer paying for higher education expenses, for the taxpayer or a spouse or child.

☞ *Analyze:* What incentives are available: exclusions, deductions, credits, deferral devices? Are the specific requirements of the statutes met? What limitations apply, particularly with respect to income levels? Don't let the taxpayer "double dip"— i.e., claim two benefits for the same dollars.

If you don't remember anything else, remember this: *The alternative minimum tax is designed to ensure that all taxpayers pay some amount of tax, even if they have tax-advantaged investments or activities.*

Exam Tips *on*
IDENTIFYING THE TAXPAYER

☛ Even though the discussion of the assignment of income doctrine comes close to the end of this book, it is conceptually one of the first questions you should ask yourself in analyzing tax questions.

☞ *Look for:* Intrafamily transfers, usually from a senior generation to a younger generation, with the opportunity to lower taxes on the overall economic unit.

☞ *Analyze:* Has there been an impermissible assignment of income from one person to another? What is the result of this assignment? Is there a judicial doctrine or statutory "fix" that prevents this assignment? Perhaps the "kiddie tax"?

☛ Use the smell test: Does it seem that the taxpayer is "getting away with something" by transferring income or property to another person? If so, the question probably involves an assignment of income problem.

☛ The assignment of income doctrine applies most often to services income.

☞ *Look for:* One person who performs services, but another receives the compensation, in money or other property. That other person just happens to be in a lower tax bracket.

☞ *Analyze:* Compensation income is taxed to the person who performs services. Then, that person is considered to have made a gift to the person who ended up with the income. However, if state, federal, or foreign law divides the income between two people—that will usually be respected.

☛ The assignment of income doctrine also applies to income arising from property.

   ☞ *Look for:* Assignments of dividends, interest, rent, royalties, etc.

   ☞ *Analyze:* Did the assignor transfer the underlying property or just the income stream? If only the income stream, it is likely to be an impermissible assignment of income.

☛ Remember two fundamental principles:

   ☞ Familial transfers are subject to particular scrutiny.

   ☞ The substance of a transaction governs its federal income tax consequences—not its form. If it seems too good to be true, it probably is.

If you don't remember anything else, remember this: *Taxpayers try to direct income to people in lower income brackets, such as children—and the IRS resists this strategy.*

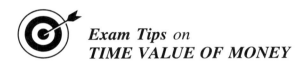

Exam Tips on
TIME VALUE OF MONEY

☛ Most law exams do not ask pure time value of money questions like Questions 156 through 159 in the "Quiz Yourself" section of the textbook. Time value of money principles are embedded in other kinds of questions.

   ☞ *Look for:* A taxpayer's choice between two alternative receipts, or an opportunity to defer income or accelerate deductions.

   ☞ *Analyze:* Discuss time value of money principles to explain why a taxpayer would choose one alternative or plan over another.

☛ The statutory rules (§§483, 7872) are all based on making a loan transaction reflect economic reality: Interest would be charged, and must be imputed if it is not stated.

   ☞ *Look for:* Loans, sales of property, etc. without an adequate stated interest rate.

   ☞ *Analyze:* Which section applies; what exactly does it impute; what are the results to the taxpayers? Analyze each side of the transaction separately.

☛ *Math anxiety?* Forget running the numbers. Discuss the theory of the time value of money, and what it causes taxpayers (and Congress) to do in a particular situation.

If you don't remember anything else, remember this: *Time value of money principles are the underpinnings of most tax strategies. If a tax can be deferred into the future, it is a "cheaper" tax than a tax paid currently.*

Exam Tips on
RECOGNIZING RELATED TAX STATUTES

☞ What kind of tax problem is being posed?

   ☞ A *reactive* problem: A transaction or series of transactions has already occurred, and the facts are given.

   ☞ A *proactive* (planning) problem: The transaction or series of transactions hasn't yet occurred, and there is time for the taxpayer to make a plan to achieve the best tax result.

   ☞ A *policy* problem: The point of the question is not a single transaction or taxpayer, but designing a method of improving the tax system for an entire class of transactions or taxpayers.

☞ Consider the call of the question carefully. In *which taxpayer's* tax consequences is the professor interested? If the professor is interested in fewer than all of the taxpayers in the transaction, focus on the others only to the extent that their tax consequences directly impact those in which the professor is interested.

☞ In solving a reactive problem, don't waste time on how the taxpayer "should" have structured the transaction, unless specifically asked to do so. Instead, fully consider the tax consequences of alternative interpretations of the facts and conclude as to which interpretation is most appropriate. Ethical issues (such as what would constitute an appropriate return position) can be embedded in this type of problem.

☞ When addressing a proactive problem for a taxpayer, consider first the taxpayer's tax and nontax goals and then consider alternative ways of accomplishing those goals, within the facts that are flexible. Propose alternative paths to solve the taxpayer's problem and analyze the tax consequences of each path. Choose the path that produces the best overall consequences for the taxpayer and explain why the other paths are less suitable. Ethical issues, including conflicts of interest and development of reasonable return positions, may well be embedded in proactive problems.

☞ When addressing a policy question, consider the factors that relate to the fairness, practicality and intended effects of a particular tax provision. What is the purpose of the statute? Does it make the tax system "fairer" or "less fair"? Will it be a nightmare or a cakewalk to administer by the IRS? What will the average taxpayer do when faced with the statute? Will he or she change any behavior? If so, in what positive and negative ways?

☞ Any set of facts can raise a large number of potentially applicable tax statutes. Which ones do you discuss on an exam? If a tax statute is clearly inapplicable, do not squander valuable time discussing it. If the facts are clearly within a statute, discuss this succinctly. But at the heart of many tax questions lies a statutory "domain problem." A domain problem exists when the statute either contains some ambiguity in its terms that raises questions about whether the facts fit within its domain, or the facts themselves are ambiguous, which also raises questions about their inclusion in the statute's domain. These types of situations usually deserve an in-depth analysis in an exam situation, engaging in the process of statutory interpretation of ambiguous terms, or discussing alternative interpretations of the facts that cause them to fall within or without the domain of the statute.

☛ In addressing the tax consequence of applying a particular concept or statute, discuss each step in your analysis carefully. If performing some arithmetic feat, show how you reached your conclusion. If you have identified some ambiguity in the statute that causes you to be uncertain as to whether it applies, be sure to discuss the effects in the alternative of falling within and without the domain of the statute.

SHORT-ANSWER QUESTIONS AND ANSWERS

SHORT-ANSWER QUESTIONS

Note: These questions are from the "Quiz Yourself" section of the full-length *Emanuel Law Outline* on *Basic Federal Income Tax*.

CHAPTER 1

GETTING STARTED IN FEDERAL INCOME TAX

1. Why would a taxpayer disclose the details of a particular return position even though not required to do so by the usual tax return reporting rules? _____

2. The IRS is assessing additional taxes, interest, and penalties against Leona. She is outraged, because in her opinion, "Only the little people pay taxes!" She is further outraged because she relied on an article in *Time* magazine and followed that advice in taking one of her return positions and disclosed that on the return. After calming her down, you must explain what authorities do and do not have "precedential value." How do you do that? _____

3. Willie received a Statutory Notice of Deficiency assessing $13,000,000 in back taxes, interest, and penalties. He hasn't a cent to his name, only a guitar, a collection of records, and an old pickup truck. If Willie wants to contest this assessment, how should he do so? _____

4. Why might a taxpayer prefer to litigate in a U.S. District Court rather than the U.S. Tax Court? _____

5. What is the difference between a Revenue Ruling and a private letter ruling?

6. Carla was surprised to hear from her tax preparer that a position she and her tax preparer had taken for years in the past needs to be disclosed on the return or the preparer can't sign the return. What is motivating this change in approach? _____

7. Why would taxpayers be subject only to the "not frivolous" position standard on their own tax returns, while tax preparers are subject to a higher standard? _____

8. Your congressman proposes a new Code provision that allows a person getting a divorce a deduction of $5,000 in the year the divorce is final. His rationale is that taxpayers have additional expenses in that year, and their taxable income should reflect that reality. You are his aide and official tax guru. What do you tell him as to the advisability of this? (Disregard revenue and budget process implications.) _____

9. Become facile in finding Code and regulations sections in your statute book *before* you need to do this in class. Can you find IRC §102(b)(2)? Or §117(b)(2)(A)? Or §108(f)(2)(C)(iii)? How about Treas. Reg. §1.61-2? Or Treas. Reg. §1.132-5?

CHAPTER 2

IDENTIFYING GROSS INCOME

10. Valley Girl Buffy asks, "*Gross* income? What's up with *that?*" Can you explain to her what "gross income" really is? _____

11. This year, Cally earned $300,000 in salary as a model. She spent $50,000 on housing, $100,000 on clothing, and $2,000 on food. She spent $100,000 on having fun: sporting events, galas, travel, and parties. The rest she invested in a Certificate of Deposit earning 2 percent. Using the Haig-Simons definition of income, what is Cally's income? _____

12. Assume that Cally (from the previous question) invested her surplus funds not in a CD but instead in EndRun Co., a high-flying stock. At the next year its value plummeted to $2,000. What effect does this have on her income in the later year, using the Haig-Simons definition of income? _____

13. Nick's grandparents pay off his student loans for him as a graduation present. Does this result in income to Nick?

14. Ken borrowed $15,000 from his credit union to buy a car. Does he have income when he receives the loan proceeds, under the economic benefit theory of income? Why or why not? _____

15. Martha is the ultimate stay-at-home mother. She raises the children, and in her spare time, she decorates the home she and her husband own, repairs their appliances if they break, creates fabulous meals on a shoestring, and gives advice on cooking, cleaning, and crafts to her many friends, neighbors, and acquaintances. What is her "income" from these activities? _____

16. Don purchased Chump Chowder, a parcel of unimproved real estate, for $500,000. His plans for building a seafood restaurant on the property never matured, and several years later, he sold it for $750,000. Assume no depreciation was claimed and no improvements to the property were made. What is Don's "income" from the sale of Chump Chowder and why? _____

17. Donna provides legal services to Mandy in exchange for Mandy's boarding Donna's dogs while she travels. Do Donna or Mandy have income from this exchange? _____

18. Lana has saved $10,000. She purchases 100 shares of ABC stock with this money. Does she have income as a result of this transaction? _____

CHAPTER **3**

SPECIFIC INCLUSIONS IN GROSS INCOME

19. Diane's employer falls on hard times. Instead of giving her the usual paycheck, the employer gives her a used car worth $3,500 and promises to pay her $3,000 in two weeks. How will Diane be taxed? _____

20. Michael, a noted basketball player, realizes that he needs a plan for his retirement. He pays a $500,000 one-time premium for an annuity, which will pay him $100,000 per year beginning on January 1 of the year he turns 65 and continuing for the rest of his life. At age 65, he is deemed to have a life expectancy of 20 years. When Michael receives his first year's payment of $100,000, must he include it in his gross income? _____

21. Assume Michael, from the previous question, died on January 30 of the year he turned 67. The terms of the annuity provide that if the annuitant dies before the end of his life expectancy, the remaining amounts that would have been received, based on his life expectancy at the time the annuity began paying, will be paid to his estate or beneficiary. What are the tax consequences if $1,700,000 is paid to the estate or beneficiary in that year? _____

22. Cindy and Bill are getting a divorce. The divorce decree says that Cindy must pay Bill $100,000 within 30 days of the entering of the decree, $50,000 on the first anniversary of the divorce, and $25,000 on the second anniversary of the divorce, unless Bill dies during this period. They have no children. Will these payments be includable in Bill's income? _____

23. Bruce and Debi are divorced. Under the divorce decree, Bruce is obligated to pay Debi $24,000 per year for ten years. Is this alimony, under the federal definition? _____

24. Aging film star Greta's mansion in Bel Air is virtually falling apart. She leaves for a trip around the world, and rents it to starving actor Harrison for $200 per month and Harrison's agreement to spend 20 hours a week fixing it up. What are the tax consequences to Greta of this arrangement? _____

25. Marc borrowed $1,000,000 from the bank. He absconded to Europe, and never paid it back. The bank determined that the amount was uncollectible, and wrote it off. The time period for collection expired. What are the tax consequences of this transaction to Marc? _____

26. Assume the same facts as in the previous question, except that Marc's mother is mortified at her son's behavior, and repays the loan. What are the tax consequences of the loan and its repayment to Marc? _____

27. Frieda owed $40,000 on her credit card. She contacted a credit counseling agency, which convinced the credit card company to accept a reduced amount of $25,000. What are the tax consequences of this transaction to Frieda? What if Frieda had been disputing

some of the charges with the credit card company at the time of the discharge?
_____

28. Rookie pitcher Greg listened to his parents' advice and purchased disability income insurance. It's a good thing he did, because in his very first major league game, he injured his shoulder and was released from the team. He receives payments from the insurance company. What is the tax treatment of these payments to Greg? _____

29. Bea was selected to win a Nobel Prize for her work in chemistry. She immediately donated the monetary prize to the Red Cross. Will she be taxed on this award? _____

30. Carlotta was a bookkeeper for ABC Corp who felt she was underpaid. She took matters into her own hands and embezzled $50,000 from the company before being discovered. She promises to repay the money as soon as possible. What are the tax consequences to Carlotta? _____

31. Of the following, which is *not* includable in an individual taxpayer's gross income?

    (a) Dividends received from corporations
    (b) Royalties received from the licensing of patents
    (c) Rent received from tenants in a commercial building
    (d) Interest on a loan made to a relative
    (e) A periodic payment received under an annuity contract

CHAPTER 4

SPECIFIC EXCLUSIONS FROM GROSS INCOME

32. Upon settlement of her grandfather's estate, Rikki received a pair of antique carved mongooses worth $50,000. Her grandfather had won these in a poker game in India many years before. What are the tax consequences of this receipt to Rikki? _____

33. Tonika sued Dump-It-All, Inc., for illnesses she contracted as a result of a toxic waste dump near her home. She ultimately prevailed, receiving reimbursement for all her medical expenses and damages for pain and suffering. What are the tax consequences of these receipts to Tonika? _____

34. DotComInc has debts of $1 million, property with a fair market value of about $50,000, (with a basis of zero), and a net operating loss of $400,000. Negotiating with creditors, DotComInc obtains cancellation of $700,000 worth of its debt. What are the tax consequences to the company of this cancellation? _____

35. Kerry worked for many years as a bookkeeper for ABC Company. Upon his retirement, the company gave him a gift of a golfing vacation. What are the tax consequences of this gift? _____

36. Sheri is a flight attendant whose employer provides certain fringe benefits, including medical insurance for herself and her husband and the opportunity to fly free on a standby

(seats available) basis for her and her family. What are the tax consequences of these fringe benefits to her? _____

37. A recent ABA newsletter reported that a major law firm is providing free breakfasts and dinners for associates, as well as a "personal concierge service," which runs personal errands for associates (such as picking up dry cleaning, standing in line for tickets, etc.). The firm explains these benefits as a way to improve morale and help associates balance work and home life expectations. What are the tax consequences of these benefits to the associates? _____

38. Travis bought a home in Year 1. He used it as his principal residence in Year 1 and Year 2. He then decided to change his life: He abandoned his career as a tax lawyer, got his private detective license, and moved onto a houseboat in Florida. The house sat empty for a couple of years, and he sold it in Year 5 at a gain of $75,000. What are the tax consequences of this sale to Travis? Assume all transactions occur on the first day of the year.

_____

39. Bob purchased Blackacre for $200,000. A friend loaned him $180,000 and he paid the rest in cash. Bob used Blackacre as his principal residence for several years. Real estate prices plummeted and Bob fell on hard times. At a time when Bob was insolvent and the outstanding principal balance of the mortgage was $140,000, Bob negotiated with his friend that he would repay only $100,000 of the loan. What are the tax consequences to Bob?

_____

40. Lisa's employer provides her and her family with health insurance, and also provides disability insurance for Lisa. In Years 1 through 5, the employer spent $10,000 on these premiums for Lisa. In Year 4, Lisa became very ill. She incurred $25,000 of medical expenses, of which the insurance company reimbursed her for $20,000. Eventually, she was determined to be disabled, and now receives $2,000 per month under the disability policy. What are the tax consequences of these events to Lisa?

_____

41. In Hamm and Brenda's divorce decree, Hamm was to pay Brenda the sum of $1,000 per month until their only child reached age 18, at which time the amount was to be reduced to $250 per month. Hamm has paid $1,000 per month for each of the past five years, and Brenda has not included any amount in her gross income. Is this the correct reporting position? _____

CHAPTER 5

DEDUCTIONS—IN GENERAL

42. Lee owns a small business, which he runs as a sole proprietorship. His view is: "What's the point of owning a business unless you can run all your expenses through it?" Therefore, he deducts all his living expenses (food, rent, vacations, etc.), in addition to his business expenses, on his Schedule C. What's wrong with that, if anything?

_____

43. On his 2009 federal income tax return, Double Dip Dan deducted the basic standard deduction and his itemized deductions. The IRS assessed additional tax. Why? _____

44. T. C. "Cat" Adorre is a congressman. He is considering proposing a tax code change that would benefit taxpayers who incur expenses in adopting animals from shelters. You are his aide and official tax guru. He asks: "Would it be more beneficial for taxpayers to allow a tax deduction or a tax credit for these expenses? What's the difference, anyway?" _____

45. Jodi runs her hair salon as a sole proprietorship. This year, she invested $50,000 in new styling equipment to be used in her business. She intends to deduct all of these costs. Is she correct? (Assume §179 does not apply.) _____

46. What is the difference between adjusted gross income and taxable income? Why do taxpayers try to minimize AGI? _____

47. Of the following, which are deductible from gross income in computing AGI and which are deductible from AGI in computing taxable income? Medical expenses, personal exemption, standard deduction, moving expenses, retirement savings, capital losses, net personal casualty losses, charitable contributions, alimony. _____

CHAPTER 6

PERSONAL DEDUCTIONS

48. Under the terms of their divorce decree, Tom will pay Nicole $10,000 per month as alimony and $1,200 per month as child support. Assume that the alimony meets the federal definition of alimony. May Tom deduct these payments? _____

49. In 2009, Dorothy has AGI (without considering the following described events) of $200,000 for past year. During the year, her home in Kansas was destroyed by a tornado. The basis of the home was $250,000 and its fair market value was $500,000. Dorothy had no insurance on the home. What are the tax consequences of this event to Dorothy? _____

50. Assume the same facts as in the previous question, except that Dorothy also received $100,000 from an insurance company attributable to the theft of a very valuable pair of shoes. She had a basis of $20,000 in the shoes. What are the tax consequences to Dorothy, considering *both* events? _____

51. Avid whale watcher Molly decides to move to Seattle. She purchases a new principal residence on the ocean there for $1.5 million. She takes out a mortgage of $1.2 million from Friendly Bank, and pays for the balance in cash. She owns no other properties. May she deduct the interest on the debt? _____

52. Sam owns a parcel of property on which he has built a new home. During construction, he lived in a dilapidated home on the property. Under applicable land use regulations, only one home suitable for occupancy may exist on this parcel. Now that the new home is ready for its occupancy permit, Sam wants to donate the older home to the local fire department (a governmental unit) for a burning-home exercise. By removing the old residence, the burning exercise will allow him to move into the new home. He intends to claim a deduction equal to the fair market value of the older home. May he do so? _____

53. Of the following, which is not deductible?

    (a) Federal income taxes
    (b) State income taxes
    (c) State property taxes
    (d) State sales and use taxes
    (e) None of the above is deductible.

54. Pete's hobby is auto racing. This year, he was in a car wreck and incurred $100,000 in medical expenses. His medical insurance company reimbursed $75,000 of these expenses this year, and he paid for the balance with a $10,000 distribution from a qualifying health savings account (HSA) and the rest with savings. His AGI is $250,000. May Pete deduct any of these medical expenses? _____

55. Tom locates, buys, and sells hard-to-find vinyl recordings for his employer, Oldies but Goodies, Inc. ("OBG"). Under the terms of his employment agreement, OBG will reimburse him for up to $2,500 of properly substantiated travel expenses associated with his sales activities. This year, Tom incurred $30,000 of such expenses, of which $2,500 was reimbursed by OBG. He also had $500 in other qualifying miscellaneous expenses. His AGI is $140,000. How should Tom treat these expenses? _____

56. Janet, a single taxpayer, has a complicated household. The following people live with her. Assume that none of these individuals plans to claim an exemption for himself or herself on his or her own tax return. For whom may Janet claim a personal exemption on her income tax return? _____

    (a) Her daughter, age 16
    (b) Her son, age 23, a full-time college student who lives at college nine months of the year
    (c) Her stepdaughter from a prior marriage, age 18
    (d) Her mother, age 86, who has Social Security benefits of $1,000 per month
    (e) Her brother, who is currently unemployed
    (f) A foster child, age 12
    (g) Her single niece, age 30, who is visiting the United States for an extended period from her home in Mexico
    (h) An unrelated boarder, who pays Janet $500 per month for room and board

57. The parents of a dyslexic child send him to boarding school. Part of the program of the school is devoted to overcoming reading disabilities. May the parents deduct the tuition, room, and board they pay to the school as a medical expense? _____

58. Catherine is employed as a nurse by DocInaBox, Inc., an outpatient clinic. DocInaBox maintains a qualified retirement plan in which Catherine participates. Her AGI is $45,000. In 2009, Catherine would like to establish an IRA. May she do so, and if so, how much will be her contribution? _____

59. Assume that in the next year, Catherine's income increased sufficiently that she could not make a deductible contribution to a regular IRA, and that she is not able to qualify for a Roth IRA. Why might she still want to make a contribution to a regular IRA, even though the contribution is not deductible? _____

60. Donald tells Maurice, *"You're fired!"* Maurice then incurs the following expenses: $10,000 in attorneys' fees in an unsuccessful attempt to sue his employer for breach of contract; $1,500 in job search expenses to obtain a similar position; $500 to a moving company to move his things out of his office at Donald's building; and $5,000 in psychological counseling to help him recover from this harrowing experience. Of these, which are deductible—and in what manner? What if Maurice says, "I've had it with this business! I'm only going to take a job in a completely different profession!"? _____

CHAPTER 7

BUSINESS AND INVESTMENT DEDUCTIONS

61. Clean Machine is a sole proprietorship operating a mobile car-detailing service. This year, the owner, Win, made a number of expenditures, as follows:

Wages to employees	$25,000
Waxes, soaps, etc.	$6,000
Licenses	$500
Parking fines	$600
Advertising	$10,000
Séance to get business advice from deceased father	$3,000
Legal fees to settle dispute with car owner	$5,000
Legal fees to quiet title to parking lot	$15,000
New van	$35,000

Which of these expenditures are deductible to Win? If not deductible, how should they be treated? _____

62. Jody purchased a rental house on July 1 of Year 1 for $55,000. She rented it for $3,000 in Year 1, and $6,000 in each of Years 2 and 3. She sold it on January 15, Year 4, for $80,000. Assuming no improvements to the home, what is her gain or loss on the sale? _____

63. Grant purchased a bagpipe store from Adam. He purchased the entire bagpipe inventory, a list of all the customers who loved bagpipe music, and obtained a promise from Adam not to engage in the retail bagpipe business for five years from the date of sale. He paid Adam $30,000 for the promise. How should Grant treat the $30,000 for tax purposes? _____

64. Baxter is a large-animal veterinarian. In 2009, he returned to his hometown to open a practice. He spent $50,000 on equipment, and on June 1 hired an assistant, Penny, to whom he paid $2,500 per month. He spent $10,000 on fixing up his leased premises and another $5,000 on various miscellaneous expenses associated with opening his business. He was finally ready to open on August 1. His expenses after that date were $35,000. Which expenses are deductible, if any? How should nondeductible expenses be treated?

_____

65. Lenore purchases the Wallflower Hotel on January 1, Year 1. She expects to be able to claim 12 months of depreciation for the hotel during Year 1. Is she able to do so? Why or why not? _____

66. Xavier makes a loan of $25,000 to Zena. Eventually, it becomes clear that Zena will never repay the loan. What is the proper tax treatment of the loan to Xavier if:

- Xavier is Zena's father? _____
- Xavier is Zena's employer? _____
- Xavier is in the business of making loans to individuals? _____

67. Bennie is a law professor. This year, he traveled across the country to teach one semester at another law school. While there, he incurred expenses for rent, food, and utilities. He also incurred traveling expenses there and back. Are any of these expenses deductible to Bennie? _____

68. Wendy owns a catering business. She is considering expanding to include a restaurant and spends $10,000 hiring experts to help her analyze this idea. She eventually does open the business. Is the $10,000 deductible? If so, when? _____

69. Richard is a law librarian. He decides to go to law school. He wants to deduct the costs of his education. May he do so? _____

70. Peter is a practicing lawyer. Bored with criminal defense work, he decides to get an LLM in tax. The program takes one year, and most students (including Peter) work almost full time during the program. Peter wishes to deduct the cost of his LLM. May he do so? What if Peter pursued the LLM right out of law school? _____

71. Bonbon owns a rental house. She was paid rental income of $10,000. Her expenses were repairs ($1,500), property management ($3,000), and taxes ($2,500). She also spent $15,000 adding another bedroom to the home. How should Bonbon report these items?

_____

72. What is the rationale for allowing depreciation or amortization deductions?

_____

73. Howard is concerned about the health and morale of his employees. He hires a yoga instructor to conduct classes twice a week in the conference room. These classes are optional for all employees, although Howard pays them for the hour they attend. Is this expense deductible? Will the employees be required to include the value of the classes in their gross income as additional wages? _____

CHAPTER 8

MIXED BUSINESS AND PERSONAL EXPENSES

74. Shady Brokerage Company is being investigated by the SEC for allegedly running a Ponzi scheme. Selena is an employee at Shady and also has fallen under suspicion. Although Selena was ultimately cleared of all charges, she incurred $75,000 of legal fees defending herself. May Selena deduct these expenses? _____

75. Tom is engaged in the practice of law as a sole proprietor. During the year, he incurs a number of meal and entertainment expenses that he would like to deduct from his business income. These are:

Country club dues	$10,000
Golf greens fees (with clients):	$850
Restaurant meals (with clients):	$1,000
Sporting event tickets (clients attended as guests):	$3,500
Sporting event tickets (Tom did not attend; clients did):	$500
Annual employee picnic:	$1,600

   May Tom deduct all or part of these expenses? _____

76. Billie, a cardiovascular surgeon, is considering buying a horse farm and several horses. She's allergic to hay, but her teenage daughters are avid riders, and she currently has to pay an expensive riding academy for her daughters to ride. Billie is a city gal, but longs for the country life. She understands that, at least in the first few years, farms are "losing propositions," but she thinks she can eventually turn a profit by having her daughters board and train other people's horses. In the meantime, she's looking forward to deducting the losses from the farm. You're her tax advisor. What do you tell her? _____

77. Ty is a lawyer. Throughout his lifetime, he has been interested in the sport of polo. He buys and sells polo ponies and plays polo whenever and wherever he can. Ty wants to deduct the losses he incurs in playing polo and trading in polo ponies against the income from his law practice. His theory is that he meets clients at polo activities, and becoming known as a wheeler-dealer in polo ponies can only help his reputation as a lawyer. Will Ty likely be successful in deducting these losses? _____

78. Rudy's principal residence is in New York City, but he has a second home in the Adirondacks. Each year, he spends four weeks there, and then rents out the home to vacationers for the rest of the year. In the past, Rudy has reported all of the rent received from the property in his gross income each year, and has deducted 100 percent of the expenses, including taxes, insurance, and repairs. He also has been depreciating the property on a straight-line basis over 27.5 years. Has Rudy's reporting position been correct? Why or why not? _____

79. Susan is a consulting psychologist in Boston. She occasionally sees patients as does a traditional psychologist, but most of her time is devoted to preparing for and testifying in trials as an expert witness. She owns a townhouse: The bottom floor is her office, and the top floor is her home. In her office, she sees patients, talks with lawyers in person and on the telephone, keeps records, bills insurance companies and lawyers, and does her research. She uses the office exclusively for work. May she deduct expenses associated with the home office? Why or why not? If she can deduct expenses, which ones are deductible? _____

80. Jeff spends most of his time playing poker, entering poker tournaments, and studying poker. This year, he earned $120,000 in winnings, and had $300,000 in losses. Last year, the reverse was true: He had much more winnings than losses. Will Jeff be able to deduct his losses from gambling from this year? If so, how? If not, why not? _____

81. Why are business meal expenses only 50 percent deductible? _____

82. Steve owns a home in Oregon, and Mike owns a home in Florida. They agree to "swap" houses for three months: Steve lives in Mike's house, and Mike lives in Steve's house, from July through September. No cash changes hands. Steve wants to deduct one-fourth (three months' worth) of repairs, utilities, depreciation, and other expenses associated with his home. Will he be successful? _____

83. Debbie is an employee of ABC Company, which makes animated films for children. She is the "voice" for all ducks and other fowl-like creatures in these films. She recently had tonsillitis, and things didn't go so well. Her employer told her that her voice was no longer sufficiently fowl-like and fired her, but she suspected—and ultimately proved—more sinister, discriminatory motives. Since then, Debbie's voice has enjoyed starring roles in other films, but she now works independently, not as an employee. Debbie sued her former employer and received $300,000 in damages for violation of a state anti-discrimination law, of which her attorney received $100,000 as her fee. May Debbie deduct these legal fees? _____

CHAPTER 9

TRANSACTIONS IN PROPERTY

84. Al and Sal are avid sports memorabilia collectors. Al owns a baseball signed by Mickey Mantle. Sal owns a football signed by Joe Montana. Both purchased these items years ago and they have appreciated in value. They trade. What are the tax consequences to them of this trade? Disregard any nonrecognition provisions of the Code. _____

85. Taylor owns a collectible sports car, which she purchased many years ago for $10,000. It has appreciated significantly in value. Melique convinces Taylor to sell him the sports car, in exchange for Melique's promise to completely remodel Taylor's kitchen. Do either of these individuals have income or loss from this transaction?

86. What is the function of "basis"? Of "adjusted basis"? _____

87. Dick owns Bleak House, a bed-and-breakfast inn for literary types. He had an initial basis of $140,000 in this property, and has claimed $40,000 of depreciation deductions over the years. He agrees to sell the property to Tom for $300,000. What are the tax consequences of this sale to Dick? _____

88. Assume the same facts as in the preceding question, except that Dick has a mortgage on Bleak House in the amount of $100,000. He agrees to sell Bleak House to Jerry. Jerry will pay Dick cash of $200,000 and assume the debt on Bleak House. What are the tax consequences of this transaction to Dick? What is Jerry's basis in Bleak House? _____

89. Courtney purchased the Emerald Apartment Building for $1 million. She financed 100 percent of the purchase price through Very Friendly Bank, which loaned her the money on a nonrecourse basis. Over the years, she properly claimed $250,000 of MACRS deductions with respect to the property. Unfortunately, the value of the property declined and became a stone around her neck. One day she simply marched into the bank, gave them the deed to the property and walked away. She had paid off only $50,000 of the debt, so her mortgage balance was $950,000 at that time. The bank ultimately sold the property for $600,000. Courtney reported a $150,000 loss on this transaction on her tax return. Was she correct? _____

90. Linda purchased The Bates Motel for $500,000, the entire amount of which she financed with a recourse mortgage from a bank. Over the years she claimed $100,000 in depreciation deductions. Some spooky things happened at the motel, and it declined in value because few visitors wanted to stay there. Linda was unable to repay the debt. Last year, when Linda had a mortgage balance of $450,000, the bank foreclosed on the property. The property was sold for $200,000, all of which was applied to Linda's loan. The bank tried to collect the remaining $250,000, but ultimately decided it was uncollectible because Linda's debts were well in excess of her assets. The bank wrote off the debt. What are the tax consequences of this transaction to Linda? _____

91. Would the result in the previous question be any different if the bank and Linda had simply agreed that she would transfer the motel to the bank in full satisfaction of the debt? _____

92. What is "tax cost" basis? Can you offer an example? _____

CHAPTER 10

NONRECOGNITION TRANSACTIONS

93. Al and Sal are avid sports memorabilia collectors. Al owns a baseball signed by Mickey Mantle. Sal owns a football signed by Joe Montana. Both purchased these items years ago and they have appreciated in value. They trade. What are the tax consequences to them of this trade? _____

94. What are the rationales for the nonrecognition sections of the Code such as §§1031 and 1033? _____

95. Katherine owns Blackacre, in which she has a basis of $40,000. It has a fair market value of $100,000. Spencer owns Blueacre, in which he has an adjusted basis of $30,000. It has a fair market value of $90,000. Both Blueacre and Blackacre are parcels of land held for investment by their owners. Both parties intend to hold the property received for investment. Katherine and Spencer trade their properties, and as part of the trade Spencer transfers a sports car to Katherine. What are the tax consequences of this trade to Spencer and Katherine? _____

96. Assume the same facts as in the previous question, except that Spencer did not hold Blueacre for investment, although he intends to hold Blackacre for investment. What are the tax consequences of this trade for Spencer and Katherine?

97. Assume the same facts again as in Question 95, except that Katherine and Spencer are married at the time of the transaction. What are the tax consequences to Katherine in this situation? _____

98. Jim owns Wineacre, a parcel of land on which he has unsuccessfully tried to grow grapes for years. The land has fallen in value, so that now his basis is $200,000 and the fair market value of Wineacre is $150,000. Jim is giving up the wine business. A friend of his is in the squash-growing business and offers to trade Squashacre for Wineacre. Jim agrees. How should he go about this transaction from a tax point of view? _____

99. Tony owns Rome Tower and Cleo owns Egypt Tower. Both are commercial office buildings. The properties have the following characteristics:

	Tony—Rome Tower	**Cleo—Egypt Tower**
Fair market value	$300,000	$180,000
Adjusted basis	$160,000	$200,000
Mortgage	$150,000	$0

Cleo transfers Egypt Tower to Tony. Tony transfers Rome Tower to Cleo, subject to its mortgage. Tony also transfers $30,000 to Cleo as part of this transaction. What are the tax consequences of this exchange to Tony and Cleo? _____

100. Let's take another look at Tony and Cleo from the previous question. Assume the following alternative facts:

	Tony—Rome Tower	**Cleo—Egypt Tower**
Fair market value	$300,000	$180,000
Adjusted basis	$160,000	$100,000
Mortgage	$180,000	$60,000

They exchange properties, each assuming the other's mortgage, with the lenders' approval. What are their tax consequences? _____

101. Harry and Sally are getting a divorce. Under the terms of their divorce decree, Sally will be deeded the marital home, which has a fair market value of $200,000 and an adjusted basis of $150,000. She will also receive stock in ABC Corporation with a fair market value of $100,000 and an adjusted basis of $175,000. Harry will receive the rest of the assets. What are the tax consequences to Harry and Sally of these transactions?

_____

102. Ivanna and Steve are getting a divorce. In the divorce decree, the marital home is given to Ivanna in her sole name, with the proviso that it must be sold within eight years and the proceeds split 50/50. In the meantime, Steve must continue to pay the mortgage, taxes, insurance, and repairs. The home is sold eight years after the divorce and the proceeds are split between Steve and Ivanna. Steve insists that he has no gross income to report on the sale transaction. Is he correct? _____

103. Don owned a commercial fishing boat in Miami in which he had an adjusted basis of $200,000. It had a fair market value of $600,000. The fishing boat was destroyed by a hurricane in December of Year 1. In January of Year 2, Don received insurance proceeds of $600,000 from the insurance company. He spent the rest of Year 2 looking for a suitable replacement. In December of Year 2, he purchased a new fishing boat for $500,000. What are the tax consequences of these events to Don? What if he decided that the commercial fishing business was an industry of the past and the new boat was designed to take tourists on deep-sea fishing trips? _____

CHAPTER 11

TIMING OF INCOME AND EXPENSES

104. Why does the U.S. income tax system use an annual accounting system?

_____

105. Jerry's business has been profitable in the past and he paid taxes in the years 2000–2007. Due to the downturn in the economy, the business produced a $100,000 loss in 2008. Jerry would like to "average" his income over the years. May he do so, and if so, how?

106. Sandy entered into a consulting contract for services with Rocky Corp. The contract said that Sandy was to be paid $100,000, but if her consulting services did not increase Rocky's sales of gravel and sand by 35 percent by the end of the next year, the consulting contract price would be reduced based on a formula. Sandy received $100,000 in Year 1, but had to repay $15,000 in Year 2. How would Sandy prefer to report the receipt of income in Year 1 and how should she do so? _____

107. Tom is a lawyer using the calendar year and the cash method of accounting. Tom performed work in December and gave the client his bill, but the customer didn't pay until January. When will Tom properly include this payment in his gross income?

_____

108. Consider Tom from the previous problem. What if Tom's client had showed up at his office on December 31 with a check but Tom refused to let him in? _____

109. Pam, a calendar year, cash-method taxpayer, wants to claim a Year 1 deduction for the following payments. Which of the following, if any, will be deductible in Year 1?

(a) Her check written and mailed on December 29, Year 1, for payment of state personal income taxes.

(b) Her check written and mailed December 29, Year 1, but postdated January 1, Year 2, for a charitable contribution.

(c) Her check written and mailed December 29, Year 1, for otherwise deductible trade or business expenses on an account for which she is aware there are insufficient funds to honor the check.

(d) Same as (c), except that because of a mistake made by her bank, of which she had no knowledge, there are insufficient funds in the account to honor the check.

(e) Her check written December 29, Year 1, for alimony that will be due January 31, Year 2.

110. Opie is a motivational speaker, using the calendar year and cash method of accounting. He paid otherwise deductible expenses of $5,000 this year, by paying $2,000 by check and $3,000 by credit card. He also owed the local office supply store $4,500 as of year end. When will Opie properly deduct these amounts? _____

111. Oils R Us, an aromatherapy store, opened the year with $10,000 of inventory on hand. It purchased another $25,000 of products from suppliers, and its year-end count shows $12,000 of inventory on hand. It had gross sales of $50,000. What is its net income considering only inventory expenses? _____

112. Adam works for BigCo. On each anniversary of his commencement of employment with BigCo, Adam receives 500 shares of BigCo stock from BigCo. However, Adam cannot sell the stock, and if he leaves BigCo prior to the fifth anniversary of receiving the stock, he must forfeit all his rights to such stock. What are the tax consequences of Adam's receipt of the stock? _____

113. GoTown Recording Studios uses the calendar year and the accrual method of accounting. It engages Soundbites Corp. to provide mixing services in Year 2 for a stated amount. GoTown will pay Soundbites in two payments, one at the end of Year 1 and the second six months later in Year 2. When will GoTown properly deduct the payments to Soundbites? _____

114. Samantha owned Hideaway Hills, a ranch in California. Samantha is not a dealer in such property and the ranch is not her personal residence. She has a basis of $300,000 in the ranch. She sold Hideaway Hills to Darin for $1,000,000. Darin will pay her $200,000 per year, plus interest at market rates, for the next five years. When will Samantha report the gain on the sale of the ranch? Is there any other income to report? _____

115. Sara paid $5,000 of state income taxes and deducted this amount on her federal tax return for Year 1. This entire amount reduced her tax. In Year 2, she received a refund of $2,000 of those state income taxes. What are the tax consequences to Sara of receipt of the refund in Year 2? _____

116. Bev, a college basketball coach, inherited an apartment building from her mother. This year, it produced a net loss for tax purposes of $40,000. Bev wants to deduct this amount on her income tax return. May she do so? _____

CHAPTER 12

CHARACTER OF INCOME AND LOSS

117. Your best friend is applying to be an IRS auditor. She's been studying for weeks and is very nervous about the upcoming test. She calls you and asks, "Why is it, exactly, that taxpayers seek to characterize income as ordinary and loss as capital?" Please answer her. _____

118. Wally is a sole proprietor engaged in the business of selling hand-carved duck decoys. Which of the following is *not* a capital asset in his hands: (1) his residence, (2) his supply of wood, (3) his stamp collection, (4) his antique tractor? _____

119. Laura won the lottery, and is entitled to receive $100,000 a year for 25 years. She did not want to wait for her money. So, just one year after the date she won, she sold her rights to receive the cash to Mr. X for $1,400,000. She claimed that the gain on sale (her lottery ticket cost $5, so her gain is $1,399,995) is capital and she is entitled to be taxed at 15 percent on the gain. Is she correct? _____

120. Regina sells the following assets on the dates given. Will she have long-term or short-term capital gain or loss? _____

Asset	Acquisition Date and Method	Disposition Date	Short Term or Long Term?
Stock	Jan. 1, Year 1, purchase	Dec. 30, Year 1	
Stock	Jan. 1, Year 2, purchase	Jan. 1, Year 3	
Land held for investment	Through like-kind exchange on Jan. 1, Year 2. Her relinquished property had been held for two years.	July 1, Year 2	
Coin collection	Jan. 1, Year 3, as gift from father	July 1, Year 3	

121. Wally (from Question 118) also owns a van in which he travels to country fairs to display his ducks. He has an adjusted basis of $35,000 in the van. He sells it for $25,000. What is the character of his loss on the sale, and how will he be taxed on it? Alternatively, what if in the same year he sold his display cabinets at a gain of $35,000? _____

122. John is a singer and songwriter. He has a collection of guitars and other musical instruments that he acquired from a famous singer many years ago. He purchased them for $50,000, and has taken $30,000 of depreciation on them. The instruments have appreciated in value and when his wife insists he get a "real job," he sells all of them for $100,000. What are the tax consequences to him of this sale? _____

123. Why are there two rates for the 15/0 percent category of net capital gain? _____

124. Michael purchased a parcel of land in Hawaii for $2,000,000. He held it for several years while he proceeded to get the proper zoning for homes of five acres or less, and put in streets and essential services, such as water and sewer lines. He then sold the entire parcel to Gwyneth for $5,000,000. Is he entitled to capital gains treatment? Why or why not? What if, instead of selling the entire parcel, he sold ten lots to people who proceeded to build homes on the property? _____

125. Corrie purchased a house for $120,000. She used it as a rental property, and properly claimed $30,000 of MACRS deductions with respect to it. In due course, she sold it for $150,000. How is she taxed on the gain or loss recognized from this transaction, and why? What if she had sold it for $80,000? _____

126. Andrea had the following transactions during the year:

(a) Sale of land held for more than one year: $5,000 loss
(b) Sale of ABC stock held for more than one year: $15,000 gain
(c) Sale of NOP stock held for less than one year: $25,000 loss
(d) Sale of stamp collection held for more than one year: $20,000 gain

What are the tax consequences of these transactions to Andrea? _____

127. Des is in the business of manufacturing basketballs. This year, the following events occurred with respect to equipment used in the trade or business:

- Property A was destroyed by fire. Loss = $30,000.
- Property B was sold. She recognized a gain of $45,000, of which $10,000 was §1245 recapture income.
- Property C was sold. She recognized a $15,000 loss on that sale.

What are the tax consequences of these transactions to Des? _____

128. In the previous question, what if Bev had experienced a net $5,000 §1231 loss in the previous year? _____

129. What are the principal arguments *for* having a tax preference for capital gain income? Against? Why are there substantial restrictions on the deduction of capital losses? _____

130. Brian, strapped for cash, sells his blood plasma. He makes two claims to reduce his taxes. First, he argues that he has no income at all from the sale because he is really worse off—he feels physically ill afterward. Second, even if he has income, it is capital gain, not ordinary income. Is Brian correct? _____

131. Why do the ordering rules for applying capital losses to reduce capital gains exist? Do they make a difference in actual tax due for taxpayers? _____

CHAPTER 13

TAX RATES AND CREDITS

132. How does a tax credit differ from a tax deduction? How does it differ from an exclusion from gross income? _____

133. In 2009, Ray, a single taxpayer, sold some stock in which he had invested many years ago. He realized and recognized a $10,000 long-term capital gain. Ray wants to know how he will be taxed on this gain. Consider the following two alternatives: (a) Ray's taxable income (not considering this gain) is $260,000, or (b) Ray's taxable income (not considering this gain) is $6,000. _____

134. What is the rationale for the AMT? Give two examples of AMT adjustments that support this rationale. _____

135. Catherine, a single taxpayer, had the following items of income and deduction in 2009:

Salary income:	$129,400
Taxable interest income:	$3,000
Alimony payments:	$12,000
Interest on private activity tax-exempt bonds:	$2,000
Home mortgage interest on condo:	$5,000
State income tax:	$9,000
Medical expenses in excess of 7.5% of adjusted gross income	$1,000
Charitable deductions:	$2,000
Miscellaneous itemized deductions in excess of 2% floor:	$3,000

Will Catherine pay AMT? Why or why not? _____

136. Catherine, from the previous example, tells you that her obligation to make alimony payments will terminate at the end of 2008. Assuming that all of Catherine's other items remain the same, and the exemption amounts also remain unchanged, will Catherine's glee in having the alimony payments terminate be dampened by having to pay AMT? _____

137. A reckless newspaper reporter wrote a story about Becky that she was negligent in her duties as an employee of a child care facility. Becky sued the reporter and the newspaper for libel, and was awarded $300,000 in damages. Under Becky's agreement with her attorney, the attorney was entitled to one-third of this amount, or $100,000. What are the tax consequences of this transaction to Becky? _____

138. Candace is a single mother of two children, ages six and eight. Her AGI is $38,000. She spends $3,000 per year on child care while she works, and another $500 for their care while she travels as a volunteer for the American Cancer Society. What are the tax consequences to Candace of these expenditures? _____

139. Jordan has earned income and modified adjusted gross income (MAGI) of $10,000 and is a single father of one child, age ten. Assume an Earned Income Amount of $8,950 and a Phaseout Threshold of $16,420. To what earned income credit, if any, is he entitled? _____

140. Kara and Jim are married, filing jointly. They have three children. Their MAGI is $25,000. Assume an Earned Income amount of $12,570 and a Phaseout Threshold of $19,540. Are they entitled to an earned income credit and if so, what is the amount of the credit? _____

141. In what significant way does the earned income credit, the paid-taxes credit, and to some extent the child credit differ from the child care credit? _____

142. Paul and Inga are married and file a joint return. Their modified AGI is $102,000. Inga is a full-time student in a graduate program in education at the local college. She paid $14,000 in tuition in 2009. Their daughter, Susan, is starting college, and they paid $20,000 in tuition and academic fees for her. She is a dependent of Paul and Inga. Assume the Phaseout Threshold is $100,000 for the Lifetime Learning Credit and $160,000 for the American Opportunity Credit. What tax credits are Paul and Inga entitled to claim on their income tax return? _____

143. Erin is thinking about buying a home in 2009. She has never owned a home before, but has found a small condo that is perfect for her. The purchase price is $150,000, and she plans to put $50,000 "down" and finance the rest with a mortgage. What tax benefits may Erin claim as a result of this transaction? _____

CHAPTER 14

IDENTIFYING THE TAXPAYER

144. What is the tax incentive for a taxpayer to "assign income"? If tax rates become more progressive, is there a greater or lesser incentive to engage in assignment of income strategies? _____

145. Danielle writes romantic novels. Her daughter Tiffany is 12 years old. Danielle requests that her publisher (the owner of the copyright to Danielle's works) pay all the royalties on the book to be published this year to Tiffany, so that Tiffany can begin saving money for college. Her publisher does so, and reports Tiffany as the taxpayer on the required Form 1099. Is this correct? _____

146. Will Danielle be successful in having the royalties taxed to Tiffany if she owned the copyright and transferred it to Tiffany? _____

147. Sam is Peter's grandfather. Peter's parents are living. Sam owns a number of bonds and regularly receives interest payments on these bonds. Sam directs the company that issued the bonds to pay Peter, rather than Sam, the interest on the bonds for two years. The company does so. Who is taxed on this interest, and why? _____

148. Assume the same facts as in the previous question, except that the bonds are tax-exempt private activity bonds. Why would it matter who is taxed on these interest payments if they are tax exempt? _____

149. Barbara is George's mother. Barbara owns a ranch in Texas. In Year 1, she transferred an undivided 50 percent interest in the ranch to George, as a gift. In Year 10, a buyer purchases the ranch for $2,000,000. Barbara and George each report one-half of the gain on the sale. Is this correct? _____

150. Brian files a lawsuit against Rob alleging defamation of character. Prior to trial, Brian's health starts to fail. He assigns his rights in the action to Steve for a payment of $500,000. The trial and subsequent appeals result in an award of $5 million. Who, if anyone, must include this amount in gross income? _____

151. Kayla, a single taxpayer, sues her employer for race discrimination. She hires an attorney on a contingent fee basis to represent her. Ultimately, the court enters a judgment of $500,000 against the employer. The lawyer's share of that is $165,000 for fees and $35,000 for costs, and Kayla receives $300,000. How should she treat this transaction for tax purposes? Assume 2009 rates, and disregard any phaseout of itemized deductions on personal exemptions for regular tax purposes. _____

152. Assume the same facts as in the previous question, except that the action was for slander rather than discrimination. What changes, if anything? _____

153. Spencer is age 12. He has a paper route, from which he makes $3,600 per year. He also has investment income of $3,000 per year from stocks and bonds given to him by relatives over the years. Spencer's parents are living. How will Spencer be taxed on his income? _____

154. Spencer's brother, Corbin, is age 20. He is a student at the local community college and has a part-time job at a local coffee house. He has investment income of $5,000 per year. How will Corbin be taxed on this income? _____

CHAPTER 15

TIME VALUE OF MONEY: PRINCIPLES AND APPLICATIONS

155. Why should (and do) taxpayers care about the time value of money? _____

156. What is the present value of a promise to pay you $10,000 in five years, if the appropriate interest (discount) rate is 5 percent? What if the interest (discount) rate were 9 percent? _____

157. How much would you have to invest today to have $10,000 in eight years, if interest rates held steady at 6 percent? At 12 percent? _____

158. If you had $3,000 to invest today, and interest rates held steady at 4 percent, how much would you have at the end of 10 years? 15 years? 30 years? _____

159. Your rich aunt gives you a choice of receiving a gift of $50,000 today or a gift of $70,000 five years from now. Interest rates are holding steady at 8 percent. Which should you choose, assuming you are a rational taxpayer? _____

160. Grandmother is considering making a gift to her granddaughter, who is heading for college in a few years. She could either give the granddaughter $5,000 or contribute the same amount to a 529 plan for the granddaughter's benefit. From a tax perspective *only*, which plan would be better for Grandmother to implement? _____

161. Beverly is a doctor with a large income taxed at the highest federal and state tax rates. She tells you about an interesting offer that she has heard about from her broker. She has an opportunity to invest in a venture to locate and communicate with alien life forms. This has dazzling commercial potential. Start-up costs would be large, and she would have to invest $75,000, but this would result in over $300,000 of losses, which would serve as deductions to her over the next five years. She could use them to offset her salary income. Beverly consults you about this idea. What do you say? _____

162. Of the following, which one is *not* an income deferral strategy?

(a) Investing in real estate
(b) Use of the cash method
(c) Categorizing payments to a former spouse as alimony rather than child support
(d) Engaging in a like-kind exchange

163. Identify two methods the Code and/or courts and IRS use to combat inappropriate income deferral strategies. _____

164. Ronald owned the Flying Z Ranch. Due to failing health, he sold the ranch to his good friend James for $900,000. The contract called for payment in a single lump sum in five years, with no provision for interest. Ronald's basis in the ranch was $400,000, so he simply reported $500,000 of capital gain in the fifth year when he received payment. At the time the contract was entered into, the applicable federal rate was 6 percent. Was Ronald's reporting position correct? What is James's basis in the ranch? _____

165. Joe's mother wants to lend Joe $10,000, interest-free. What will be the tax consequences of this loan? What if the loan were $100,000? $1 million? _____

ANSWERS TO SHORT-ANSWER QUESTIONS

1. In order to avoid the substantial understatement penalty of §6662, the taxpayer might choose to fully disclose the details of a transaction.

2. Precedential value means, in the tax world, that authorities can be cited as precedent in the Tax Court and that, if they are administrative guidance, the IRS will be bound by such rulings. Court opinions, temporary and final regulations, revenue rulings, and revenue procedures all have precedential value and all bind the IRS except for some court opinions (it is bound by the Supreme Court's opinions, and appellate courts' opinions for tax controversies appealable to that circuit). Authorities that do not have precedential value and do not bind the IRS: private letter rulings and Technical Advice Memoranda addressed to other taxpayers; Chief Counsel Advice; proposed regulations; the Internal Revenue Manual; and forms and instructions issued by the IRS. Also (need it be said?) *Time* magazine—while possibly a source of tax information—does not generate opinions with precedential value.

3. Willie has two alternatives. He can file a petition in the U.S. Tax Court, if he files within 90 days of the date of the Statutory Notice of Deficiency. If he does so, he won't have to pay the tax unless and until the Tax Court decides against him. But he might want to consider coming under the wing of the Bankruptcy Court—this will stay enforcement proceedings. There is no guarantee that the taxes will be dischargeable in bankruptcy, but maybe he could get to keep his guitar and truck.

4. In a U.S. District Court, a taxpayer has the right to a jury trial, while cases in the U.S. Tax Court are tried to a judge, not a jury.

5. Both private letter rulings and Revenue Rulings address the application of the tax laws to a particular set of facts. But a private letter ruling is a form of written determination by the IRS, which is addressed to a particular taxpayer in response to the taxpayer's request. It is binding only with respect to that taxpayer. It cannot be used or cited as precedent. A Revenue Ruling is a statement of the law issued by the IRS not addressed to any particular taxpayer, and has precedential effect.

6. It appears that the tax preparer is concerned that the tax return position previously taken would not pass muster under the standards of §6694, which imposes penalties on tax preparers who take unreasonable positions. In order to comply, the preparer must conclude that the position taken has a reasonable basis, and if the position is not disclosed on the return, it must be supported by substantial authority. It appears that in this situation, the position that the tax preparer wishes to take is supported by a reasonable basis (or the tax preparer could not take the position at all), but the preparer appears concerned that the higher substantial authority standard might not be met.

7. Taxpayers are not expected to have the same access to or experience with the various administrative interpretations of the Code as tax professionals, so taxpayers would not be able to evaluate whether a particular position met the "reasonable basis" or "more likely than not" standards. However, taxpayers are expected to determine if the positions they are taking are frivolous, a relatively low standard to meet.

8. In advising the congressman, you would focus on the fairness, administrative practicality, and economic effects of this provision.

Fairness: Does it treat persons similarly situated, as to their ability to pay, in a similar fashion? Doubtful. Certainly the good congressman is correct that many people getting a divorce have extra expenses associated with that divorce, and this reduces their ability to pay. But the proposal has two faults (at least) in the fairness arena. The first problem is the reach of the statute. It is not limited to people who really have extra expenses, nor does it distinguish the year in which those expenses actually occur. Second, divorce expenses are clearly personal expenses. While some personal expenses are deductible (such as certain medical expenses and casualty losses), in all of these cases you can be pretty sure that the taxpayer is really "out" a significant amount of money. Not so with divorces—in fact, some people (those married to compulsive shoppers, for example) may be saving money by getting a divorce.

Administrative practicality: It seems to be easy to administer, at least in its current form. The year of divorce is easy to identify, and the people getting a divorce are also easy to identify. However, one might wonder how to distinguish between real divorces and those designed to take advantage of this deduction (see below).

Economic effects: Here is where you tell your congressman that "this dog won't hunt." Not only does it appear he is supporting divorce, he may in fact appear to be creating an economic incentive for people to get a divorce. It's a political dead end because of these unintended effects.

9. [No answer required.]

10. "Gross income" is the term used in §61 to mean all income, from whatever source derived. It is the beginning place for the calculation of taxable income, the tax base on which the income tax is levied. You can tell Buffy that the "gross" in "gross income" refers to the fact that no deductions are taken in determining it.

11. The Haig-Simons definition of income defines income as the sum of (1) all rights exercised in consumption, plus (2) the change in value of property rights from the beginning to the end of the taxable period. Cally exercised $252,000 in consumption rights. She also had a net increase in property rights of $48,000 (the CD) plus the interest accrued on that amount during that year ($960). Thus, her total income (under this theory) is $300,960 for the year, exactly the same as what she earned.

12. Cally started with a property right worth $48,000 and ended with a property right worth $2,000. In the Haig-Simons definition of income, the net decrease in property rights ($46,000) is a reduction in her income for that year.

13. Yes, anyone's payment of Nick's obligations results in an economic benefit to him, and so he has income in the Haig-Simon sense. Later chapters will discuss specific exclusions for gifts.

14. Ken does not have an economic benefit from taking out the loan, because he has an offsetting obligation to repay the loan. It doesn't matter what the loan was for; the loan and the purchase of the car are two different transactions.

15. Imputed income is the value of the use of property one owns, or the services one performs for oneself. The value of all of Martha's activities that she performs for herself and family (child care, decorating, cooking, etc.) constitute imputed income. Also, one-half of the rental value of her home is imputed income to her (the other one-half is imputed to her co-owner, her husband). The advice she gives to others is not imputed income, as it is not services she provides for herself (nor does she appear to be receiving income for this activity). However, under our system of taxation, imputed income is not included in gross income. This avoids the difficult question of how to value these services.

16. Don's income from the sale of Chump Chowder is $250,000, the difference between the sales price ($750,000) and his cost of the property ($500,000). Don is entitled to recover his capital investment in the property and be taxed only on the gain he experiences on the sale.

17. Both have income. This is a barter transaction, in which the value of the services exchanged will be income to both parties. It will probably be easier to value the services based on the standard fee for boarding dogs, so each will have income equal to that fee.

18. No. Lana has simply transformed money into property; she has had no increase or decrease in income under any theory. However, if she receives dividends on the stock, that would be income to her.

19. Internal Revenue Code §61(a) provides that gross income includes all income from whatever source derived, including income from services. Diane has gross income of $3,500, which is the value of the car she received from her business, which she must include in her gross income. She is not taxed on the mere promise to pay in the future, so the promise to pay $3,000 is not income to her until she receives it, in cash or in kind.

20. Michael must include some of each payment in his gross income. IRC §72 determines the amount to be included. Michael must multiply each payment by the "exclusion ratio," the numerator of which is his investment in the contract and the denominator of which is the expected total return of the contract. The resulting number will be the nontaxable amount (his capital recovery) and the rest he must include in gross income. The expected total return is calculated by taking Michael's life expectancy and multiplying it by the annual payment on the contract ($100,000 × 20 years = $2,000,000). In Michael's case, the exclusion ratio produces the following result for each payment:

$$\$100,000 \times \frac{\$500,000}{\$2,000,000} = \$25,000 \text{ (nontaxable)}$$

The remaining $75,000 of each payment is included in Michael's gross income.

21. If Michael died on January 30 of the year he turned 67, let us assume that he received a payment of $100,000 in each of the years in which he turned 65, 66, and 67. Thus, he had recovered $75,000 of his total $500,000 investment in the contract ($25,000 per year × 3 years). Let us assume also that the remaining amount of $1,700,000 (17 years × $100,000) is paid in the year of death to his estate or beneficiary. In that case, the estate or beneficiary is able to claim an exclusion of $425,000 of the total amount received, which is Michael's unrecovered investment in the contract at the time of his death. Thus, of the $1,700,000 received, only $1,275,000 is includable in the estate or beneficiary's gross income.

22. These payments appear to meet the requirements of alimony: They are made in cash and received under a divorce decree; the parties aren't living together; the payments stop if the recipient dies; and they are not disguised child support. Thus, they should be included in the gross income of the recipient, Bill. However, because the payments vary by more than $15,000 per year, they will be considered "front-end loaded" and be subject to the special rules of §71(f). This section requires that the amount of so-called excess alimony payments be included in the income of the payor in the third post-separation year. To determine the excess alimony payment, a rather complex calculation must be completed, as follows:

Step 1: Compute the excess payment for the second post-separation year. (IRC §71(f)(4))

Alimony paid Y2 − (Alimony Y3 + $15,000)

$50,000 − ($25,000 + $15,000)

$50,000 − $40,000 = $10,000 = Excess payment for second post-separation year.

Step 2: Compute the excess payment for the first post-separation year. (IRC §71(f)(3))

$$\$100,000 - \left\{ \left[\frac{((\$50,000 - 10,000) + \$25,000)}{2} \right] + \$15,000 \right\}$$

$100,000 − ($32,500 + $15,000)

$100,000 − $47,500

$52,500 = Excess payment for first post-separation year.

Step 3: Add the two excess payments together:

```
   $10,000 second year
+   52,500 first year
   $62,500 total
```

The total amount is the amount that will be included in Cindy's gross income and deducted from Bill's gross income in computing AGI in the third post-separation year.

23. It is tempting to label this as alimony: It is payable in cash, pursuant to the divorce decree, and presumably the couple are living separately. However, there is no indication that the payments will stop upon the death of the recipient. If they are not required to cease at that time, the payments will not be alimony.

24. Greta has income. But how much? Focus on the exchange: Greta is providing a home for Harrison, and thus what she receives in exchange is properly considered rental income. This would be $200 per month plus the fair market value of the services Harrison would perform. The best way to measure this is to determine the fair rental value of the house, or, if that is not possible because there simply isn't a rental market for dilapidated mansions, by determining the hourly rate for carpenters.

25. Marc did not have income in the year of the loan because of the offsetting obligation to repay it. However, in the year it is forgiven (written off by the bank) he has discharge of indebtedness income in the amount of $1,000,000 (plus any accrued interest left unpaid).

26. Marc does not have discharge of indebtedness income if his mother repays the loan. This is a benefit to him, which would be income, but would probably be considered a gift, which would be excluded from his gross income.

27. Frieda has $15,000 of discharge of indebtedness income that is included in her gross income unless she can fall within any of the exceptions of IRC §108(b), such as the insolvency exception. If Frieda had a legitimate basis for disputing any of these charges, however, the discharge attributable to those amounts would not constitute discharge of indebtedness income under the disputed liability doctrine. Allocation of the discharge among disputed and accepted items is a question of fact.

28. If Greg paid for the disability insurance premiums with after-tax dollars (money he has after he pays income taxes), the amounts received would be excluded from his gross income. If the employer paid for the premiums, with before-tax dollars (these amounts were paid as a fringe benefit, so they never entered Greg's gross income), the amounts received under the policy are includable in Greg's gross income.

29. Bea may exclude the prize from her gross income: She didn't do anything to enter the competition; she need not perform any services; and she immediately transferred the award to charity. IRC §74.

30. Carlotta must include the $50,000 in her gross income. Her promise to repay the funds does not affect this result. In fact, it is very unlikely that any embezzler will be able to meet the four requirements of *James v. United States*, 366 U.S. 213 (1961).

31. (e). At least for a portion of the payment. Not all of the annuity payment will be included in gross income. When the taxpayer receives a periodic payment from an annuity, a portion of it is generally a tax-free return of capital (the amount paid for the annuity) and the rest is included in gross income. All of the other items (dividends, rents, royalties, and interest) are included in gross income.

32. Section 102(a) excludes from gross income bequests and inheritances. Rikki can exclude from her gross income the value of the carvings. (Her basis in the carvings will likely be their fair market value as of the date of her grandfather's death.)

33. Tonika may exclude amounts received as reimbursement for medical expenses, unless she previously deducted them and obtained a tax benefit as a result. Amounts received for physical injuries are also excludable from gross income (§104(a)) and thus all of these receipts are excludable from Tonika's gross income.

34. The adjustment in the amount of this indebtedness results in $700,000 of discharge of indebtedness income to DotComInc. However, because it is insolvent (liabilities exceed assets) it may exclude the discharged amount from gross income under §108(a), up to the amount of insolvency (which, in this case, is greater than the discharged amount). However, it must reduce its net operating loss to zero as a result of this discharge.

35. Although the company may view this as a "gift" in the sense that it was not required as a condition of employment, this is definitely included in Kerry's gross income. Section 102(c) provides that any transfer made from an employer to an employee is not considered a gift. Even if the transfer was made immediately after the employment relationship

ended, it related to the employment relationship and therefore would not be excluded as a gift.

36. Sheri may exclude from gross income the medical insurance premiums paid by her employer for her and her family (§106) and may exclude as a no-additional-cost fringe benefit (§132) the value of standby flights.

37. If the meals are provided for the convenience of the employer, the value of the meals is excluded from gross income. In this case, the employer's explanation does not support a "convenience of the employer" argument in the usual sense, and it is not clear whether the associates are "on call" during these meal times, as in *Benaglia v. Commissioner*, 36 B.T.A. 838 (1937), acq. 1940-1 C.B. 1. Unless these services were considered "de minimis" under §132, the concierge service will be included in the gross incomes of the associates who use the service, and the amount included will be the fair market value of such services (presumably valued by reference to the cost of such services in the market). "De minimis" in this context might include the occasional use of an office staff person for personal errands, but an entire program of such services provided on a regular basis would not qualify.

38. Section 121 requires the taxpayer to own and use the home as a principal residence for at least two of the past five years in order to exclude the gain on sale from gross income. Travis's use of the home qualifies and therefore he may exclude the $75,000 of gain from his gross income. (This assumes that he has not used the exclusion during the past two years.)

39. Bob has discharge of indebtedness income of $40,000. However, because the discharge relates to principal residence indebtedness—Bob's mortgage was to acquire his home—§108(a)(1)(E) applies to exclude this discharge of indebtedness income from Bob's gross income. He must, however, reduce the basis of the home by $40,000. A related question, which would change the result, is whether Bob's friend intended the discharge as a gift; if so, the discharge would be excluded under §102 and there would be no effect on basis.

40. Lisa may exclude the value of her employer's provision of insurance (both health and disability) from her gross income. IRC §106. She also may exclude the $25,000 of insurance reimbursements as they were for medical expenses. IRC §105(b). (The excess $5,000 not reimbursed by the insurance company may be deductible under IRC §213.) The disability payments she receives will be included in her gross income because her employer paid the premiums. IRC §105(b).

41. The payments from Hamm to Brenda should have been bifurcated into alimony ($250/month) and child support ($750/month). The latter is child support because it is tied to the child reaching age 18. Assuming the other requirements for alimony are met, the amount allocable to alimony should have been included in Brenda's gross income. The amount that is child support is excluded from her gross income.

42. Section 262 disallows a deduction for all "personal, living, and family expenses" unless they are deductible under a specific statute. Most of Lee's living expenses (food, rent, etc.) will not be the subject of any statute allowing deduction. In any event, personal expenses (if deductible) would not be deductible on Lee's Schedule C as part of his business expenses, but elsewhere on his return (Schedule A). They also would be subject to all of the restrictions associated with these deductions. Incidentally, this is the kind of unreasonable return position that could result in penalties, even fraud charges, against Lee.

43. Dan is entitled to deduct *either* the standard deduction *or* the itemized deduction, but not both.

44. A deduction is a subtraction from income in computing taxable income, and its benefit to a taxpayer is equal to the taxpayer's tax rate multiplied by the amount of the deduction. A tax credit is a dollar-for-dollar reduction in a taxpayer's tax. Neither is absolutely "better" than the other, but a deduction does benefit higher income taxpayers (who are in a higher tax bracket) proportionately more than lower income taxpayers. By contrast, a tax credit generates the same dollar benefit for all taxpayers who are entitled to it.

45. Jodi's purchase of equipment is a capital expenditure, not a deductible expense. Therefore, she cannot deduct it in the year of acquisition, but instead must recover the cost over time, through MACRS deductions, although §179 may apply to accelerate these deductions.

46. Adjusted gross income is the amount computed by subtracting certain items from gross income. Tax is not imposed on AGI, but instead on taxable income, which is the amount computed by subtracting certain items from AGI. Because AGI serves as a measurement for many other tax computations, such as phaseouts for certain tax benefits (e.g., personal casualty losses or medical expenses), reducing AGI tends to increase the likelihood that a taxpayer will benefit from these other reductions.

47. *Deductible in computing AGI:* moving expenses, retirement savings, capital losses, and alimony. *Deductible in computing taxable income:* personal exemption, standard deduction, charitable contributions, medical expenses, and net personal casualty losses.

48. IRC §215 allows Tom a deduction for alimony paid during the taxable year; this is a deduction from gross income in computing AGI. The child support is not deductible.

49. Dorothy's loss on her home is a personal casualty loss in the amount of $250,000 (the lower of basis or value). However, personal casualty losses are subject to two limitations. First, in computing the deduction, each loss is reduced by $500 (in 2009; however, in future years the "deductible" may return to its historic $100 amount). Second, personal casualty losses are deductible only to the extent they exceed 10 percent of AGI. Dorothy's AGI is $200,000, so the personal casualty loss of $249,500 is deductible to the extent it exceeds $20,000. Thus, her personal casualty loss is $229,500. This is a deduction on Dorothy's itemized return—i.e., available only to her if she itemizes, and therefore as a deduction from AGI in computing taxable income.

50. The theft of the shoes and receipt of the insurance proceeds is a constructive sale of that item, so Dorothy realizes $80,000 of gain on that transaction. This is a personal casualty gain. Personal casualty gains offset personal casualty losses, so that the net result is the net personal casualty gain (income) or net personal casualty loss (deduction). The net loss is $249,500 minus $80,000, or $169,500. To the extent this exceeds $20,000 (10 percent of Dorothy's AGI) it is deductible. Thus, $149,500 is deductible as an itemized deduction— i.e., available to her only if she claims the itemized deduction, and therefore as a deduction from AGI in computing taxable income.

51. Assuming that the property secures the debt, the interest on the acquisition indebtedness, up to $1,000,000 of debt, is deductible. Molly also may deduct the interest on an additional amount of debt ($100,000) as home equity indebtedness. The remaining interest will be nondeductible.

52. Sam is attempting to take a charitable deduction under §170 of the Code. Normally, a deduction for the fair market value of the property would be available to him (and it would be his burden to prove the value by appraisal). However, in this case, Sam appears to be receiving something of value. Without the burn, he would be in violation of the land use laws, and would have to remove the older home in some way to make way for the new home. By donating the home, he avoids this cost and places his property in compliance with local law. Although this is a close case, Sam probably is not entitled to a deduction for this donation. However, if Sam could show that the costs of removal were nominal, he may be able to claim a deduction for the property donation.

53. (a). A taxpayer must choose to deduct either state sales and use taxes *or* state income taxes.

54. The amount Pete received as reimbursement for medical expenses is not included in his gross income. The $10,000 distribution from the HSA is not includable in his gross income. The remaining $15,000 is deductible as an itemized deduction as medical expenses to the extent it exceeds 7.5 percent of his AGI. This 7.5 percent of AGI is $18,750, and because his remaining expenses are less than that amount, Pete may not deduct any amount as medical expenses as an itemized deduction.

55. The amounts Tom received as reimbursements of travel expenses are not included in his gross income. The excess amount ($27,500) is potentially deductible on his return. However, unreimbursed employee business expenses are deductible by the taxpayer only to the extent that they—along with all other expenses in this category of miscellaneous expenses—exceed 2 percent of the taxpayer's AGI. This amount is $2,800 ($140,000 × 2%). Thus, combining the $500 of miscellaneous expenses and $27,500 of unreimbursed expenses produces $28,000 of expenses. These are deductible only to the extent that they exceed $2,800. Therefore, $25,200 of these expenses is deductible. This is a deduction on Tom's itemized return—i.e., available to him only if he itemizes, and therefore as a deduction from AGI in computing regular taxable income. These deductions, however, will be limited in computing AMT and might subject Tom to this tax.

56. In order to claim a personal exemption for any of these people, they must qualify as Janet's "dependent," which requires that they either be a "qualifying child" or a "qualifying relative." Janet may claim an exemption for her daughter as a "qualifying child," assuming that the daughter lives with Janet for at least half the year and doesn't provide over half of her own support. The stepdaughter will likely not qualify, because Janet is no longer married to the stepdaughter's father. None of the others qualify as a "qualifying child" because of the residence test (the son) and the relationships test (everyone else).

The foster child and the boarder are not "qualifying relatives" because of the lack of formal family relationship to Janet. However, her son, brother, mother, and even her niece may qualify, assuming that their gross incomes are less than the exemption amount ($3,650 for 2009) and that Janet provides over half of their support. Although it would appear that Janet's mother's income is greater than the exemption amount, only a certain amount of her Social Security benefits will be included in gross income, and it is not clear how much that would be; further investigation is necessary. Even though Janet's niece may be a nonresident alien, she is domiciled in Mexico, and therefore she could be a qualifying relative.

57. Usually, the cost of tuition, room, and board would be a nondeductible personal expense, even if part of the program is involved in treating a medical disorder. This is because the taxpayer is purchasing education, not medical care. See *Barnes v. Commissioner*, T.C. Memo 1978-339. If, however, the taxpayer can show that a portion of the fees paid are directly connected to remediation of the child's medical condition, and would not be paid but for that condition, this portion could qualify as a medical expense.

58. Catherine may establish either a Roth IRA or a regular IRA and may contribute up to $5,000 to it, unless she is age 50 or older, in which case her contribution could increase to $6,000. If Catherine establishes a regular IRA, she may deduct contributions to it, because although she participates in her employer's qualified retirement plan, her AGI does not exceed the threshold at which no deductible contributions can be made to it ($55,000 for 2009). Most taxpayers seem to prefer the Roth IRA, because distributions from the Roth are not includable in the taxpayer's gross income.

59. If Catherine contributes to a regular IRA, the contribution will grow tax-free until it is distributed to her after retirement. Distributions from the regular IRA will be included in her gross income, but she may believe that the combination of tax-free growth in the IRA and her anticipated lower tax rate in retirement still makes the regular IRA a good deal.

60. Maurice may deduct (but only if he "itemizes"—i.e., claims the itemized deduction) the following: $10,000 of legal fees, $1,500 in job search expenses, and probably the $500 in moving costs to remove his items from Donald's office. All of these will be miscellaneous itemized deductions subject to the 2 percent floor. The $5,000 in counseling will be a medical expense, which will be deductible as an itemized deduction to the extent it exceeds 7.5 percent of Maurice's AGI. Maurice's job search expenses will be deductible only if he is looking for a position in his current occupation. Expenses for looking for a position "in a completely different profession" will be capital in nature and nondeductible.

61. Section 162 allows a deduction for all of the ordinary and necessary expenses of carrying on a trade or business. Win's expenses for wages to employees, waxes, soaps, etc., and advertising would certainly fit within this category. The legal fees incurred in the dispute with a car owner would also qualify; even though they might be unique in Win's experience, legal fees are of the usual type of expenses incurred by businesspeople, and therefore considered "ordinary." Similarly, license fees are usually deductible, although there may be some question of when these are deductible (we don't know Win's method of accounting). Parking fines are not deductible, because §162(f) prohibits a deduction for fines or illegal payments. The fees for the séance are almost certainly not deductible; although courts generally don't substitute their judgment for those of businesspeople, in this case, the expenditure would probably not be considered "ordinary" or "necessary." The legal fees to settle the dispute about title to the parking lot are properly capitalized; they are not deductible, but instead become part of the basis in the asset (fee title or lease). Similarly, the van is a capital asset that must be capitalized. However, a portion of the expense may be deducted under IRC §179, which allows up to $250,000 (in 2009) to be deducted instead of capitalized.

62. Jody's basis in the rental home must be adjusted downward to account for MACRS deductions allocable to it. Residential real property is deductible on the straight-line basis, over 27.5 years. Therefore her annual depreciation deduction is $2,000 ($166.66 monthly). She is entitled to the following depreciation (MACRS) deductions:

Year 1	5.5 months	$917
Year 2	12 months	$2,000
Year 3	12 months	$2,000
Year 4	0.5 month	$83
Total		**$5,000**

As a result, her adjusted basis is $50,000, and the gain on sale is $30,000.

63. The promise from Adam is a "covenant not to compete," one of the so-called §197 intangibles that must be amortized over 15 years—regardless of the actual term of the promise. Therefore, Grant will take a deduction of $2,000 per year for 15 years attributable to the covenant.

64. The amount that Baxter paid for equipment is a capital expenditure that, except for amounts properly deductible under §179, must be capitalized and depreciated under MACRS. The leasehold improvements are amortizable on a straight-line basis over 15 years. Of his $10,000 of pre-opening expenses ($5,000 to his assistant and $5,000 of miscellaneous expenses) only $5,000 is deductible in the year of opening. The rest is amortizable over 15 years. The expenses incurred after opening are deductible, assuming that they otherwise meet the requirements of being ordinary and necessary.

65. When a taxpayer acquires real property, he or she is deemed to have acquired it on the midpoint of the month it is acquired, regardless of the day on which it is actually acquired. The function of these conventions is to simplify MACRS calculations. Therefore, Lenore will be able to claim 11½ months of depreciation for Year 1, not a full 12 months.

66. Xavier would like to take a deduction for the bad debt. Ideally, he would like the debt to be a business bad debt, because that leads to an ordinary deduction, rather than a capital loss.

- If Xavier is Zena's father, the first question is whether there is a debt at all, or if there were a debt, whether the "badness" of it is really the father making a gift to the daughter. If the debt is bona fide, and it is really a bad debt, it would be a nonbusiness bad debt, as it is family oriented, not related to the business (absent other facts).
- If Xavier is Zena's employer, there is a possibility that this could be considered a business bad debt if Xavier's primary motivation in making the loan was to further the business. If his primary motivation was to be a "nice guy," the debt is a nonbusiness bad debt.
- If Xavier is in the business of making loans, the debt is a business bad debt.

The distinction between a business and nonbusiness bad debt is important because business bad debts are deductible from gross income in computing adjusted gross income, while a nonbusiness bad debt is deductible only as a short-term capital loss.

67. Assuming Bennie's tax home is and remains at his home institution, his visit at the other school is a temporary job away from home. Therefore, Bennie traveled away from home on business, and is entitled to deduct his reasonable expenses while away from home, including rent, food (to a certain extent), and other expenses. These expenses are considered unreimbursed employee business expenses, deductible if he itemizes, but subject to the 2 percent limitation.

68. Wendy will probably be considered as creating a capital asset, because the restaurant is a separate and distinct asset from the catering business. As such, these expenses must be capitalized, but some or all of them may qualify as pre-opening expenses, in which case up to $5,000 is deducted in the year of opening and the rest is amortizable over 180 months.

69. If Richard's job required him to earn a law degree, he would be able to deduct the costs of his law school education. However, if his employer did not require it, the cost would not be deductible because it would qualify him for a new profession. In the latter case, Richard's argument that his information would help him better carry out his current duties would probably fall on deaf Tax Court ears. See *Galligan v. Commissioner*, T.C. Memo 2002-150.

70. A practicing lawyer who goes back to school to get an LLM can usually deduct these costs because that lawyer is in a trade of business. See *Ruehmann v. Commissioner*, T.C. Memo 1971-157. So, if Peter returns to school to get the LLM, he will likely be able to deduct the cost of the program. If Peter is seeking the LLM right out of law school, however, he probably will not be able to deduct the cost. Although Peter may argue that his wages from working show that he is in a trade or business and thus should be able to deduct the cost of the education, he may be viewed as experiencing an uninterrupted period of education rather than the establishment of a trade or business. A temporary law job occurring while the person is continuing his or her education may be more akin to education than a job, and thus would not create a trade or business for the student. See *Weyts v. Commissioner*, T.C. Memo 2003-68.

71. Bonbon must report the rental income as part of her gross income but may deduct the expenditures for repairs, property management, and taxes as ordinary and necessary expenses of the production of income under IRC §212. Thus, her net income, not considering MACRS deductions, will be $3,000. She will not be able to deduct the costs of the addition, as this is a capital expenditure. She will be able to claim MACRS deductions of some amount for the home and the addition, but these cannot be determined from the facts given.

72. Depreciation is allowed for capital assets—i.e., those that will last more than one year. To allow a deduction in the year of acquisition would result in a mismatch of income and the costs of producing the income over time—accelerating the deductions while the income would be reported over a number of years. Depreciation deductions match the "using up" of the asset to the income it produces over time. However, the schedule for depreciation (or amortization, for that matter) rarely matches up with the actual fall in value of the asset (if any). It is, at best, an approximation and Congress frequently tinkers with MACRS and §179 deductions to achieve non-tax economic goals.

73. Putting aside any employment law issues Howard may face, the cost of the yoga instructor (and the wages of employees while they take the class) is likely deductible as an ordinary and necessary business expense. The expense is ordinary (employers often expend amounts to improve employees' health and morale), the business connection is sufficient, and there is nothing to suggest that the expenditures are excessive or unreasonable. The employees would likely be able to exclude the value of the class as a fringe benefit under the de minimis exclusion of IRC §132(e)(1).

74. The origin of the expense rule determines whether an expense is personal or business related. *United States v. Gilmore*, 372 U.S. 39 (1963). In this case, the origin of the expense is Selena's activity as an employee—i.e., her trade or business. While the consequences could have been intensely personal (jail time), it is the origin, not the consequences, of the expense that is relevant. Therefore, the legal expense should be potentially deductible. However, this expense is an unreimbursed employee business expense, which is subject to the 2 percent floor of §67. This expense will be deductible for regular tax purposes to the extent that it, combined with all of her other miscellaneous expenses, exceeds 2 percent of Selena's AGI. It may be limited in computing the alternative minimum tax as well.

75. Tom's expenses can be analyzed in the following categories:

    (a) Country club dues of $10,000: ***nondeductible.***
        Section 274(a) provides that dues to social clubs are nondeductible. Tom may not deduct this amount.

    (b) Meals and entertainment $5,350: ***may be partially deductible.***

Golf greens fees (with clients):	$850
Restaurant meals (with clients):	$1,000
Sporting event tickets (clients attended as guests):	$3,500

Meals and entertainment expenses must run a gauntlet of requirements in order to be deductible. First, they must be "ordinary and necessary business expenses" as determined under §162. In this case, these are obviously ordinary expenses, as they are frequently incurred by business owners. They are of the type most business owners view as appropriate to their ability to obtain and retain business, and thus are "necessary." Tom is clearly carrying on a trade or business so there is no problem with pre-opening capitalization, and they do not create a specific benefit beyond the close of the taxable year, so they should not be capitalized under principles of *Indopco.*

Section 274, however, imposes additional requirements. First, with respect to meals, these must not be lavish or extravagant. The lavishness is, of course, a question of fact. It appears that Tom was with the clients at the meals, so no restriction will apply because of his absence. Next, with respect to the tickets, only the face value of the tickets may be deducted. No facts exist to determine whether the amount is in excess of the face value. The requirement of §274 that may create problems is the "business connection" test. Tom may find it difficult to meet the "directly related" test because both sporting events and golfing provide the kind of significant distraction that would preclude meeting that test. However, if he can show that he had a specific expectation of generating income, that he engaged in an active business discussion during the event, and that in light of all the facts and circumstances, it was primarily a business meeting, he can meet the test. However, Tom may meet the less stringent "associated with" standard if he can show that he had a clear business purpose in engaging in the activity, and that a substantial and bona fide business discussion occurred in connection with the activity. It is more likely that he will meet this test.

If he can meet either business connection test, the amounts expended will still be subject to the 50 percent limit: Only 50 percent of the amount will be deductible.

(c) Sporting event tickets for events that Tom did not attend but clients did of $500: ***nondeductible in full; possible partial business gift deduction.***

This expense might not even be considered an "ordinary and necessary business expense" under §162 because it appears to lack any connection to Tom's business. Assuming Tom could establish some connection sufficient to justify the expense under §162, the expense must nevertheless qualify under the more stringent provisions of §274. In the case of sporting event tickets where Tom did not attend, but clients did, it will be impossible for Tom to establish his right to deduct any part of the item as a meal and entertainment expense because the business connection test cannot be met—Tom cannot show a substantial and bona fide business discussion when he wasn't even there. However, Tom may be able to claim a business gift deduction for these tickets, subject to the limitations imposed on business gifts ($25 per person).

(d) Annual employee picnic of $1,600: ***fully deductible.***

This type of expense is clearly an "ordinary and necessary business expense" under §162 (see discussion above). Moreover, it is not likely that this would be considered a "lavish" event given the amount expended. Expenditures for employee picnics and similar events are exempt from the business connection tests and from the 50 percent limitation. Therefore, 100 percent of the cost of this event would be deductible.

76. Billie should be aware that the IRS may well challenge the deduction of losses from the horse farm as "hobby losses" under §183 of the Code. This provision denies a deduction for expenses in excess of income for activities not undertaken "for profit." Whether an activity is engaged in for profit depends on the taxpayer's intention, as evidenced by the nine factors outlined in the regulations. No one factor is determinative. However, a number of factors may work against Billie, including:

- *Time and energy spent on the activity:* As a surgeon, Billie probably has limited time to devote to the business. Relying on teenagers to handle the business is probably not a businesslike plan in the long run. She would need to engage a manager to handle the farm business.
- *Similar success:* Billie apparently has no experience in these matters.
- *Financial situation:* Billie has substantial income from other sources and doesn't need income from the farm to support her family. In fact, she could be expected to seek tax benefits from this activity.
- *Personal enjoyment:* Billie "longs for the country life." She seems to want to support her daughters' wish to ride horses, which would suggest a personal, not profit, motive. On the other hand, she is allergic to hay, which would suggest little pleasure in a horse farm.

If Billie is to make the best possible case for deducting any loss, she should ensure that she takes a businesslike approach to this endeavor, researching best practices and getting the professional help she needs to run the operation. She should be able to show that the farm will increase in value, and that these operations can and do produce profits, even if her particular farm does not. It would be helpful not to have many years of losses in a row.

77. This question raises the issue of when activities can be combined. If Ty can combine the law practice and polo activity, the deductions generated by the polo activity will offset his law income. Moreover, if he can combine the activities, he is more likely to qualify for a presumption of profit motive for the combined activity under the two-out-of-seven-years test. In deciding whether two activities can be combined, the courts will examine the closeness of the economic connection between the two, the similarity of the endeavors, the business purpose for conducting the two activities together or separately, and all of the other facts and circumstances of the situation. Treas. Reg. §1.183-1(d)(1). In this situation, it will be difficult for Ty to make a successful argument that the two activities should be combined. Ty's argument that he meets clients through polo would have to be substantiated by proof that in fact he relies on polo to generate significant fees, and even then, his argument is likely to fail because law practice and polo are not similar, nor is there any compelling business reason to operate them together. See *Mendoza v. Commissioner*, T.C. Memo 1994-314. For whether the polo activity, alone, would qualify, see Question 76.

78. Rudy has been reporting the results of the summer home incorrectly. He is correct in including all of the income from the rental of the property. However, because the property is used partially for personal purposes, the expenses must be allocated between personal and business use. The deductible expenses attributable to the rental (other than expenses deductible without regard to the rental) cannot exceed the total expenses (other than expenses deductible without regard to the rental) multiplied by the percentage of the year the home is rented. While Rudy will be able to deduct all of the property taxes, because these taxes are deductible regardless of rental activity, the rest of the expense will be limited.

79. Susan would like to deduct the expenses of her home office, and it appears that she can do so. She uses the home office exclusively on a regular basis as the principal place of business for her practice. A home office qualifies as a taxpayer's principal place of business if (1) the taxpayer uses the office to conduct administrative or management activities of the taxpayer's trade or business, and (2) there is no other fixed location of the trade or business where the taxpayer conducts substantial administrative or managerial functions of the business. This would appear to be the case for Susan; although she travels to trials, her administrative work is done at the home office and there is no other *fixed* place of business for her practice. As to which expenses are deductible, Susan can already deduct (regardless of the home office) the interest on her mortgage and her property taxes on the property. But because it is a home office, she may also deduct repairs made to that portion of the property and, perhaps most important, she can depreciate that portion of the dwelling. Of course, when she sells the home, she will not be entitled to the exclusion of §121 on the gain from the sale of a principal residence for the portion used as a home office and depreciated.

80. The fact that Jeff spends most of his time playing poker, studying poker, and entering tournaments suggests that he is a professional gambler. If so, he may deduct the poker losses for the year against the poker winnings for the year. He would report the winnings and losses on a Schedule C. However, the net loss for the year is not deductible. If Jeff is not a professional gambler, he may still deduct the poker losses, but again the loss would be limited to the poker winnings. In that case, Jeff would include his winnings as gross income and would deduct the gambling loss as an itemized deduction.

81. Meal expenses are one of those mixed personal and business expenses: while sharing a meal with a client or business associate may certainly further a taxpayer's business, it is also meeting a basic personal need. Moreover, when this limit was imposed, there was

some thinking that this would help curb the lavishness of such expenses that could not easily be monitored through use of the "ordinary and necessary" requirements of §162.

82. To answer this question fully, you may want to review the materials on barter. Steve and Mike have "bartered" their homes—i.e., traded in-kind use of the homes. Steve and Mike would be required to include in gross income an amount equal to the fair market value of the rental. If they did so, then each would be able to deduct expenses associated with that rental, subject to the limitations of §280A. Without including this amount in gross income, it is not possible to take the corresponding deduction.

83. Yes, probably—but how? These are not the kind of legal fees that Debbie could deduct as an above-the-line deduction, because the origin of the claim was state law, not federal anti-discrimination law. Debbie would like to deduct them on her Schedule C because they would be fully deductible. But they relate not to her trade or business that she is carrying on now, but instead to her relationship as an employee. Therefore, they are properly deductible on Schedule A as a miscellaneous expense subject to the 2 percent floor. This will likely hurt Debbie when she calculates her AMT because these expenses are not deductible in computing AMT.

84. As a result of this trade, Al and Sal both have realization events: What they received was different, qualitatively, than what they had before; they have different legal rights after the trade. Each has realized gain in the amount of the difference between the fair market value of what was received, and the basis of what was transferred. That gain will be recognized unless they can find a nonrecognition statute that applies.

85. This barter transaction results in income to both Taylor and Melique. Taylor has sold the sports car, and will recognize gain on that transaction equal to the difference between the fair market value of the sports car and its basis in Taylor's hands. (The value of the car is probably easier to determine than the value of the remodel.) Melique has received payment for services to be rendered, and must include the fair market value of the car in his gross income. Both Taylor and Melique would be wise to agree upon the fair market value of the sports car and report their two transactions consistently.

86. Basis represents the initial economic investment a taxpayer has in an item of property (or his or her deemed investment, as in the case of property received as a gift or from a decedent). Adjusted basis reflects the initial basis, plus or minus, respectively, the capital recovery claimed or improvements made to the property after acquisition. In both cases, basis or adjusted basis is the starting point for measuring the capital recovery deductions a taxpayer may claim, and is the way of measuring gain or loss on ultimate disposition of the property.

87. Dick has a realized and recognized gain of $200,000, which is equal to his amount realized ($300,000) minus his adjusted basis in the property of $100,000 ($140,000 − $40,000).

88. Dick has a realized and recognized gain of $200,000, which is equal to his amount realized of $300,000 ($200,000 in cash plus assumption of the $100,000 mortgage) minus his adjusted basis in the property of $100,000 ($140,000 − $40,000). Jerry's basis is $300,000, which is equal to his purchase price: $200,000 in cash plus the assumption of the mortgage.

89. No. Courtney is thinking that her loss is equal to the difference between the fair market value of the property ($600,000) and her adjusted basis ($750,000). But this is incorrect. She should have reported a *gain* of $200,000. Under *Tufts*, Courtney is deemed to have sold the property and the amount realized is equal to the amount of the outstanding loan ($950,000). Her adjusted basis in the property is $750,000 ($1,000,000 − $250,000 of MACRS deductions). This produces a gain of $200,000.

90. Linda has two transactions in the year of foreclosure and write-off. First, she has a sale of the property for $200,000. She had an adjusted basis of $400,000 in the property (her cost minus her depreciation deductions). This results in a $200,000 loss to her, which should be deductible under IRC §165(c). However, she also has $250,000 of discharge of indebtedness income. This may be excludable from Linda's gross income, however, if she meets any of the exceptions of §108(a), such as the insolvency exception.

91. The result would be the same, assuming that the value of the motel were $200,000 on the date of transfer.

92. When a taxpayer receives property and must include its fair market value in gross income, the basis of the property is its "tax cost," or the amount included in gross income. An example of tax cost basis is when a taxpayer is paid for services with property. The taxpayer includes the fair market value of the property in gross income, and takes the property with a basis equal to the amount included in gross income.

93. Al and Sal have realized gain attributable to the trade. However, assuming that these properties are held by Al and Sal "for investment," §1031 will probably apply to defer recognition of the gain. The football and baseball are properties of a like kind, and not the kind of property ineligible for like-kind exchange treatment (unless Al or Sal are in the business of collecting and trading memorabilia, in which case these items would be inventory to that person, and thus ineligible). If §1031 applies, Al and Sal will not recognize the gain associated with the trade, and will take a basis in the new item equal to the basis in the old item.

94. All of the nonrecognition provisions of the Code are about deferring the time at which gain or loss will be toted up and will appear on an income tax return. For like-kind exchanges, involuntary conversions, and divorce transfers, there is a sense that the time is not ripe for taxing gains and allowing losses: The taxpayers have stayed in the same investments or kind of investments and no cash has changed hands (and if it does, recognition of gain can occur). For like-kind exchanges, there is the added rationale that nonrecognition combats the "lock-in effect," the tendency to hold on to property to avoid the adverse income tax consequences. (Perhaps this rationale could be extended to divorce transfers as well—a different kind of "lock-in.") For involuntary conversions and divorce transfers, there is the added rationale of not kicking someone when they are down—waiting until a better time, when property is actually sold, to assess the taxpayer's true gain or loss.

95. Spencer and Katherine's tax consequences are analyzed separately.

- *Katherine's tax consequences assuming qualification as like-kind exchange:*

Realized gain: $60,000 = ($90,000 + $10,000) − $40,000
Recognized gain: $10,000 (the value of the sports car)
Basis in Blueacre: $40,000

- *Spencer's tax consequences assuming qualification as a like-kind exchange:*

Realized gain: $60,000 = $90,000 − $30,000
Recognized gain: -0-
Basis in Blueacre: $40,000 = $30,000 + $10,000

The fair market value of the sports car must be $10,000 if the transaction is to involve a trade of value for value. If Spencer's basis in the sports car were different from its fair market value, he would realize gain or loss on the transfer of the car. Realized gain would be recognized, but it is doubtful that loss would be recognized. Katherine's basis in the sports car would be $10,000 (its fair market value).

96. If Spencer did not hold Blueacre for investment, all of his realized gain would be recognized because the transaction would not qualify as a like-kind exchange. This does not affect Katherine's ability to qualify for like-kind exchange treatment.

97. If Katherine and Spencer are married, §1041 prevents the recognition of *any* gain on the transaction for either party. Katherine will take any property she receives with the same basis as it had in the hands of Spencer.

98. If Jim trades Wineacre for Squashacre, his loss will not be recognized. Therefore he should not trade properties; he should *sell* Wineacre and *purchase* Squashacre.

99. This is a qualifying like-kind exchange. Therefore, the parties' tax consequences are as follows:

- *Tony's tax consequences:*

Realized gain/loss: $140,000 = $330,000 − $190,000
Recognized gain: $120,000 = $150,000 − $30,000
Adjusted basis in Egypt Tower: $160,000

- *Cleo's tax consequences:*

Realized gain/loss: ($20,000) = $330,000 − $350,000
Recognized gain/loss: -0-
Adjusted basis in Egypt Tower: $320,000

100. Notice in this case that because the "equity" in each property is the same ($120,000) there will be no transfer of the additional $30,000 from Tony to Cleo. The tax consequences to Tony and Cleo are summarized in the table below.

	Tony	**Cleo**
Realized gain/loss	$140,000 gain	$80,000 gain
Recognized gain/loss	$120,000 (net relief from liability)	-0- (no net relief from liabilities)
Basis of new property	$160,000 old basis + 120,000 gain recognized − 180,000 Cleo's A/L + 60,000 Tony's A/L $160,000	$100,000 old basis + 0 gain recognized − 60,000 Tony's A/L + 180,000 Cleo's A/L $220,000

	Tony	**Cleo**
Is this correct?	If sold for FMV ($180,000), using this basis, Tony would recognize the realized gain that was not recognized: $20,000.	If sold for FMV ($300,000), using this basis, Cleo would recognize all of the gain that went unrecognized: $80,000.

101. The transfers of property are almost certainly incident to a divorce, and therefore §1041 applies to defer recognition of any gain or loss. Neither Harry nor Sally will have income as a result of these transactions, and each will take the property he or she receives with the basis it had immediately prior to the transfer. Therefore, Sally will receive the marital home with a basis of $150,000 and the ABC stock with a basis of $175,000.

102. Steve is probably right. Remember that §1041 applies as between the parties to a divorce, not to sales to third parties. Who owns the property is a question of fact, and in this case, Steve has a strong case that Ivanna was the owner of the property so that its sale to a third party generated income to her, not to Steve. The division of the proceeds of the sale would probably be governed by §1041, however, resulting in no income or a deduction to either party. Ivanna would probably be able to claim an exclusion under §121, which Steve would not be able to do because he did not live in the home or own it for the time periods required. See *Suhr v. Commissioner*, T.C. Memo 2001-28.

103. The destruction of the fishing boat is a constructive sale of the fishing boat, in which Don realizes a gain of $400,000, which is the difference between the amount received from the insurance company ($600,000) and his adjusted basis in the boat ($200,000). However, he may defer recognition of this gain if he meets the requirements of §1033. In order to qualify, he must reinvest the proceeds in similar property within two years. In this case, he probably qualifies, as he has purchased a commercial fishing boat within the requisite period. However, he did not fully invest the proceeds. Therefore, he will recognize $100,000 of gain, and his basis in the boat will be his old basis ($200,000) plus the gain recognized ($100,000), or $300,000. If he reinvests in a tourist fishing boat, he runs the risk that this will not be considered property similar in use, and therefore he may have to recognize all of the gain. This is a close case, and the IRS would be likely to assert that commercial fishing and tourist deep-sea fishing tours are not "similar" uses.

104. The government needs some way to measure a taxpayer's income and collect the tax in predictable, objective, and fairly frequent intervals. The taxable year concept provides that technique.

105. Income averaging *per se* is not possible, but Jerry may carry back his net operating loss to previous years or forward to future years. Although the usual rule is that losses can only be carried back two years, if Jerry's business is an "eligible small business," he can carry back the 2008 loss three, four, or five years at his option. He does this by filing amended returns, and this carryback has the result similar to "averaging" his income.

106. Sandy would like to report no income until the contingency is resolved, and defer that income to the future. However, Sandy had a colorable legal claim to $100,000 and must include that amount in income in the year of receipt. In the next year, she can invoke §1341 to pay the lower of the tax resulting from (a) computing the tax in Year 1 as if the

$15,000 had never been included; or (b) including the income in Year 1 and deducting the repayment in Year 2.

107. Because Tom is a cash method taxpayer, he will include the payment in gross income in the year he receives it—Year 2. When he performed the services and sent his bill is irrelevant.

108. Tom would be in constructive receipt of payment, because he had access to the money and refused to take it.

109. These questions address the proper timing of deductions for a calendar year, cash method taxpayer. A cash method taxpayer deducts amounts when paid.

    (a) For tax purposes, a timely mailing is a timely payment, so unless other factors exist that would prevent a deduction, Pamela may deduct payments made by check and mailed in Year 1 for otherwise deductible personal income taxes.

    (b) By postdating the check January 1, Year 2, Pamela prevents the check from being presented for payment until Year 2, and so the payment is not deductible until Year 2.

    (c) If the taxpayer is aware (or should be aware) that there are insufficient funds in the account on which the check is drawn, the mailing of the check does not constitute payment.

    (d) If the taxpayer had no knowledge (or reason to know) of the mistake and insufficient funds, mailing constitutes payment even if the check is dishonored.

    (e) Because the alimony isn't due until Year 2, Pamela cannot accelerate the deduction by prepaying it in Year 1.

110. Opie will deduct $5,000 for payments made, and it doesn't matter if they are made by check or credit card. He cannot deduct amounts owed at the end of the year because he has not yet paid them.

111. Oils R Us is required to account for inventories because it sells merchandise. It has $50,000 of gross income. Its cost of goods sold is computed by taking beginning inventory ($10,000), adding purchases ($25,000), and subtracting ending inventory ($12,000). Its cost of goods sold is $23,000. Therefore, its net income, considering only inventory costs, is $27,000 ($50,000 − $23,000).

112. Adam has received property for services, a transaction that generates compensation income to him. However, this property is "restricted": Adam cannot sell it and may forfeit his rights to the stock if he leaves BigCo. Under §83, Adam will include the fair market value of the stock in his gross income (and the employer, BigCo, will take a deduction) on the first date at which the stock is transferable or the forfeiture provisions lapse. For example, if Adam receives 500 shares on January 2, Year 1, the transferability and forfeiture provisions will lapse on January 2, Year 6, and Adam would be required to include in his gross income the fair market value of the shares in his gross income in Year 6 (at their value in that year). Adam can make a §83(b) election to include the value of the shares in his gross income when he receives them, which would be a good choice if he expects the value of the BigCo shares to increase in value.

113. As an accrual method taxpayer, GoTown generally deducts expenses when all events have occurred that determine the fact of the liability and the amount of the liability can be determined with reasonable accuracy. This test would normally lead to GoTown deducting the expense in Year 1. However, the economic performance rules are an overlay on the all events test. They provide that deduction cannot occur prior to economic performance. For the purchase of services, economic performance occurs when the services are provided. Therefore, GoTown may not deduct the payment until Year 2, when Soundbites provides the services.

114. Unless Samantha elects out of the installment method, she will report the gain realized on the transaction over the five-year period of payments. The portion of each payment that is income is determined by multiplying the payment ($200,000) by a fraction, the numerator of which is the gross profit ($1,000,000 − $300,000) and the denominator of which is the total contract price ($1,000,000). Thus, 70 percent of each payment, or $140,000, will be income. Moreover, Samantha must include the interest paid by Darin in gross income in the year it is received, assuming she is a cash method taxpayer.

115. Under IRC §111, the refund of the state income taxes is a recovery that may lead to inclusion of amounts in Sara's gross income. The exclusionary amount—the amount of the total $2,000 recovery that can be excluded from gross income—is the amount of the original deduction that did not reduce tax in the prior year. Since the entire amount reduced her tax, the entire amount of the recovery is included in gross income.

116. This is a passive activity loss, as it is produced from the activity of rental real estate. Therefore, Bev may deduct it against passive income, and depending on her AGI, Bev may be able to claim $25,000 of it as a deduction (§469(i)). If she cannot deduct the loss, it will be suspended and will carry over to the future until she can use it against passive income or she sells the apartment building.

117. Tell her (gently) that she's got it backwards: Taxpayers seek to characterize income as capital and loss as ordinary. Capital gain income is eligible for lower tax rates, as compared to the rates on ordinary income. On the deduction side, there are restrictions on the ability of taxpayers to take deductions for capital losses, while ordinary losses offset ordinary income. Therefore, taxpayers try to characterize income as capital and losses as ordinary.

118. The wood is part of his inventory or supplies and is therefore not a capital asset.

119. Several courts (see, e.g., *United States v. Maginnis*, 356 F.3d 1179 (9th Cir. 2004)) have held that a taxpayer who sells his or her right to lottery payouts does not qualify for capital gain treatment. The theory is that if Laura had not sold the rights, she would have received ordinary income over 25 years, and so selling the rights is merely an acceleration of that income, and does not transform it from ordinary to capital.

120.

Asset	Acquisition Date and Method	Disposition Date	Short Term or Long Term?
Stock	Jan 1, Year 1, purchase	Dec. 30, Year 1	Short term—she held it for less than one year.
Stock	Jan 1, Year 2, purchase	Jan 1, Year 3	Long term—she held it for at least one year.

Asset	Acquisition Date and Method	Disposition Date	Short Term or Long Term?
Land held for investment	Through like-kind exchange on Jan 1, Year 2. Her relinquished property had been held for two years.	July 1, Year 2	Long term—her holding period of her relinquished property is added to her holding period of the replacement property.
Coin collection	Jan 1, Year 3, as gift from her father	July 1, Year 3	Long term, assuming the father held the coin collection for at least six months; donee tacks the donor's holding period on to her own.

121. The loss on the sale of the van is a §1231 loss because it is attributable to the sale of a depreciable asset used in Wally's trade or business. If §1231 losses exceed gains, the net loss is deductible as an ordinary loss. If §1231 gains exceed losses, they are taxable as capital gain. In this case, if there is only a loss on the sale of the van, it will be an ordinary loss for him. If gains on the sale of the displays exceed the loss on the sale of the van, the gain will be considered capital gain (probably 15/0 percent gain).

122. The hidden question here is whether these are "collectible" instruments, in which case they do not depreciate in value and John should not have taken depreciation on them in any event. However, without more facts, let's assume that John properly claimed depreciation. John has an $80,000 gain on the sale of the instruments. This would be considered §1231 gain, which would normally be taxed as a capital gain, since there is no reported §1231 loss. However, §1245 will require recapture of the depreciation of $30,000 as ordinary income. The rest would be capital gain, and probably would be considered 15/0 percent gain.

123. The capital gains tax rate is supposed to be less than the rate for ordinary income. For taxpayers in the 15 or 10 percent bracket, a 15 percent capital gains rate would not be lower. Therefore, the 0 percent rate (formerly 5 percent) is available for taxpayers in brackets up to 15 percent.

124. The question for Michael is whether he has capital gain or ordinary income on the sale of the property—i.e., whether the property is a capital asset. If the property is a capital asset in his hands, it will generate capital gain. However, if the property is inventory in his hands, it is not a capital asset, and he would have ordinary income on its sale. If he sells the parcel as a whole, he probably would not have ordinary income; he probably has a good argument that the parcel is an investment, not inventory. However, the more activity he engages in—installing services, plotting the lots, etc.—the closer he gets to the edge. When he subdivides and sells the lots individually, he has likely crossed the line into the world of "inventory," especially if he takes all the usual steps to sell the lots, such as advertising, meeting with customers, etc. However, there are no bright lines in this area. Section 1237 would have provided him with a bright line, but it appears that it is too late for Michael to take advantage of it.

125. The rental home is a capital asset in Corrie's hands. Her adjusted basis in the property is $90,000 ($120,000 – $30,000). Her gain on the sale is $70,000. None of this is §1250 recapture, so the amount treated as 25 percent long-term capital gain is equal to the depreciation deductions previously claimed, or $30,000. The remaining $40,000 is 15/0 percent long-term capital gain. Assuming no other transactions, she will be taxed at 25 percent on $30,000 of the gain ($7,500) and at either 15 percent or 0 percent on the remaining $40,000 gain. If Corrie's sales price had been $80,000, she would have recognized a $10,000 loss on this property, which would have been a 15/0 percent capital loss. No amount is treated as 25 percent gain or loss, as that category is triggered only when the taxpayer recognizes certain kinds of gain.

126. Andrea has the following results:

Net short-term capital loss:	($25,000)
Net long-term 28% gain:	$20,000
Net long-term 25% gain:	-0-
Net long-term 15%/0% gain:	$10,000

To apply losses against gains, the $25,000 short-term capital loss is applied first to the 28 percent gain, completely eliminating it. Then, the remaining $5,000 of short-term capital loss is applied against the long-term 15/0 percent gain, reducing it to $5,000. When this process is complete, Andrea has a $5,000 long-term capital gain, taxable at the 15/0 percent rate.

127. All of these assets appear to be §1231 assets: They are depreciable property (equipment) used in the taxpayer's trade or business. Des's casualty losses exceed casualty gains, so the loss is excluded from the computation of §1231 gains and losses. The gain on Property A is netted against the loss on Property B, but only $35,000 of the gain on Property A is included in the computation, because the recapture income is ordinary income and cannot be §1231 gain. The netting process produces a net gain of $20,000, which is considered capital in nature.

128. If Des had experienced a $5,000 loss in the previous year that was characterized as an ordinary loss under §1231, a portion of her gain in the current year—up to that amount of loss—would be considered ordinary. Thus, $5,000 of her gain would be ordinary and the remaining $15,000 would be capital.

129. The principal arguments for having a capital gains preference (a lower tax rate on capital gain income) are: (1) a reduction in the tax rate on investments will increase savings, investment, and economic prosperity; (2) a capital gains preference is said to reduce lock-in (the tendency to hold on to assets rather than putting them to their best economic use) by reducing the tax associated with sale; (3) because capital gains often accrue over many years, requiring the gain to be recognized in a single year (the "bunching" effect) can result in the taxation of gain at the highest marginal rate in the year of recognition, even though the incremental gains might have been taxed at lower rates had they been recognized in the years they accrued, so a capital gains preference reduces the bunching effect; and (4) because the recognized gain upon sale of a capital asset may not represent real gain, but instead may represent inflationary gains, the capital gains preference mitigates the impact of inflation by lowering the tax in the year of sale.

The principal arguments against a capital gains preference is that it introduces new heights of complexity into the tax code, and of course, that it may not have the effects described above.

The rationale for a limitation on capital losses is that allowing a taxpayer to deduct capital losses without limitation would arguably give the taxpayer too much discretion to adjust his or her taxable income by selling only those capital assets that have declined in value.

130. Brian is thinking like a tax lawyer—he would prefer an exclusion from gross income, but if he must have income, he'd like it to be taxed at a lower capital gains rate, rather than as ordinary income. Unfortunately for Brian, several courts have held that the sale of plasma and other body parts generates income, and no one has (yet) been successful in claiming that the sale is of a capital asset, as it is more likely to be considered "inventory." See *Green v. Commissioner*, 74 T.C. 1229 (1980) (taxpayer claimed "depletion allowance"— a kind of capital recovery—to offset ordinary income on the sale of her rare blood, but the court rejected her claim).

131. With the proliferation of categories, some ordering rule is necessary to prevent chaos. The long-term loss/gain ordering rules are relatively taxpayer friendly, allowing losses to be applied to reduce gains, first, on the kinds of capital gain subject to the highest rates (28 percent and 25 percent). Thus, the overall rate of tax on capital gains should be lower than if the reverse applied—losses were first applied to the 15/0 percent category. The ordering rule that puts short-term capital losses at the end of the line—they cannot be applied against long-term capital gain until all long-term losses have been applied— makes it more difficult for taxpayers to use (or generate) short-term losses to offset long-term gains. The ordering rules work against taxpayers who have long-term losses and short-term gains, as the former cannot offset the latter.

132. A tax credit is a dollar-for-dollar reduction in the amount of tax due, while a deduction is a reduction in the amount of gross income or adjusted gross income, upon which the tax is calculated. An exclusion ensures that some amount of what would otherwise be income never becomes part of the tax calculation at all. A deduction or exclusion potentially saves the taxpayer the amount equal to his or her rate multiplied by the dollar amount of the deduction or exclusion, while a tax credit potentially saves the taxpayer one dollar for every dollar of tax credit. Moreover, some tax credits are refundable—i.e., they generate a refund if the credits exceed the tax, which is not a characteristic of deductions or exclusions.

133. In 2009, the lowest tax rate on ordinary income is 10 percent, which in turn causes the capital gains rates potentially to fall to zero (instead of 5 percent) for taxpayers in that bracket. Ray's long-term capital gain is properly categorized as 15/0 percent gain. If his taxable income, not considering this gain, is $260,000, he is in the 33 percent marginal bracket and this gain will be taxed at 15 percent. If his taxable income not considering the gain is only $6,000, he is in the 10 percent bracket and the gain will escape taxation altogether.

134. The rationale for the AMT is that every taxpayer—even those with activities that generate significant tax benefits in the form of deferred or excluded income or significant deductions—should pay some tax. For example, certain kinds of tax-exempt interest (from private activity bonds) are included in gross income for AMT purposes, while exempt

for regular tax purposes. Also, depreciation on equipment is required to be claimed on a longer, slower schedule for AMT purposes than for regular tax purposes. Thus, taxpayers whose activities generate significant amounts of MACRS deductions, which reduce their taxable income and tax for regular tax purposes, will have larger AMTI in the early years of capital recovery.

135. To answer a question like this, it is helpful to have at hand certain figures that vary from year to year. To address Catherine's situation, it is helpful to know the personal exemption amount for 2009 ($3,650), the AMT exemption amount for single taxpayers ($46,700), and the regular tax rates for the year.

To determine whether Catherine is subject to the AMT, first compute taxable income and tax for regular tax purposes, as follows:

Salary income:	$129,400
Plus taxable interest income:	+3,000
Gross income:	$132,400
Minus alimony payments:	−12,000
Adjusted gross income:	$120,400
Minus itemized deductions	
Home mortgage interest:	5,000
State income tax:	9,000
Medical expenses in excess of 7.5% of adjusted gross income:	1,000
Charitable deductions:	2,000
Miscellaneous itemized deductions in excess of 2% floor:	−3,000
Total itemized deductions:	(20,000)
Minus personal exemption	−(3,650)
Taxable income for *regular* tax purposes:	**$96,750**

Catherine's regular tax liability of $20,810 is equal to $16,750 plus 28 percent of the amount by which her taxable income ($96,750) exceeds $82,250.

To determine whether Catherine will have to pay AMT, her taxable income is adjusted as follows to produce alternative minimum taxable income:

Taxable income for *regular* tax purposes:		**$96,750**
Plus:		
Tax-exempt interest on private activity bonds:	1,000	
State income taxes:	9,000	
Miscellaneous itemized deductions:	3,000	
Medical expenses:	1,000	
Personal exemption:	3,650	
Total adjustments:		+17,650
AMTI		**$114,400**

Because Catherine's AMTI is greater than $112,500, the regular exemption amount to which she would otherwise be entitled ($46,700) is reduced by 25 percent of the amount by which her AMTI exceeds $112,500. (($114,400 − $112,500) × 0.25 = $475). Thus, Catherine's exemption amount is $46,225.

AMTI	$114,400
Minus exemption amount	− 46,225
Tax base for AMT	68,175
Times tax rate for AMT (26%)	× 0.26
AMT	**$17,726**

Because Catherine's regular tax liability ($20,810) is more than her alternative minimum tax liability ($17,726), she will not pay AMT. (However, this does not excuse her from calculating the AMT liability to determine if she is subject to this surtax.)

136. No, elimination of the deduction for alimony won't increase Catherine's chances of being caught in the AMT net. It is not one of the tax preference items that trigger AMT concerns. If, however, Catherine were to use the $12,000 to invest in certain kinds of investments (private activity bonds, or perhaps equipment for her business that generates a large MACRS deduction in the first year), the AMT could be triggered.

137. All of the award must be included in Becky's gross income, and her $100,000 of attorneys' fees is deductible on Schedule A as a miscellaneous itemized deduction for regular tax purposes, to the extent that these fees, plus any other miscellaneous itemized deductions, exceed 2 percent of her AGI. She cannot claim these as an above-the-line deduction because the award was not pursuant to the relatively limited category of claims that generate attorneys' fees eligible for such a deduction. For purposes of calculating her AMTI, however, none of the attorneys' fees are deductible because they are a miscellaneous itemized expense. This event, therefore, can potentially generate significant AMT liability for Becky.

138. Candace can't deduct these personal expenses. IRC §262. However, she may be entitled to a nonrefundable tax credit for dependent care expenses. She appears to qualify: She maintains a household with children; they are under the age of 13; she incurs expenses to care for them while she works. The amount expended for child care while she works as a volunteer ($500) would not be eligible for the credit. The amount of the credit will be a percentage of the lesser of her earned income, child care expenses, or the specified dollar amount of the statute based on the number of children ($6,000 for two children). The percentage is based on AGI. In Candace's case, she will be entitled to claim 23 percent of her actual expenses of $3,000, or $690, as the child care credit.

139. Jordan is entitled to claim the earned income credit because his income is within the earned income limitation. He has one qualifying child, and thus will be entitled to a credit of $3,043.00, computed as follows:

34% × $8,950	=	$3,043
− 15.98% × (10,000 − 16,420)	=	-0-
Available earned income credit	=	**$3,043**

140. Kara and Jim may claim an earned income credit of $4,506. This is computed as follows:

$$
\begin{aligned}
45\% \times \$12,570 &= \$5,656 \\
-21.06\% \times (25,000 - \$19,540) &= \$1,150 \\
\hline
\text{Available credit} &= \mathbf{\$4,506}
\end{aligned}
$$

141. The difference between these two categories of credits is whether they are refundable or not. Some tax credits are refundable—i.e., they generate a refund if the credits exceed the tax. The taxes-paid credit, the earned income credit, and, potentially, part of the child credit are refundable. If these credits exceed taxes due, the taxpayer may receive a refund. The child care credit is not refundable; if the taxpayer has more credit available than taxes, the excess credit goes to waste.

142. All of these payments for tuition and fees are potentially available for the American Opportunity Tax Credit (formerly the Hope Scholarship Credit) and Lifetime Learning Credit. Susan's tuition is not available for the American Opportunity credit, because she is not in her first two years of postsecondary education. However, she can take the Lifetime Learning Credit for these expenses. Her credit would be equal to 20 percent multiplied by the maximum amount of expenses available in 2009 ($10,000), but may be limited by the family's AGI. In this case, the family's AGI exceeds the amount at which phaseout begins ($100,000). Thus, the credit would be reduced, and calculated as follows:

$$\$10,000 \text{ expenses} \times 20\% = \$2,000 \text{ (otherwise available credit)}$$

$$\text{Reduction amount} = \$2,000 \times \frac{(102,000 - 100,000)}{\$20,000} = \$200$$

Available credit:

Otherwise available credit	$2,000
− Reduction amount	− 200
Available credit	$1,800

Paul and Inga may also take a credit for Susan's tuition. This is allocated to the American Opportunity Credit, so that only $2,500 of credit is potentially available. The amount of the credit is 100 percent of the first $2,000 of qualifying educational expenses and 25 percent of the next $4,000 of such expenses. Therefore, the maximum available credit is $2,500. This credit is not reduced, because Paul and Inga's AGI does not exceed the phaseout threshold amount.

143. Erin will be able to claim deductions for the home mortgage interest and real property taxes that she pays every year with respect to her home. Also, if she purchases the home between January 1 and December 1, 2009, she will be able to claim a first-time home-buyer's credit, which is a credit equal to up to 10 percent of the purchase price, with a cap of $8,000. For purchases in 2009, Erin will not be required to "pay back" the credit each year or upon sale, unless she sells the home within 36 months of purchase. This essentially reduces the cost of the home to $142,000.

144. Taxpayers "assign" income in order to direct it to a person in a lower tax rate than their own and to avoid paying gift taxes. If a father is in the 33 percent bracket for ordinary income and his son is in the 15 percent bracket, it makes sense for the father to try to direct income to the son, as the family as a unit will save 18 percent in taxes if the attempt is successful. As tax rates become more progressive (i.e., there is a larger spread between the lowest and highest rates), there is a greater incentive to engage in assignment of income strategies.

145. Danielle has probably engaged in an inappropriate assignment of income. She transferred income from services (transformed into "property"—the intellectual property that gives rise to the income) to her daughter, who did not perform the services. However, she would argue that there is no impermissible assignment because she transferred 100 percent of the income stream. However, without also transferring the intellectual property that gives rise to the income, she retains power over that income stream that would defeat her argument.

146. If Danielle can transfer the intellectual property (the copyright) to Tiffany, she will be able to direct the income to Tiffany as well. Of course, the transfer of the copyright to Tiffany will be a gift (not includable in Tiffany's income for income tax purposes (IRC §102), but a gift for gift tax purposes).

147. Sam is taxed on the interest. He cannot give away just the interest element. If he wants Peter to be taxed on the interest, then Sam must give Peter the bonds.

148. If the income is tax-exempt interest, it won't matter who is deemed to own it for regular tax purposes. But this kind of interest income may be included in alternative minimum taxable income, and therefore the assignment of income doctrine is relevant.

149. It is probably correct. Although the case of *Salvatore v. Commissioner*, 29 T.C.M. 89 (1970), might raise questions, in this case (1) the length of time between gift and ultimate sale; and (2) the absence of facts suggesting that Barbara's share was uncertain supports the taxpayers' position that the transfer was bona fide and that the substance of the transaction is a sale by both Barbara and George of the property.

150. Brian's assignment of his claim will probably not result in an assignment of income because the claim is contingent and doubtful at the time of transfer. Thus, the transferee will properly include the amount in gross income. Because Steve has a basis in this action of $500,000, he will include only $4,500,000 in gross income; the rest will be a return of capital. Steve will argue that this is capital gain, but is unlikely to prevail.

151. Under *Banks v. Commissioner*, 543 U.S. 426 (2005), Kayla must include the entire amount of the award ($500,000) in her gross income when she receives it. (IRC §104(a) doesn't apply to exclude this award because this is a nonphysical injury.) However, Kayla will be allowed an above-the-line deduction (a deduction from gross income in computing AGI) for her attorneys' fees and costs.

152. In this case, Kayla must still include the $500,000 in her gross income, but is not allowed an above-the-line deduction in computing AGI for her attorneys' fees and costs. Instead, she can claim these as a miscellaneous itemized deduction, subject to the 2 percent floor of IRC §67. Assuming she had no other income or deductions that year, here are her tax consequences:

Regular Tax Liability		**AMT Liability**	
Gross income	$500,000	Taxable income	$306,350
Minus:		*Plus:*	
Itemized deductions	(190,000)	Itemized deduction:	190,000
Personal exemption	(3,650)	Personal exemption	3,650
Taxable income	$306,350	AMTI	$500,000
Regular Tax	$ 86,254*	AMT	$482,500**

Total Tax Liability:

$ 86,254	Regular tax
50,246	AMT
$136,500	**Total tax**

*From tax tables

**26% of $175,000 + 28% of $375,000 (Kayla's AMTI is too high for her to enjoy any exemption amount).

153. Spencer will probably file his own tax return, but he does have the option of filing with his parents. His regular tax rate (10 percent) will apply to his earned income and up to $1,800 of his investment income. But the remaining amount of investment income will be taxed at his parents' marginal rate.

154. Corbin's situation is a little more difficult to analyze than Spencer's. At his age, for the kiddie tax to apply, Corbin must be a full-time student for at least five months of the year and must not provide more than one-half of his support during the year in question. If those two conditions apply, the kiddie tax will apply to Corbin and all of his investment income in excess of $1,800 will be taxed at his parents' rate. If not, Corbin's regular tax rate will apply to all of his income, both earned and investment.

155. Taxpayers should (and do) care about time value of money principles, because these principles affect the amount of tax they owe—specifically, by affecting the timing of taxes. Taxpayers typically seek to defer income as far into the future as possible (while still having access to it) in order to defer the tax on this income. Taxpayers want to contribute money to tax-deferred savings vehicles such as IRAs for this reason. Taxpayers can always hope the tax will never be paid (consider the impact of §1014), but if it is, the present value of that future tax is less than its face amount. Taxpayers also want to accelerate deductions as much as possible, because these deductions reduce the taxes owed currently.

156. The present value of a promise to pay you $10,000 in five years if the appropriate interest rate is 5 percent is **$7,840.** If the appropriate rate is 9 percent, the present value is **$6,500.** The appropriate interest rate should take into account the riskiness of the promise. A promise by the United States federal government (as in a savings bond) is essentially risk-free and would have a low interest rate. By contrast, a promise by a deadbeat (high risk) would carry a higher interest rate.

157. This is just another way to ask for the present value of a future sum. If you know you have a debt to pay in eight years of $10,000, you might set aside the present value of that debt (assuming an interest rate) and let that sum grow during the term so that you would have just the right amount to pay off the obligation. This is often how people save for college

educations for children or for their own retirement, although they generally do that through periodic savings rather than putting aside a lump sum. At 6 percent, the amount you would have to put aside is **$6,270.** At 12 percent, you would only have to put aside **$4,040.**

158. If interest rates held steady at 4 percent, you would have:

10 years:	$4,437
15 years:	$5,405
30 years:	$9,740

159. To answer this question, you must compare the present values of the two gifts: the present value of $70,000 five years in the future or $50,000. Because gifts are not included in gross income, there are no taxes to figure into the equation on the gift itself. You should take the gift today because the present value of the future gift is $47,670, less than the current gift. The present value is calculated as follows:

$$PV = \frac{FV}{(1 + i)^n}$$

$$PV = \frac{\$70,000}{(1 + 0.08)^5}$$

$$PV = \$47,670$$

This can also be calculated by using a PV table: multiply the future gift by the number at the intersection of 8 percent and five years, or 0.681. This produces the same number. (It's a relatively close case. You should also consider whether the stated interest rate doesn't reflect the riskiness of this gift—your rich aunt might "forget" to make it! The riskier the promise, the higher the interest rate properly used in calculating present value, and the lower the present value of the future gift.)

160. Putting aside nontax issues such as whether the granddaughter is mature enough to handle a $5,000 gift, Grandmother should seriously consider using the 529 Plan. If the granddaughter invests the money, she will be taxed (perhaps at her parents' rate) on the income from the gift. If the money is placed in a 529 Plan, it can grow tax-free and this income will not ever be taxed if the money is used for educational purposes. However, in making that decision, Grandmother should consider any fees associated with the plan and the likely rate of return in the plan.

161. Beverly should run—not walk—away from this so-called opportunity. Leaving aside the wisdom of such a venture, she will not be able to use the losses from the venture to offset her income from private practice. This would constitute a passive activity because it is certain that Beverly, a doctor, will not be actively involved in the business of contacting alien life forms (plus, the structure of the investment will probably ensure that it is a passive activity for her). The passive loss rules prevent a taxpayer from using "passive losses" to offset nonpassive income, so that the deductions from the venture would be useless to her until she disposes of the activity.

162. (c) is not an income deferral strategy. Investing in real estate takes advantage of the realization principle: Increases in the value of the real property are not taxed until the property is disposed of in a realization event. Use of the cash method can defer income until it is received. A like-kind exchange defers the gain on the exchange of property until the replacement property is sold. But the characterization of a payment to a former spouse as alimony results in a deduction to the payor (thus, a deduction strategy) and the payee spouse must include it in gross income when received.

163. Each Code section that allows for potential deferral (e.g., like-kind exchanges under §1031) contain myriad rules to confine the technique to its intended scope. The doctrine of constructive receipt is an example of a non-Code method of preventing inappropriate use of the cash method to defer income. A cash method taxpayer cannot exclude income if he or she has the right to it, even if he or she does not claim it.

164. No. The Code will impute interest to this transaction. There are three potentially applicable Code provisions (§483, §7872, and §1272 and its related statutes). Of these, §483 applies because this involves a sale or exchange of property for which the purchase price is less than $1 million.

Section 483 provides that the unstated interest must be calculated by subtracting from the total deferred purchase price the present value of the future payments, using the applicable federal rate. In this situation, the AFR is 6 percent. Using present value formulas (or the chart on page 338), the unstated interest is calculated to be $227,700, and therefore the purchase price for the ranch is $672,300. Ronald's gain on the transaction is $272,300 (the sales price minus his basis.). James's basis in the ranch is $672,300, the same as Ronald's selling price.

165. Joe's mother may lend him a total of $10,000 without interest because of the de minimis exception for gift loans. IRC §7872(c)(2)(A). If the loan is $100,000 or less, the transaction will be cast as a gift of the forgone interest (calculated at the applicable federal rate for long-term obligations) but the amount treated as included in the mother's income will be limited to Joe's investment income (i.e., his total of dividends, interest, etc.). If the loan is $1 million, neither of these exceptions apply. In that case, each year Joe's mother will be deemed to have made a gift of the forgone interest to Joe, who in turn transfers it to his mother as interest, which she must include in her gross income.

ESSAY EXAM QUESTIONS
AND ANSWERS

ESSAY EXAM QUESTIONS

QUESTION 1

Calvin and Sue divorced in Year 1. They agreed to the following financial arrangements:

Calvin received all of the assets of the sole proprietorship business that he owned during the marriage. They continued the arrangement they had established during their marriage: Sue continued to work in the business, and Calvin paid her $2,500 per month. The divorce decree referred to this amount as alimony, and required it to continue for ten years, or her death, if earlier. Calvin also gave her a lump sum of $20,000 on each of the first, second, and third anniversaries of the divorce, which was required by the divorce decree if she survived for that period.

Sue received the marital home, for which they paid $150,000. It was worth $200,000 on the day of the divorce. She also received stock in XYZ Corporation, in which the couple had a basis of $500,000, but which was worth $250,000 on the date of the divorce. Finally, Sue received a coin collection, which Calvin had assembled over many years. It was worth $75,000 on the day of the divorce and Calvin estimated that his basis was $25,000 in the collection.

It is now Year 3. In Years 1 and 2, Sue included the $2,500 per month in her gross income as alimony and Calvin has deducted it. In both years, Sue worked in the business. Calvin also deducted the $20,000 payments in each of Years 1 and 2, but Sue did not include them in her gross income. In Year 3, Sue sold the XYZ stock for $150,000 and the coin collection for $175,000. Sue calculated a loss of the $100,000 on the sale of stock and used this loss to offset the gain on the coin collection, so that she only reported $50,000 of long-term capital gain, taxable at the 28 percent rate.

Did Sue properly report all of these transactions? If not, what should she have done?

QUESTION 2

Beatrice, a single woman, owned a home that was her principal residence for many years. It was located in an area of the country where home prices had fallen significantly in the past several years. She tried for two years to sell her home. Beatrice had paid $125,000 for this home. It had been appraised at a value of $350,000 prior to the drop in prices in her area.

After trying for more than two years to sell the home, she hit upon a brilliant plan, which she immediately implemented.

Beatrice designed a writing competition, which she advertised over the Internet and in magazines. Each entrant in the competition would have a chance to win the house. Each entrant had to write a 200-word essay on why he or she would be the best new owner for this particular house. Each entrant was required to pay a $100 "processing fee" to enter the competition. Beatrice considered the contest to be successful—she received 3,000 entries.

Beatrice had appointed a committee of friends to read all the essays. They selected Xavier as the winner, and Beatrice transferred ownership of the property to him after he was declared the winner. He was thrilled to receive a home worth $300,000 for a mere $100 and a 200-word essay. He immediately gave up his day job and embarked upon his longtime dream of a writing career. (What he didn't know was that after reading half the essays, the committee gave up and threw all the entries in a hat and selected one at random.)

What are the tax consequences of this transaction to Beatrice and Xavier?

QUESTION 3

Brian owns Whiteacre, an apartment building. He has an adjusted basis of $400,000 in White-acre, and it is subject to a mortgage of $260,000. Anita owns Blueacre, a commercial office building. It is worth $800,000 and is subject to a mortgage of $350,000. Anita has an adjusted basis of $400,000 in Blueacre.

A. Brian and Anita exchange Whiteacre for Blueacre and, in addition, Brian transfers a collectible painting, worth $10,000, in which he had a basis of $2,000, to Anita. Brian had held the painting for many years. Each assumes the other's liabilities. What are the tax consequences of this exchange to each taxpayer?

B. Would your answer change if Anita had recently acquired Blueacre as an inheritance?

QUESTION 4

Spencer, a cash-method taxpayer, is the owner of an Internet research business organized as a sole proprietorship. As of December 31 of the year in question, he had received $125,000 in payments from customers and $25,000 in oral promises to pay within 30 days from clients. He also incurred the following expenses:

Compensation to employees	$25,000
Advertising	$5,000
Rent	$12,000
Telephone & Internet	$2,500
Taxes	$2,000
Business entertainment	$1,000
Insurance	$3,500

With respect to equipment, Spencer had an interesting year:

- He purchased a computer for $5,000 for exclusive use in the business.
- He sold Equipment A, which had a basis of zero, for $1,500. He had originally purchased the computer for $10,000.
- He sold equipment B for $3,500. It had an original cost of $3,000 and an adjusted basis of $2,800.
- Equipment C, which had a fair market value of $1,500 and basis of $2,500, was stolen. He received no insurance proceeds for this loss, as it was below his deductible amount for theft.
- A flood destroyed Equipment D, which had a basis of $5,000. His insurance company paid him $8,300 for this loss. Assume no cost recovery deductions had been claimed for Equipment D.

Spencer had a $200 unrecaptured §1231 loss from prior years.

Please advise Spencer on the tax consequences of these transactions.

QUESTION 5

In Year 1, Steve transferred $500,000 to Barney, a respected investment adviser. Barney and Steve agreed that Barney would invest this money on Steve's behalf. Steve was pleased when he received quarterly statements from Barney showing a steady increase in the value of his account. In most years, Steve allowed the account to continue to grow, but he withdrew funds in a couple of years. At the end of each year, Barney sent Steve the proper forms so that Steve could include the correct amounts of income (dividends, interest, and capital gains) in his gross income. Steve properly reported these amounts in accordance with those reports.

The following is a summary of Steve's account for Years 1 through 5, as shown on the statements:

Year	Beginning Balance	Dividends, Interest, and Capital Gains Earned	Withdrawals	Ending Balance
1	$500,000	$ 50,000	$ -0-	$550,000
2	550,000	60,000	-0-	610,000
3	610,000	70,000	100,000	580,000
4	580,000	100,000	-0-	680,000
5	680,000	120,000	100,000	700,000
6		**$400,000**	**$200,000**	

In Year 6, Steve was horrified to learn that Barney has allegedly been running a Ponzi scheme. (In a Ponzi scheme, new investors' money is used to pay existing investors. The scheme continues as long as there are new investors, but when the flow of money from new investors' money dries up, the house of cards comes tumbling down.) It appears from press reports and the SEC investigation that Barney did not make any investments on Steve's (or any other investor's) behalf, and in fact all the quarterly statements that Steve received were pure fabrications. There is no money to be distributed to Steve (or anyone else). There may be some insurance available to investors, up to $100,000 for each investor, but that is uncertain. Various investors (but not Steve) have commenced litigation against Barney, the accounting firm that audited Barney's company, and others tangentially involved in the scheme. The outcome of that litigation is uncertain and in any event will not be resolved for many years. In the meantime, Barney has been indicted by a federal grand jury and is under house arrest in his Manhattan apartment. He has filed for bankruptcy.

Steve's AGI (without considering these events) is $120,000. He wants to know how to report this event for tax purposes. What would you tell him?

ESSAY EXAM ANSWERS

SAMPLE ANSWER TO QUESTION 1

The fundamental issues of this question are: Did Sue have income or loss as a result of the divorce and sale transactions, and if so, did she properly report this income or loss for tax purposes?

The divorce payments: Sue had an accession to wealth when she received the $2,500 per month, the annual $20,000 payment from Calvin, Calvin's half of the marital home and XYZ stock, and Calvin's coin collection. All of these are considered income within the meaning of §61. **See Figure 2, Boxes [1] → [2] → [4].**

Do any exclusions potentially apply to exclude these amounts from Sue's gross income?

(a) *$2,500 per month: Sue's treatment appears to be correct.* Sue did not claim that the $2,500 per month payments were excluded from her gross income, and because that payment appears to meet the definition of alimony (made in cash; pursuant to the divorce decree; ending with her death not designated as nondeductible/nonincludable; and does not appear to be child support), it appears to be includable in Sue's gross income. **See Figure 2, Boxes [5] → [6] → [14].**

A subsidiary question is whether these payments are alimony or compensation. Does it matter? Both are includable in Sue's gross income, but the IRS could quibble about it because alimony is not subject to employment taxes, while these taxes must be paid on compensation. The fact that she is working for Calvin strongly suggests that is it compensation income, but nothing in the decree apparently requires her to work (she would presumably still get the payment even if she didn't work). Note that this issue is important, but employment taxes, fortunately, are beyond the scope of most basic tax courses.

(b) *$20,000 payments: Sue's treatment appears to be incorrect.* This payment also appears to meet the definition of alimony (made in cash; pursuant to the divorce decree; not to be made after her death; not designated as nondeductible and nonincludable; and does not appear to be child support). **See Figure 2, Boxes [5] → [6] → [14].** Thus, Sue should have included the $20,000 payments in her gross income in each of Years 1 and 2 and should include it in Year 3. The total alimony payments do not vary by more than $15,000, so the front-end-loaded alimony rules do not apply.

(c) *Home, XYZ stock, and coin collection: Sue's treatment appears to be correct.* Because these assets are not cash, they cannot constitute alimony, and therefore are a property settlement, which is not income to Sue (they are treated as a gift under §1041(b)(1)). There is no limit on the excludable amount. **See Figure 2, Boxes [5] → [6] → [11] → [12].**

The sale of assets: In order to answer this question, Sue's basis in these assets must be determined.

Sue received property—the XYZ stock and the coin collection—in a divorce, and therefore her basis is determined under §1041. She takes these properties with a basis equal to the basis of the property in the hands of the married couple. Therefore, her basis is $500,000 for the XYZ stock and $25,000 for the coin collection (although she might need more proof than Calvin's "estimate" to establish the basis of the collection). Neither the stock nor the coin collection is the type of asset that is subject to adjustment to basis for depreciation or amortization, and no facts suggest any additions to basis. **See Figure 5, Boxes [1] →[3] → [12] → [13] → [14].**

Once Sue's basis is determined, it is possible to calculate her realized gain or loss on the transactions. Her amount realized is the sales price she received for each asset, and her realized gain or loss is equal to the amount realized minus her adjusted basis in the asset. No nonrecognition provisions appear to apply for these sales for cash. **See Figure 7, Boxes [1] → [3] → [4] → [5] → [6] → [11].** The result:

Stock: $350,000 loss ($150,000 amount realized minus $500,000 basis)

Coin collection: $150,000 gain ($175,000 amount realized minus $25,000 basis)

Figure 7, Box [13] poses the question "What is the character of this gain or loss?" Figure 10A answers this question.

Sue's sales result in a realization event in which gain or loss was recognized. The assets appear to be capital assets in Sue's hands—i.e., they are not the type of assets described in §1222. No special recharacterization rules (such as recapture) recast gain or loss as ordinary. Therefore, the nature of the gain or loss is capital. **See Figure 10A, Boxes [1] → [3] → [4] → [5] → [8].**

Figure 10A, Box [9] asks the question "What kind of capital gain is this?" Figure 10C answers this question. None of the gain or loss is from a nonbusiness bad debt. Sue has held the assets for more than one year. The coin collection was a collectible, so that gain is a 28 percent capital gain. The loss from the sale of XYZ stock is 15/0 percent gain, as it does not fit within any of the other categories. Sue has no other gain or loss in these categories (or in other categories), so she has a net $350,000 long-term net 15/0 percent loss and a net $150,000 net long-term 28 percent gain. **See Figure 10C, Boxes [1] → [3] → [4] → [8] → [9a] → [9b].**

Because Sue has both capital gain and loss, the next question is whether the loss can offset the gain. The net loss from the 15/0 percent category is applied to completely eliminate the net gain in the 28 percent category, and the net result is a $200,000 net long-term capital loss carryover in the 15/0 percent category. **See Figure 10C, Boxes [15] → [16] → [17].**

Therefore, Sue overreported the gain on these transactions and should file an amended return to eliminate the reported gain and record her capital loss carryforward.

SAMPLE ANSWER TO QUESTION 2

The beginning point for answering this question is this: What is the nature of the transaction into which Beatrice has entered? Beatrice believes she has sold her home for $300,000 (3,000 entries at $100 each). If so, her realized gain of $175,000 ($300,000 amount realized minus her basis of $125,000) would be excluded from her gross income under §121, because she owned and lived in the home for the requisite two-year period. **See Figure 7, Boxes [1] → [3] → [4] → [5] → [6] → [11] for calculation of gain and loss. See Figure 2, Boxes [1] → [2] → [4] → [5] → [9] → [12] for the §121 exclusion.**

However, the IRS might have a different perspective on the nature of the transaction. Beatrice might be viewed as organizing and running a raffle, and if so, the proceeds of the raffle would be included in her gross income as ordinary income. **See Figure 2, Boxes [1] → [2] → [4] → [5] → [14].** The sale of the home would therefore generate a realized loss of $174,900 (her basis of $150,000 minus Xavier's purchase price of $100). However, because the home is held for personal purposes, she may not deduct the loss under IRC §165(c). **See Figure 7, Boxes [1] → [3] → [4] →[5] → [6] → [11] for calculation of gain or loss.**

But was the home really worth $300,000? Prices had dropped in Beatrice's area, and this purported "sale" did not establish the fair market value of the home, as do most sales between unrelated parties. For example, if the home had been worth only $200,000, a middle ground is possible: Beatrice would treat the sale of the home as a sale for $200,000, and thus her realized gain would be $74,900 (again, excluded under §121) and her proceeds for the raffle would be $100,000.

To avoid this ambiguity (and to comply with any applicable state laws prohibiting this kind of raffle), Beatrice could organize this sale in a different way. She could give a charity an option to purchase the home for $300,000, and the charity would run the raffle. Then, if the raffle were successful, the charity would exercise its option to purchase the home and would then transfer it to the winning entrant. The charity would retain the excess proceeds of the raffle, if any. If not enough entries were received, the charity would not exercise its option to purchase the home. In this scenario, Beatrice would be viewed as selling the home and would not take any charitable deduction (she has made no contribution to charity). See Rev. Rul. 83-130, 1983-2 C.B. 148.

In either case, it is tempting to view Xavier as purchasing a home for $100. However, he has won a raffle-type gamble, and therefore he must include the fair market value of the home as ordinary income. **See Figure 2, Boxes [1] → [2] → [4] → [5] → [14].** Then, his basis in the home is his $100 investment plus the amount he included in gross income (this is called "tax cost basis"). **See Figure 5, Boxes [1] → [3] → [10] → [11].** Xavier may be surprised to discover that he must pay tax on his "winnings" even though he has no cash with which to pay the tax.

SAMPLE ANSWER TO QUESTION 3

A chart of the parties' tax consequences is included at the end of this answer.

The first step is to calculate the parties' realized gain or loss on the exchange of the properties. **See Figure 7.** Anita's equity in Blueacre is $450,000 (its fair market value of $800,000 minus the debt of $350,000). Therefore, Whiteacre must be worth $700,000, because Brian will trade Whiteacre (with equity of $440,000) plus a painting worth $10,000 for Blueacre. Each party will calculate his or her amount realized and adjusted basis, and compute realized gain or loss. **See Figure 7, Boxes [3] → [4] → [5] → [6].**

Brian's realized gain or loss: Brian's amount realized is the fair market value of Blueacre plus the benefit of release of $260,000 of liabilities. His adjusted basis in Whiteacre is $400,000, to which he also adds his additional investment in obtaining Blueacre—i.e., the assumption of Anita's liabilities of $350,000 and the fair market value of the painting ($10,000) he gives to Anita. Brian's realized gain or loss is $300,000.

Anita's realized gain or loss: Anita's amount realized is the fair market value of Whiteacre ($700,000) plus the amount of liabilities from which she is released ($350,000) plus the fair market value of the painting ($10,000). Her adjusted basis is $400,000 in Blueacre plus the amount of liabilities she takes on ($260,000). Anita's realized gain is $400,000.

The next step is to determine whether any nonrecognition rule applies to defer recognition of gain for Brian or Anita. This question obviously focuses on like-kind exchanges. **See Figure 7, Boxes [6] → [7] → [8], and Figure 9.**

A taxpayer will not recognize gain or loss on an exchange of property if the requirements of §1031 are met. A qualifying like-kind exchange occurs if there is an exchange of qualifying property, of like kind, when the taxpayer has held the surrendered property for investment or for use in a trade or business and intends to hold the property received for investment or in a trade or business. **See Figure 9, Boxes [1] → [2] → [3] → [4] → [5] → [6].**

A. The two properties are like kind (real property for real property), and this kind of property qualifies for a like-kind exchange. Assuming that each of these taxpayers held the properties for investment or for use in a trade or business and intends to hold the acquired properties for either of these uses, these requirements are met. If so, neither taxpayer will recognize gain or loss, except to the extent of nonlike-kind property received (boot). Net relief from liabilities is treated as boot. (However, each taxpayer is analyzed separately—one taxpayer might meet the like-kind exchange requirements, while the other might not.)

Brian's tax consequences: Brian, who had a net assumption of liabilities (he was relieved of $260,000 and took on $350,000) is not deemed to have received boot. Because he did not receive boot, Brian does not recognize any of his realized gain or loss on the like-kind exchange. **See Figure 9, Boxes [8] → [11].** (Notice that no calculation of his gain or loss is technically required if no gain or loss recognition is required. Nevertheless, it is good practice to calculate his realized gain in a testing situation.) His basis in Blueacre is equal to the basis of the property he transferred, plus the gain recognized, minus the fair market value of the boot received, plus any boot paid. **See Figure 9, Box [13].** For basis purposes, the assumption and relief of liabilities are both taken into account. Brian's basis in Blueacre is $500,000 (see chart). However, although Brian does not recognize any of his realized gain on the disposition of Whiteacre, he is treated as having sold the painting in a separate transaction when he used it to "purchase" Blueacre from Anita. His amount realized is the fair market value of the painting ($10,000) and his adjusted basis in it is $2,000. The difference is his realized gain of $8,000. No nonrecognition rules apply to avoid recognition of this gain. **See Figure 7, Boxes [1] → [3] → [4] →[5] → [6] → [11].** The character of that gain is capital, and is likely in the 28 percent collectible category. **See Figure 10A, Boxes [1] → [3] → [4] → [5] → [8] and Figure 10C, Boxes [1] → [3] → [4] → [5].**

Anita's tax consequences: Anita received nonlike-kind property (the painting, with a fair market value of $10,000, and net relief of liabilities of $90,000), thus she received $100,000 of boot. Therefore, it is necessary to calculate her realized gain or loss in order to determine the tax consequences of this receipt of boot. Anita recognizes her realized gain up to the amount of the boot received, or $100,000. **See Figure 9, Boxes [9] → [10].** The rest of the gain is not recognized. **See Figure 9, Boxes [9] → [11].** Her basis in the property received, Whiteacre, is equal to the basis of the property she transferred, plus the gain recognized, minus the fair market value of the boot received, plus any boot paid. **See Figure 9, Box [13].** For basis purposes, the assumption and relief of liabilities are considered. Her basis in Whiteacre is therefore $400,000 (see chart).

The tax consequences to the two taxpayers are summarized as follows:

	Brian	Anita
Amount realized	$ 800,000 Blueacre + 260,000 A/L **$1,060,000**	$ 700,000 Whiteacre 350,000 A/L + 10,000 painting **$1,060,000**
Basis in property surrendered	$400,000 Whiteacre 350,000 A/L + 10,000 painting **$760,000**	$400,000 Blueacre + 260,000 A/L **$660,000**
Realized gain or loss	**$300,000 gain**	**$400,000 gain**
Recognized gain or loss	**$8,000 painting** (28% capital gain)	$ 10,000 painting + 90,000 net liability relief **$100,000** (likely 25% or 15%/0% capital gain)
Basis of property received	$400,000 basis of Whiteacre − 260,000 A/L + 350,000 A/L + 10,000 painting **$500,000 basis of Blueacre**	$400,000 basis of Blueacre + 100,000 gain recognition − 350,000 A/L + 260,000 A/L − 10,000 painting **$400,000 basis of Whiteacre** **$10,000 painting**

B. If Anita had received the office building as an inheritance, the theoretical question arises of whether she held it for investment or for use in a trade or business. There is no definitive answer to this; it depends on her intentions as revealed by her use, the period of time she held the property, and similar factors. However, it may not matter (or matter much) to Anita, because if she had recently received Blueacre as inheritance, her basis would be the fair market value on the date of death, and therefore she would have little if any gain or loss in the property. Anita's situation does not affect Brian's potential ability to qualify his side of the transaction as a §1031 exchange; each taxpayer's situation is analyzed independently.

SAMPLE ANSWER TO QUESTION 4

This question raises issues regarding the proper reporting of income and expenses for tax purposes for a taxpayer engaged in business. In general, sole proprietors report the income and deductions attributable to their businesses on Schedule C of their tax returns. Net income from business is includable in gross income (§61(a)(2)), and net loss generates a deduction (§165(c)(1)), subject to some limitations.

Spencer begins by including in his gross income his receipts from sales of information. **See Figure 2, Boxes [1] → [2] →[4] → [5] → [14].** Because he is a cash-method taxpayer, Spencer will include in his gross income all amounts received during the year, actually or constructively.

But he does not include in his gross income mere promises to pay by customers. **See Figure 2, Box [13].**

In order to qualify for any deduction, the expenditure must fall within the domain of a specific deduction statute. Spencer must, of course, substantiate his deductions.

Ordinary and necessary business expenses—in general: Section 162 allows a deduction for all "ordinary and necessary business expenses." This requires that the expenditure be usual in the trade ("ordinary"), have a reasonable likelihood of generating profit ("necessary"), be incurred for business and not personal reasons, and be incurred while the taxpayer is engaged in a trade or business ("trade or business"), and not be a capital expenditure ("expense"). Spencer's expenditures for compensation (if reasonable in amount), rent, advertising, insurance, and telephone/Internet would all seem to meet this requirement. No special limitations apply to these kinds of expenditures. **See Figure 3B, Boxes [1] → [3] → [5] → [7] → [8] → [9] → [10] → [12] → [13].**

Figure 3B, Box [14] poses the question "In which year will items be deductible?" Since Spencer uses the cash method of accounting for his business, he will properly claim deductions in the year they are paid for these expenses. "Payment" includes payment by credit card, even if Spencer does not pay the balance to the credit card company. Thus, he should deduct those expenses that have been paid during the year, whether in cash or by credit card.

Business entertainment: While business entertainment may also seem to fall within the category of §162 expenses, special rules limit deductions for business entertainment. First, Spencer must establish that the entertainment item was "directly related to" the active conduct of his trade or business, or if the activity immediately preceded or followed a bona fide business discussion, was "associated with" the active conduct of his trade or business. §274(a). Even if he meets this requirement, only 50 percent of the amount expended will be deductible. §274(n). **See Figure 3B, Box [12]** for the bifurcation of these expenses into their deductible and potentially nondeductible portions. Any nondeductible portion should be tested to see if it could qualify as a personal deduction or an investment deduction, but these expenses are not of the type that will likely qualify.

Taxes: Section 164 allows a deduction for income, real property, personal property taxes, and sales taxes, at least in some years. It is not clear what kind of tax Spencer paid, and further information is necessary to determine the deductibility of this expense.

Purchase of computer: The purchase of the computer is an outlay for a capital expenditure, because the computer is a separate asset likely to generate benefits beyond the close of the taxable year. §263. Thus, Spencer cannot take a deduction under §162 for this outlay. He may, however, deduct the cost of such items up to the lesser of $250,000 (in 2009) or the net income of the business disregarding this expense. §179. If he elects to deduct the cost of the computer under §179, its basis will be reduced by the amount of the deduction (if he fully deducts the amount, the basis will be zero). If he is not eligible for §179 deduction, he may claim MACRS deductions for this purchase, and must determine the class of property, its depreciable period, and the proper convention for calculating MACRS in the year of acquisition. He will then choose a method of recovery, such as double declining balance or straight line. **See Figure 3B, Boxes [5] → [6] and Figure 6, Boxes [1] → [3] → [5] → [6] → [12] → [13] → [14].**

Sale of equipment: Figures 4, 7, 10A, and 10B are helpful in addressing this part of the question. Figures 4 and 7 assist in the calculation of recognized gain or loss on these events.

See Figure 4, Boxes [1] → [3] → [5] → [7], and Figure 7, Boxes [1] → [3] → [4] → [5] → [6] → [9] → [11]. The results are summarized in the following chart.

Equipment	Adjusted Basis	Fair Market Value	Disposition	Realized Gain or (Loss)	Recognized Gain or (Loss)
A	-0-	$1,500	Sale	$1,500	$1,500
B	$2,800	$3,500	Sale	$ 700	$ 700
C	$2,500	$1,500	Theft	$2,500	($2,500)
D	$5,000	?	Casualty	$8,300	$3,300

The focus of this part of the question is the character of these gains and losses, given the special rules of §1245 and §1231. Spencer's sales of Equipment A and Equipment B in his business constitute sales of §1231 assets. However, we must first apply the recapture rule of §1245 to recast as ordinary income any amount of depreciation claimed on the computer before turning to the special rules of §1231. For Equipment A, the facts do not tell us what this amount is, but it is reasonable to assume that all ($10,000) of the difference between the initial purchase price and the basis is a result of capital recovery—§179 or MACRS deductions. Thus, the entire gain, which is less than the previously claimed depreciation, is treated as ordinary income. **See Figure 10A, Boxes [1] → [3] → [4] → [10].** For Equipment B, we know that $200 is attributable to previous depreciation claimed, and that amount will be treated as recapture (ordinary) income, and the rest of the gain ($500) will be treated as gain on the sale or exchange of a §1231 asset. **See Figure 10B, Boxes [1] →[3] →[4] → [10] → [5] → [6] → [7].**

For the portion of the gain on Equipment B, and for all of the gains or losses on the constructive dispositions of Equipment C and D, we must add up the §1231 gains and losses for the year, netting the two. The first step is netting casualty/theft gains and losses on §1231 property. **See Figure 10B, Boxes [1] → [3a] → [3b].** Spencer had a theft loss of Equipment C, which had a basis of $2,500 and a fair market value of $1,500. If property used in a trade or business or for the production of income is totally destroyed, and if the fair market value of such property immediately before the casualty is less than its adjusted basis, the adjusted basis of such property is the amount of the loss. Reg. §1.165-7(b)(1)(ii); Reg. §1.165-8(c). Therefore, Spencer's loss is $2,500 on the theft. He also had a casualty gain of $3,300 due to the flood. These are netted, as follows:

Theft loss:	$2,500 loss
Flood gain:	$3,300 gain
NET	**$800 gain**

Because Spencer's casualty gains are greater than his casualty losses, both are included in his netting of §1231 gains and losses. **See Figure 10B, Boxes [4a] → [4b].** Added to the net $800 gain is the $500 gain on the sale of Equipment B, creating a $1,300 net §1231 gain. Spencer had $200 of unrecaptured §1231 loss from prior years, so $200 of this gain is characterized as ordinary. The rest is capital. **See Figure 10B, Boxes [5] → [6] → [7].**

This capital gain income would be taxed at 15 percent, or 0 percent depending on Spencer's income. Because Spencer's net income from business (ordinary income) exceeds the amount that would be subject to the 10 percent regular tax rate, this capital gain will be taxed at the 15 percent rate.

SAMPLE ANSWER TO QUESTION 5

This is a difficult question for which not all the answers are clear. In addition, the IRS has recently issued Rev. Rul. 2009-9, 2009-14 I.R.B. 735, and Rev. Proc. 2009-20, 2009-14 I.R.B. 749, which address the tax consequences of this kind of transaction. In particular, Steve may want to take advantage of the "safe harbor" provided in Rev. Proc. 2009-20, which may, if certain requirements are met, allow him to claim a loss despite the ambiguities of the situation discussed below. The following analysis, however, assumes that he does not use the safe harbor.

Figures 4A–4C are helpful in answering this question. **Figure 4A, Box [1]** poses the question "Has Steve experienced a loss?"

He originally invested $500,000, and has received $200,000 back from Barney, resulting in a net $300,000 loss in this investment. In addition, however, in each year Steve included amounts in his gross income attributable to interest, dividends, and capital gains that he believed he had earned through this investment—even though these were not real. These must be accounted for in the loss analysis.

In a six-year time frame, it is likely that at least a couple of the years are "closed"—i.e., the time has passed for filing an amended return and obtaining a refund. For these years, the phantom income is best viewed as creating an "asset" with a tax cost basis. In other words, the basis of the asset is the amount of income included by Steve.

For years that are not closed, the same approach can be used. An alternative approach is worth considering, however. An argument can be made that Steve was not in constructive receipt of this income, because the payor, Barney, had no ability or intention of paying it. Under this theory, Steve could file amended returns that reduce gross income by the amount previously (and erroneously) included. Whether this is the correct approach however, depends on whether Barney really had the cash and intention to pay (a factual question that may never be determinable). Moreover, it flies in the face of a basic tax principle: An income tax return is prepared based on the facts as they existed and understood on the last day of the taxable year.

Let us assume that Steve chooses not to amend the returns, and takes the approach of treating the phantom income as having a tax basis, or $400,000. If so, his total loss is $700,000.

The following analysis tracks **Figure 4A, Boxes [3] → [4] → [5] → [7] → [9].** Whether the loss was incurred in a closed and completed transaction is a bit unclear. The press reports and the SEC investigation suggest that there is no money, but what is the factual basis for that conclusion? Is it correct? Steve will bear the burden of proof on this fact. **Figure 4A, Box [3].**

Assuming that there is a loss, in order to claim a tax loss, there must be no reasonable prospect of recovery. There may be a claim for $100,000 of insurance, which could reduce the loss to $600,000. What about the litigation? Steve will bear the burden of proof to show that the litigation will not result in any reasonable prospect of recovery. **Figure 4A, Box [4].**

Assuming that there is no reasonable prospect of recovery, it is tempting to treat the loss as a worthlessness of a capital asset, which would be a deemed sale, generating capital gain or loss. But in this case, Steve did not give Barney stock or securities; he gave Barney cash. The theft of the cash does not constitute a sale or exchange of property. **Figure 4A, Box [5].**

Steve is not in the trade or business of investing, and so this would not be a loss incurred in a trade or business. However, he did have a profit motive—he intended (and thought) that Barney would invest his funds for profit. **Figure 4A, Boxes [7] ➔ [9].**

As a result, the next stop is **Figure 4C.**

Steve's loss was incurred in a profit-oriented activity that was not a trade or business.

While Steve probably now believes it was a gamble (and not one with good odds), "gambling" means games of chance—not investments—in the tax world. The activities listed in Section 62(a) do not include theft losses other than those incurred in a trade or business, so the loss is not deductible above the line. It is an itemized deduction. Is it subject to the 2 percent floor? Section 67(b)(2) provides that casualty and theft losses under IRC §165(c)(2) or (c)(3) are not subject to the 2 percent floor. Rev. Rul. 2009-9 confirms this conclusion. **See Figure 4C, Boxes [1] ➔ [3] ➔ [5] ➔ [8].**

The result is that, making the assumptions described above, Steve may claim a theft loss of $700,000 as an itemized deduction in the year in which the theft is discovered. To the extent that this loss is not fully utilized in that year, it can potentially be carried back or forward to other years under §172.

Finally, theft losses such as this are not disallowed for AMT purposes, and so claiming this loss should not trigger AMT problems for Steve.

Glossary

Above the line.   For a deduction, a subtraction from gross income in computing adjusted gross income. See §62.

Accrual method.   A method of accounting many businesses use that requires the taxpayer to include income when the taxpayer has a right to it (whether or not received) and to deduct expenses when the taxpayer becomes obligated for them (subject to certain restrictions).

Adjusted basis.   The taxpayer's initial basis in an asset, adjusted downward for MACRS or other capital recovery. See §1016.

Administrative practicality.   A criterion for evaluating the merits of a tax statute that focuses on how a tax statute would be administered by the IRS. Would administration be easy or difficult? Would it require more or less intrusion into taxpayer's lives? Would the cost of administration be worth the advantages of the statute, even if they include increased fairness, certain economic behaviors, or increased revenue?

Alimony.   A payment made by a former spouse to the other former spouse that meets the requirements of §71, regardless of how it is labeled for state law purposes.

Alternative minimum tax (AMT).   This is a surtax designed to ensure that taxpayers who enjoy special tax benefits that reduce regular taxable income do pay some tax. See §55.

American Opportunity Credit.   Formerly known as the Hope Scholarship Credit, this is a tax credit allowed for expenditures for higher education. See §25A.

Amortization.   The common term for capital recovery for intangible assets used in a trade or business or held for investment.

Amount realized.   With respect to the disposition of an asset, the sum of the amount of money received, the fair market value of property received, and the liabilities of the taxpayer assumed by a buyer in the transaction. See §1001.

Amounts at risk.   For purposes of determining whether a taxpayer may claim a loss with respect to an activity, the amount of money or property that the taxpayer could lose if the activity fails. See §465.

Annual accounting.   The principle that income and deductions are to be reported on an annual (12-month) basis and that taxpayers report the tax results of activities as the facts exist on the last day of such annual period, even if circumstances change later.

Assignment of income.   A strategy employed by taxpayers to attempt to direct income to related persons in a lower tax bracket.

Barter.   The exchange of goods and/or services without a cash payment.

Basis.   The taxpayer's initial economic investment in an item of property.

Below-market loan.   A loan that does not include a market rate of interest, as established from time to time by the IRS, and with respect to which interest may be imputed. See §7872.

Below the line.   Referring to a deduction, a subtraction from adjusted gross income in computing taxable income. See §63.

Bonus depreciation.   "Extra" depreciation that Congress sometimes allows taxpayers as a method of encouraging taxpayers to make purchases of capital equipment. See §167.

Calendar year.   The 12-month period for reporting income and deductions; begins on January 1 and ends on December 31.

Capital asset.   Any asset other than those listed in §1221.

Capital expenditure.   An expenditure incurred by a taxpayer that creates a separate asset, or the benefit of which is likely to extend beyond the close of the taxable year. See §263.

Capital gain.   Recognized income from the sale or exchange of a capital asset. See §1222.

Capital loss.   Recognized loss from the sale or exchange of a capital asset. See §1222.

Capital recovery.   With respect to an asset, the process by which the taxpayer is allowed to recoup his or her investment in the asset in order to be taxed only on the income on the disposition of that asset. Capital recovery may be allowed upon acquisition (see §179), over the period that the asset produces income (see MACRS), or upon disposition of the asset (see §1001). The timing of capital recovery is a matter for Congress.

Cash method.   An accounting method used by most individuals that requires taxpayers to include income when received (actually or constructively) and deduct expenses when paid (subject to certain restrictions).

Character.   The nature of income or loss as capital gain or loss or ordinary income or loss.

Charitable contribution.   The donation of cash or property to a qualifying charitable organization; potentially generates an itemized deduction. See §170.

Claim of right.   The principle that a taxpayer must include items of gross income to which the taxpayer has a reasonable claim of right, even if later the taxpayer must repay all or any part of that amount. See §1341.

Collectible.   A type of capital asset that generates 28 percent capital gain or loss, such as a coin collection.

Compensation. Income received for the performance of services, whether as an employee or otherwise, and whether received in the form of cash or property. See §61(a)(1).

Constructive receipt. An overlay on the cash method of accounting principle, under which cash method taxpayers must include income in their gross incomes when they have the right to receive it, even if they choose not to do so.

Cost basis. A taxpayer's initial purchase price for an item of property, including the cash paid for the item, the fair market value of property transferred to obtain the property, and the liabilities of the seller assumed by the taxpayer. See §1012.

Deduction. A subtraction from gross income in computing adjusted gross income, or a subtraction from adjusted gross income in computing taxable income.

Deference. The principle that a court should defer to the IRS's prelitigation, published position on a tax matter.

Deferral of income. A strategy employed by taxpayer to save taxes by delaying the receipt of income until a future year.

Dependent care credit. The tax credit available for up to 30 percent of certain amounts paid for the care of dependents while the taxpayer earns income. See §21.

Depreciation. The common term for capital recovery for tangible assets used in a trade or business or held for the production of income. The method of depreciation currently in use is MACRS.

Discharge of debt. The action by a creditor that excuses a debtor from paying all or part of a debt and which can generate gross income unless excluded under §108.

Discount rate. The percentage rate used in determining present or future value and which is determined by a number of factors, including the expected interest rates that will prevail in the applicable period and the riskiness of the payments.

Earned income credit. The refundable tax credit available to taxpayers with low amounts of earned income that varies with the number of children the taxpayers claim as dependents. See §32.

Economic benefit. Any benefit to a taxpayer of a pecuniary nature, whether in cash or in another form, as opposed to a purely intangible benefit.

Economic effects. A criterion for evaluating the merits of a tax statute that focuses on the likely effects of the statute on taxpayer behavior. Will taxpayers be likely to engage in the kind of activity encouraged by the statute? Would they engage in other, undesirable behaviors? Would these effects justify the cost of administration of the statute, its effects on fairness of the system, and the impact on revenue?

Education savings accounts.   Accounts established for savings for higher education under §530 that allow deferral and possibly the exclusion of earnings on such accounts.

Exclusion.   Characteristic of an item of income that is excluded from gross income—i.e., it never becomes part of the base on which the federal income tax is levied.

Fairness.   A criterion for evaluating the merits of a tax statute, which focuses on whether the statute makes the tax system more or less able to reflect each taxpayer's relative ability to pay. If a statute increases the fairness of the system, the questions are whether such an increase justifies any increased cost of administration, and whether the statute would affect revenue and taxpayer behavior in positive ways.

Fiscal year.   A 12-month period other than a calendar year for reporting income and deductions.

First-time homebuyer's credit.   A credit of up to $8,000 for taxpayers purchasing homes between January 1 and December 1, 2009. See §36A.

Fringe benefit.   A benefit provided by an employer to an employee, such as parking. See §132.

Future value.   The projected value of a sum invested today, and which earns interest over a stated period at a stated rate.

Gambling.   Games of chance, such as poker, slots, and other games.

Gift.   A transfer made with detached and disinterested generosity—i.e., without expectation of any quid pro quo. See §102.

Gross income.   The starting place for the calculation of the federal income tax—i.e., all "income" from whatever source derived. See §61.

Health savings account.   An account to which taxpayer may make contributions and the earnings on which accumulate tax-free and may be distributed tax-free to pay for medical expenses. See §223.

Hobby losses.   The common term for losses incurred in activities that are arguably not undertaken for profit, even though they may generate income, such as horses or racecars. See §183.

Holding period.   The period of time a taxpayer holds an asset; used for computing capital gain or loss. See §1223.

Home office.   An office used in a taxpayer's trade or business that occupies a portion of the taxpayer's principal residence. See §280A.

Imputed income.   The value of property one owns and uses, or the value of services one performs for oneself and one's family.

Imputed interest. The amount of a payment characterized as interest rather than some other payment based on the principle that loans must carry an adequate amount of interest.

Individual retirement account (IRA). A savings vehicle that allows taxpayers to contribute funds to an account on a potentially deductible basis, and the earnings on which will be deferred until withdrawn in retirement. See §408.

Installment method. A method of reporting income from the sale of property other than inventory and for which at least one payment is received after the close of the taxable year in which the sale occurs. See §453.

Interest. The compensation that a lender receives for making a loan; generally taxable as ordinary income.

Internal Revenue Code. Also known as the Code, Title 26 of the United States Code.

Internal Revenue Service. Also known as the IRS or the Service, a bureau of the Department of the Treasury charged with the administration of the tax laws.

Investment income. Income from dividends, rents, royalties, and similar items.

Involuntary conversion. The condemnation of property, or its destruction by fire, storm, earthquake, or other disaster.

Itemized deduction. The sum of a taxpayer's itemized deductions—i.e., those taken on Schedule A and taken in lieu of the standard deduction. See §63.

Kiddie tax. The tax imposed on certain young taxpayers with significant amounts of investment incomes and which raises their tax rate to that of their parents'. See §1.

Life insurance. A contract between a purchaser of a life insurance policy and the insurance company in which, upon the death of the named insured, the company will pay the beneficiary a stated or determinable sum. See §102.

Like-kind exchange. An exchange of qualifying properties that qualifies under §1031.

Loan. A promise to repay a certain sum within a certain period, with or without interest.

Long term. Referring to the holding period of assets, one year or longer. See §1223.

Loss. The excess of deductions over income, or the excess of a taxpayer's adjusted basis over the sales price of an asset, or an event that results in the theft or other casualty of property. See §165.

MACRS (Modified Accelerated Cost Recovery System). The method of capital recovery in use for tangible property, whether personal or real. See §167.

Making Work Pay Credit. A refundable credit equal to the lesser of 6.2 percent of the taxpayer's modified AGI or $400 ($800 for married taxpayers filing jointly). See §36A.

Matching principle. The principle that deductions should be matched in the same taxable year with the income produced by such expenditures in order to best reflect the taxpayer's income for that period.

Meals and entertainment expenses. Expenses associated with business that are potentially subject to special limitations under §274.

Medical expense. Expenditures for the treatment, diagnosis, and amelioration of disease or injury that are potentially deductible if the expenses meet certain requirements. See §213.

Miscellaneous itemized deductions. A category of itemized deductions that are deductible to the extent that, collectively, they exceed 2 percent of a taxpayer's adjusted gross income. See §67.

Moving expense. Expenditures to move the taxpayer, the taxpayer's family and the taxpayer's personal effects, which are potentially deductible if the move meets certain requirements. See §215.

Net operating loss. The excess of deductions over income for a trade or business or income producing activity; can carry back 3 years or forward 20 years. See §172.

Nonrecognition provisions. A number of Code provisions that allow or require a taxpayer to defer recognition of income, or require deferral of recognition of loss. Examples are like-kind exchanges and involuntary conversion.

Nonrecourse debt. Debt for which the debtor does not have personal liability.

Nonrefundable credit. A tax credit that does not reduce the tax due below zero—i.e., it cannot generate a tax refund. An example is the Dependent Care Credit.

Ordinary and necessary. The requirement for deduction of business expenses that focuses on how regular and appropriate the expenditures are in the conduct of business. See §162.

Ordinary income. Income that is other than capital gain. See §64.

Origin test. The principle that it is the origin or purpose of an expenditure, not its effects, that determines its proper categorization as personal or business. See §162.

Passive loss. A loss incurred in an activity that constitutes a trade or business, but with respect to which the taxpayer did not materially participate. See §469.

Personal casualty loss. A loss incurred by a taxpayer with respect to property held for personal use that is destroyed by fire, storm, earthquake, or other disaster, or by theft. See §165(c)(3).

Personal exemption. The below-the-line deduction to which each taxpayer is entitled and which is based on a standard amount per individual. See §151.

Personal expense. An expenditure the origin of which is the taxpayer's personal life, as opposed to his or her business activity, and which is normally nondeductible unless a specific statute applies. Medical expenses are an example. See §262.

Pre-opening expense. An expenditure incurred by a taxpayer conducting a business before the business is ready to serve customers—i.e., before it opens. See §195.

Present value. The projection of the value now of a sum or sums to be received at a specified time or times in the future, after making certain assumptions as to the appropriate discount rate.

Principal residence. The taxpayer's home where he or she usually lives. See §121.

Property settlement. A transfer of property that is pursuant to a divorce decree and that potentially qualifies under §1041.

Qualified dividend income. Certain dividends received from domestic companies that qualify for the special 15 percent rate as opposed to the regular rates on ordinary income. See §1.

Qualified residence interest. Interest on debt incurred to acquire a principal residence, and interest on certain home equity loans. See §164.

Realization event. A transaction in which a taxpayer receives something qualitatively different than what he or she transferred. See §1001.

Recapture. Upon the sale of an asset held for use in a trade or business or for the production of income, the casting of what would otherwise be capital gain as ordinary income in order to reverse the benefit of previous deductions against ordinary income by the taxpayer with respect to the assets. See §1245.

Recognition. Including an item of income on a tax return or deducting a loss.

Recourse debt. Debt for which a taxpayer is personally liable.

Refundable credit. A tax credit that can reduce the tax due below zero—i.e., generate a tax refund. An example is the earned income credit.

Restricted property. Property received in exchange for the performance of services; subject to a substantial risk of forfeiture. See §83.

Revenue Ruling. Published authority by the IRS that applies the law to a stated set of facts and upon which taxpayer may rely.

Section 179 expense. A deduction for the purchase of tangible personal property to be used in a trade or business or income-producing activity, subject to certain requirements. See §179.

Section 529 plan. An account established for the funding of a taxpayer's higher education expenses in which earnings from the account are deferred or excluded from gross income. See §529.

Section 1231 asset. Tangible assets used in a taxpayer's trade or business and described in §1231. Equipment is an example.

Section 1231 gain or loss. Gain or loss from the disposition of tangible assets used in a taxpayer's trade or business and described in §1231.

Short term. Referring to the holding period (less than one year) of assets for purposes of calculating capital gain and loss.

Standard deduction. Taken in lieu of itemized deduction, the sum of the taxpayer's basic standard deduction and certain other standard deductions, such as sales tax on the purchase of a new vehicle in 2009. See §63.

Taxable income. The base on which the federal income tax is imposed—i.e., gross income minus all available deductions. See §63.

Taxable year. The 12-month period during which a taxpayer reports income and deductions; can be a calendar year or a fiscal (non-calendar) year.

Tax cost basis. A method of determining a taxpayer's basis in property that relies on the amount of income a taxpayer included in gross income.

Tax credit. A tax benefit that reduces tax on a dollar-for-dollar basis, such as the Dependent Care Credit.

Tax rate. The percentage defining the tax on an item of net income. Examples are 10 percent or 28 percent.

Time value of money. The principle that a sum of money is more valuable the sooner it is received. A dollar received in the future is worth less than a dollar to be received today, because a dollar invested today can earn interest.

Timing. The principle that income and deductions must be assigned to the correct year. Taxpayers try to use timing strategies to defer income and accelerate deductions.

Trade or business. The activity of holding oneself out as providing goods and services to customers, or engaging in gambling as a profession. See §162.

United States Tax Court. The court assigned to adjudicate tax cases, to which a taxpayer may make a petition without first paying the tax.

Unrecaptured §1231 loss. For purposes of §1231, a loss in a previous year that would otherwise have been a capital loss, but which was characterized as ordinary because of §1231. Net §1231 gains are classified as ordinary to the extent of such losses.

Table of Cases

Table of Internal Revenue Code Provisions

Page numbers are used for references to the Flow Charts, Capsule Summary, and Exam Tips. References to the Short-Answer Questions and Answers are indicated by "S" plus the question number. References to the Essay Questions and Answers are indicated by "E" plus the question number.

Table of Regulations and Other Authorities

Index

Page numbers are used for references to the Flow Charts, Capsule Summary, and Exam Tips. References to the Short-Answer Questions and Answers are indicated by "S" plus the question number. References to the Essay Questions and Answers are indicated by "E" plus the question number.

Study hint: Use this index to test your recall of tax concepts. Do you know what each term means? Can you match the concept with its Code section?